CW00420762

BETWEEN FREUD AND KLEIN

BETWEEN FREUD AND KLEIN

The Psychoanalytic Quest
for Knowledge and Truth

Adam Limentani

Foreword by
Otto F. Kernberg

Foreword to this edition by
Harold Maxwell

London
KARNAC BOOKS

First published in Great Britain in 1989 by
Free Association Books

© 1989 Adam Limentani

This edition published in 1998 by
H. Karnac (Books) Ltd.
58 Gloucester Road
London SW7 4QY
by arrangement with the estate of Adam Limentani

The rights of Adam Limentani to be identified as the author of this work have been asserted in accordance with §§ 77 and 78 of the Copyright Design and Patents Act 1988.

British Library Cataloguing in Publication Data
A C.I.P. record for this book is available from the British Library.

  ISBN 1 85575 145 3

10 9 8 7 6 5 4 3 2 1

Printed in Great Britain by Polestar Wheatons Ltd, Exeter

For my family

CONTENTS

Adam Limentani was a distinguished member of the Independent Group of British psychoanalysts. He was therefore well placed to explore the space 'between Freud and Klein'. Born in Italy and trained as a psychiatrist before becoming a psychoanalyst in Britain, Limentani had an international perspective. He held the highest offices in the profession as president of both the British Psychoanalytical Society and the International Psychoanalytical Association, and he worked for many decades in the area of sexual disorders.

Limentani's collected papers, written with great compassion, reflect the breadth of his work and clinical experience. They are about psychic pain and about the different kind of pain associated with the discovery of truth and knowing. In each of his studies he offers a careful and reflective view of the prevailing psychoanalytic ideas and then presents his own clinical material and his original contributions. Sometimes he questions cherished tenets of psychoanalysis: he sees that acting out can have value as communication, or be an alternative to psychosomatic symptoms; he questions the prevalence of castration anxiety. Most of the papers are concerned with sexual disorders—perversions, deviancy, transsexualism, bisexuality, violence. Others address themselves to broader issues in the field of psychoanalysis as a culture, as a way of maintaining standards and as a set of interrelated training institutions.

FOREWORD TO THIS EDITION
by Harold Maxwell, MD, FRCPsych

This further edition would have delighted Adam Limentani. It was his last book, and as indicated by his choice of title, it exemplified many aspects of his personality, wherein he would emulate what he saw and admired as a characteristic of his adopted country: to try to find an acceptable path between disparate factions and ideas, in this case the fiercely disputing divisions of the contemporary British Psychoanalytical Society.

Indeed he was one of the leading members of what came to be called the 'Middle Group' of analysts in London, having come here from Italy in the late 1930s, when, following the publication of the Anti-Semitica decrees, which excluded many loyal and established citizens who happened to be Jews from public life, he recognized that both his professional and his personal life would become impossible.

Reading the original text again recalls for me a valued teacher and dear friend, and his humane and generous spirit will be readily apparent. As for the content, the views of the American analyst Harold Searles writing of the formulations of Klein and her followers seem particularly germane: 'It is not a matter of having to choose between irreconcilable theoretical concepts, but rather to determine in which phase of the patient's ego development each is more useful to use. . . .'

In the decade since the first edition of this work, there are some signs that dialogue and mutual acceptance of the groups within the British Psychoanalytical Society have advanced. This collection of essays by Adam Limentani has surely made a significant contribution to a welcome happening.

September 1998

FOREWORD
by Otto F. Kernberg, MD

T HIS BOOK is most aptly titled. Adam Limentani's professional life developed in the swirl of controversies between Melanie Klein and Anna Freud within the British Psycho-Analytical Society. His work is inspired by what he still lovingly calls the 'middle group', now officially calling themselves the 'Independent Group'. This group aimed to evaluate critically the views of both camps, select what seemed the most valid from each, and thereby enrich psychoanalysis.

And a true synthesis is what Limentani has accomplished in this book. One cannot fail to be impressed by the breadth of both its perspective and the issues examined within its pages. One is equally impressed by the open-minded, self-critical, sometimes almost excessively modest, self-questioning attitude of its author. Limentani accomplishes that most difficult task of confronting controversial issues without sounding polemical. While integrating concepts from differing orientations, he never takes the easy road to simplistic eclecticism. Instead he draws attention to points of conflict and then offers his own views. His positions are invariably those of a clinician with vast experience, one who allows the answers to emerge from the nature of the clinical data. I found it particularly pleasing that this highly respected psychoanalyst accords psychotherapy the dignity it deserves, rather than relegating it to a second-class status.

Limentani's style is refreshingly readable – simple and informal. He possesses an enviable capacity for presenting complicated ideas clearly and succinctly. The contents of his book reflect the diversity of his interests and experience.

In his chapter on acting out, Limentani presents an original classification of the clinical functions of that phenomenon. He points to the problems posed by patients who do not act out at all, and examines the relationship between acting out and psychosomatic illness; he sees both acting out and somatization as potentially dangerous but also informative avenues of escape from an emotional reality that cannot be tolerated in the intrapsychic realm. In the chapter on the assessment of analysability, Limentani traces the persistent problems of psychoanalytic practice in relating the initial assessment of patients to their capability to undergo psychoanalysis and to improve with psychoanalytic treatment. His recognition of the importance of a careful initial evaluation of a patient before indicating psychoanalysis and of prognostic indicators, should serve as a refreshing stimulus for further research in this area.

In examining the problems related to the 'institutionalization' of psychoanalysis in terms of the bureaucratization of psychoanalytic training, Limentani stands – correctly, I believe – firmly against the tradition of training analysts 'reporting' on candidates. He underlines the importance of training analysts not being involved in influencing the educational progression of their candidates, and stresses that regardless of any particular arrangements, the psychoanalysis of candidates is not the same as the ordinary psychoanalytic experience.

The chapters on bisexuality, homosexuality, and perversion are a major contribution of this thought-provoking volume. Limentani analyses the relationship between the psychological predisposition to bisexuality and the actual clinical symptom of bisexual behaviour. He convincingly concludes that clinical bisexuality usually reflects severe character pathology, narcissistic and/or other borderline conditions. He proposes a classification of homosexual patients into a first group with neurotic structure – with particularly severe oedipal conflicts and castration anxiety and relatively good prognosis; a second group in which homosexuality is employed as a defence against primitive anxieties and dread of disintegration; and a third group, represented by occasional homosexual behaviour within certain restrictive social environments.

Limentani radically departs from the traditional assumption that all homosexualities indicate a severe perversion: it is only in the second group that we find cases with severe character pathology – including narcissistic personality disorders, homosexuality as a defence against severe depressive states, and homosexuality as a defence against paranoid states. He also believes that those who practice occasional homosexuality in situations of stress, prisons, and special social and cultural surroundings that blend with the general field of bisexuality need to be differentiated from truly bisexual individuals who usually present severe psychopathology.

In a comprehensive review of the psychodynamics of case material from the Portman Clinic in London, where Dr Limentani carried out psychotherapy of patients with sexual deviations, he re-evaluates the psychoanalytic contributions to the study of transsexualism, and in the process proposes an original, highly sophisticated frame of reference for the psychoanalytic understanding of these extreme conditions.

In his final chapter on perversions, Limentani shares with us his experience over many years regarding treatable and untreatable cases. Here we find a truly penetrating contribution to the study of transference and countertransference in the psychoanalytic treatment of sexual deviations. The author's critical review of contemporary psychoanalytic theories of perversion and of the dynamics of sexual deviation constitutes a major contribution to our understanding of these conditions.

Between Freud and Klein presents a wealth of ideas, expressed with admirable clarity, bearing all the hallmarks of having their origin in the consulting room and – especially the ideas about sexual deviations – the Portman Clinic in London. This book is a masterful synthesis of an outstanding clinician's experience – a major contribution to what Limentani's 'middle group' has produced.

Acknowledgements

1 'Between Freud and Klein' was first published in Italian in *Riv. Psicoanal.* 1983, 29: 434–49 as: 'Tra Anna Freud e Melanie Klein'.

2 'The Orpheus myth as reflected in problems of ambivalence and reparation in the oedipal situation' was given to the '1952 Club', a private psychoanalytic club in London, in 1964. A shorter version appeared in Italian under the title 'Problemi di ambivalenza, riparazione e le situazioni edipiche. Il mito di Orfeo' in *Riv. Psicoanal.* 1967, 3: 253–67.

3 'A re-evaluation of acting out in relation to working through' was published in *Int. J. Psycho-Anal.* 1966, 47: 274–82, and in Spanish in *Rev. Psicoanal.* 1969, 26: 841–64 under the title 'Una reevaluación del acting out'.

4 'The assessment of analysability: a major hazard in selection for psychoanalysis' was published in *Int. J. Psycho-Anal.* 1972, 53: 352–61.

5 'The training analyst and the difficulties associated with psychoanalytic training' is an expanded version of a paper published in *Int. J. Psycho-Anal.* under the title 'The training analyst and the difficulties in the psychoanalytic training situation', 1974, 55: 71–7, and in *Nouvelle Rev. Psychanal.* 1973, 5: 223–34, under the title 'L'analyste didacticien et les difficultés rencontrées dans l'analyse de formation'.

6 'Object choice and bisexuality' first appeared in *Rev. Fr. Psychanal.* 1975, 5: 858–67 and in *Int. J. Psychoanal. Psychother.* 1975, 5: 206–17.

7 'Clinical types of homosexuality'. An earlier version of this paper was given to the Royal College of Psychiatrists in London in 1974. It was published in *Br. J. Med. Psychol.* 1977, 50: 209–16, under the title 'The differential diagnosis of homosexuality'. A shorter version was published in *Sexual Deviations*, ed. I. Rosen, 1979, Oxford: Oxford

University Press, pp. 195–205.

8 'Affects and the psychoanalytic situation' was published in *Int. J. Psycho-Anal.* 1977, 58: 171–97 and in the same year in Spanish in *Rev. Psicoanal.* 34, 1: 389–415, under the title: 'Los affectos y la situación psicoanalítica', and in German: 'Die Affekte und die psychoanalytische Situation', in *Psyche* 36: 660–79.

9 'The significance of transsexualism in relation to some basic psychoanalytic concepts' was published in *Int. Rev. Psycho-Anal.* 1979, 62: 379–99.

10 'On some positive aspects of the negative therapeutic reaction' was published in *Int. J. Psycho-Anal.* 1981, 62: 379–99.

11 'From denial to self-awareness: a 20 years' study of a case of childhood delinquency evolving into adult neurosis' was published in *Br. J. Med. Psychol.* 1981, 54: 175–86.

12 'To the limits of male heterosexuality: the vagina-man' was published in *J. Analytic Psychotherapy and Psychopathology* 1984, 2: 115–29.

13 'On some aspects of human violence'. This paper was given to the Department of Psychotherapy, University of Naples, in 1984.

14 'On the psychodynamics of drug dependence' was published in *Free Associations* 1986, 5: 48–65.

15 'Perversions: treatable and untreatable'. This paper was given as the 10th Glover Lecture at the Royal Free Hospital School of Medicine, under the auspices of the Portman Clinic, London, in 1986. It was published in *Contemporary Psychoanal.* 1987, 23: 415–37.

16 'Variations on some Freudian themes'. This was the Presidential address at the 34th Congress of the International Psychoanalytical Association in Hamburg in 1985. It was published in *Int. J. Psycho-Anal.* 1986, 67: 235–43, and in Spanish in *Rev. Psicoanal.* 1985, 4: 711–26, under the title 'Variaciones sobre algunos temas freudianos'.

I wish to thank Dr Ralph Layland for his helpful suggestions concerning the selection of the papers for this book. I owe a debt of gratitude to Miss Nancy Dunlop for her unfailing support and patience during the preparation of the manuscript. I am also very grateful to the editorial staff of Free Association Books for their guidance and help.

BETWEEN FREUD AND KLEIN

INTRODUCTION

WHEN I BEGAN to go through my papers for this collection, I was at first inclined to divide them into three groups: relating to psychoanalysis, psychotherapy and applied analysis. It was suggested to me that it would be better to place the papers in chronological order, as this would be more likely to demonstrate changes in my thinking. I was happy to adopt this suggestion, which conferred a sense of greater freedom in the presentation. Having decided upon this arrangement, I promptly created an exception to it: the first paper in the collection is 'Between Freud and Klein' which appeared as late as 1984. The reason for this is that the paper is to some extent autobiographical, as it takes me back to the early struggles in pursuing a career in psychotherapy which was to lead me to becoming a psychoanalyst.

My emigration to England in 1938, forced upon me by political circumstances in Italy soon after I had acquired a medical degree in Rome, the city of my birth, had caused only a brief interruption in my desire to take up a psychiatric career.

Although I do not believe that a medical qualification is an essential preparation for the work of a psychoanalyst, I have no regrets about having spent many years working in psychiatric hospitals and clinics. My prolonged exposure to the impact of British psychiatry, with its practical no-nonsense and somewhat pragmatic approach, has proved more than useful. I believe that this prolonged experience sharpened my capacity to assess the value or uselessness of the many forms of treatment which were, at that time, fast becoming available. My attempt to use analytic psychotherapy in a busy out-patient department of a famous London medical school, surrounded by a majority of sceptical or frankly hostile colleagues, was an unforgettable and profitable experience. It forced me into self-criticism and a constant reappraisal of the method of my choice.

At the same time I was able to observe the considerable limitations of other approaches, which were marked by the frequent relapses and lack of response on the part of patients to drug and behaviour therapy in the absence of supportive psychotherapeutic measures. Furthermore, my observation of the denial and clear disavowal of unconscious processes on the part of intelligent colleagues reinforced my belief in what I was hoping to achieve.

I did my training in the British Society within the Middle group which, to my regret, was renamed 'The Group of Independent Analysts'. The original term seemed to me to reflect so well the position in which some fifty per cent of members of the British Society found themselves in the immediate post-war period; a position which allowed them to hold the balance of psychoanalytic opinion between the well entrenched Freudian group and that of the fast-growing Kleinians. As a member of the Middle group it was also easily understood that one might be more inclined towards one end of the analytic spectrum than the other.

Here I can hardly do better than quote from a statement by Susan Isaacs in the course of the 'Controversial discussions' of 1943 in the British Psycho-Analytical Society;

> It does not matter who discovers the truth provided that all truths are shown and acknowledged, that no group of workers claims to have dogmatic and private possession of the innermost secrets of truth and that all this nonsense about Kleinians and Freudians is given up. The scientific freedom to oppose and dispute the details of new discoveries or new theories carries with it the obligation to admit mistakes and to acknowledge any change of view. It is not allowable to accept other people's contributions tacitly whilst openly asserting that their views are radically wrong or unorthodox. (1943a, p. 154)

The degree of psychoanalytic expertise on display at any Wednesday meeting of the British Society during the 1950s could only inspire a sense of awe. Perhaps that is also the reason why I did not become a devotee of any of the many charismatic figures of that period. I must nevertheless acknowledge that in the early years following my qualification as an analyst I was deeply influenced by Sylvia Payne and Paula Heimann, and to some extent by the writings of Melanie Klein.

My earlier involvement with clinical psychiatry was soon replaced by a deep interest in clinical psychoanalysis and the many problems related to it in terms of selection for analysis. The years spent as a consultant to the London Clinic of Psycho-Analysis are reflected in the paper on analysability. The inclusion of a paper which touches on training issues is also a reflection of my activities within the Education Committee of the Society, which provided experience that was to prove invaluable in my subsequent participation in the running of the International Psychoanalytical Association.

I have had no hesitation in including some papers on psychotherapy, which at one time took up a quarter of my professional life. This is not the place to discuss the obvious differences between psychoanalysis and psychotherapy, but I should mention that I have always held the view that the two disciplines can contribute to and enrich one another. My colleagues and patients know that I am uncompromising in insisting that the transference and countertransference have a prominent place in psychotherapy, and that in order to exploit this it is necessary to apply the model of the psychoanalytic setting. The need of a patient to sit up should not be taken as an excuse to turn the session into a social encounter, involving the exchange of confidences. The impact of psychotherapy on my psychoanalytic views has certainly been considerable as a result of my prolonged association with the Portman Clinic, London, which specializes in the treatment of sexual deviations. Whilst a psychoanalytic study of one or two cases of a perversion may throw light on the psychopathology of the condition, it must be obvious that the experience of seeing a large number of cases of sexual deviation, in all their infinite varieties, is bound to influence one's conceptualization of the intricate factors involved in their establishment and development.

Old theories have their usefulness but in a continuously changing world we must be prepared to examine old problems in a new light. For example, as I was reviewing my paper on bisexuality, I realized that I have underestimated its prevalence, as is shown by recent statistics in connection with the AIDS epidemic. It is indeed more than likely that many psychoanalytic concepts, related not only to sexuality in all its manifestations but also to aggression and the life and death instincts, will need to be reviewed in the light of this catastrophe, which seems to be associated with an almost bizarre disregard not only for the personal safety of the subject but also for that of others.

There is some comfort in writing for a professional section of the public as it is not necessary to enlarge upon certain aspects of our work. I am thinking here of the difficulty of describing to someone who is unfamiliar with our way of working exactly what a psychoanalyst is attempting to do.

Basically I believe that our task is to make a fellow human being aware of that internal psychic reality which has no resemblance to external reality although it has a considerable bearing on it. Thus our task is not only to impart a better understanding of the conscious information he already has about his past or present life, to help a person to achieve a better degree of integration or to make the unconscious conscious; but also to guide him towards knowing more about himself and to know what the real truth is about himself and his inner world.

Knowing is of course a subjective experience that is close to awareness, but the two must not be confused; we may be aware of something without actually knowing what it is or why we feel the way we do. The exploration of such phenomena in a causal or statistical way is better left to the psychologist, just as we may only have a peripheral interest in the philosopher's approach to the investigation of the nature of belief. The psychoanalyst needs to understand that there are limitations to current human knowledge. We may know many things, but there will always be a patient who will make us aware that we do not know everything.

1   BETWEEN FREUD AND KLEIN*

TO BE INVITED to speak in memory of Anna Freud, or if I preferred, on Melanie Klein's contribution to British psychoanalysis, presented me with an almost impossible choice which provoked a wave of memories as distant as they were still alive in myself.

I owe it mostly to chance to be in the position of being someone who appreciated the qualities and gifts of these two exceptional leaders, without the tie of loyalty that goes with the full acceptance of an orthodox system such as the Freudian or the Kleinian. As far as Anna Freud is concerned, the support given to me by colleagues over the years allowed me to meet her to an extent which could not occur with Melanie Klein. In this presentation, however, I wish to offer my impressions, gathered over many years from the time I was a candidate in training to the drastically different position of being a psychoanalyst nearing the end of his career.

I shall also attempt to expose some of those anxieties and indecisions attributable to belonging to the Independent group of the British Psycho-Analytical Society, also known as the Middle group.

To make this account a little more coherent I shall go back to the initial stages of my career. My psychiatric life began at the Neuropsychiatric Clinic of the University of Rome, directed by Ugo Cerletti, the well known neuropsychiatrist, who achieved fame as the inventor of electroconvulsive therapy. Shortly after my emigration to England and the resumption in 1939, at the Maudsley Hospital, London, of my abruptly interrupted

* This paper was given at a meeting of the Italian Psychoanalytical Society in May 1983, as part of a commemoration of Anna Freud, and on the occasion of the centenary of Melanie Klein's birth.

training, I spent the next few years working in various hospitals as a psychiatrist. I had soon grown tired of the physical method of treatment prevalent in those years, and it seemed natural that I should experiment with narcoanalysis. Discussing it with one of my early teachers, Aubrey Lewis, later to become one of the most eminent psychiatrists in the Anglo-Saxon world, I expressed my doubts to him. He promptly voiced his objections, noting that if my orientation was towards a dynamic approach, there seemed to be no need to turn to the 'truth drugs' in order to get at the truth.

That was my first confrontation with an inner need to search, if not to hunt, for the truth. Even today, I assume that that was the strongest motivation for directing my efforts towards psychoanalysis.

When I presented myself at the London Institute of Psycho-Analysis, having applied for training, I had by then read something written by Freud and Jung, the easier essays. But I had also discovered, quite by chance, the existence of a small volume entitled *Love, Hate and Reparation*. It consisted of a series of lectures given by Melanie Klein and Joan Rivière in 1937, to appear later as *Love, Guilt and Reparation* (1975). The lectures aimed at the presentation of Klein's new ideas on depressive states. In this first account, the infant is held responsible for the damage caused to the object by his hate, but the reparative tendencies prevail, as they were established at the same time as the insurgence of hatred.

Although I had some difficulties in applying these new ideas to infants, I was nevertheless very impressed by the writings. I had, by the way, also read a less than informative account of the accusations and counter-accusations addressed to each other by the two main schools led by Anna Freud and Melanie Klein.

I should add that, until then, I had not failed to notice the tensions, often acute, which seemed to develop between colleagues who were already in training.

In possession of such a limited knowledge of psychoanalysis, I was not exactly ready to answer a question put to me by Winnicott: 'What kind of analysis do you wish to have?' I eventually blurted out that, having had enough of political extremism, I was hoping for something different, but I certainly did not wish for anything not quite Freudian. To this Winnicott answered with ill-concealed impatience: 'But we are all Freudians', adding after a pause, 'more or less'. And this is how I was referred to a Middle group analyst, a term which seemed to irritate some people, whilst it offered others the temptation to use it contemptuously – not that I could yet understand why.

In the years immediately following the Second World War, the London Institute was an oasis of tranquillity and co-operation, compared with the stormy and unprecedented years 1943 and 1944, when the famous 'Controversial discussions' took place. This apparent peace was the direct result of the 'Gentlemen's agreement' which had emerged from those discussions; on this base was laid the foundation of the equal representation of the three groups: the Freudian, the Kleinian, and the Independent, to be found in all sections of the administrative organs of the Society.

Psychoanalytic education was taking place under the aegis of two separate courses, with very few lectures devoted to the teaching of the three groups together. In practice the 'B' course was reserved exclusively for the Freudians, whilst the 'A' course was attended by both Kleinians and Independents. Only after a great many years was this particular type of teaching (course 'A') divided between the Independent and Kleinian groups.

The life of a so-called Independent candidate was rather hard, a fact that became undeniable as soon as I realized that my colleagues in the other two groups were united in their desire to make us feel that we lacked a proper system based on precise rules, as resulting from purely Kleinian or Freudian analyses; and I shall unhesitatingly admit that this was a source of considerable envy. How many hours did I spend on the analytic couch complaining of the absence of clear-cut directions, which would have enabled me to understand 'everything' about my patients? Indeed, in my somewhat naive state of mind, I often thought of the English proverb which says: 'The grass is greener on the other side of the stream.' The analytic grass of the Independent group appeared to me arid and full of weeds. To be told that I had the advantage of being able to choose what seemed to me to be true and more utilizable amongst the various offerings in the scientific field, was hardly reassuring. It was a relief, therefore, to discover what was going on outside course 'A'.

Anna Freud, when she was still taking an active part in the life of the British Psycho-Analytical Society, held twenty-four seminars for candidates in the first year of training. Having volunteered to attend, I was given permission to do so for only one term. When the relationship between Anna Freud and myself became considerably different, I felt very uneasy about that discourtesy on my part, as it was well known that taking the whole series, extended over three terms, was an expression of commitment, to be expected of anyone who claimed to be interested in psychoanalysis. The seminars dealt with the early contacts with patients, and looking back I am still impressed by the humanity of our seminar leader and her understanding of our inexperience. For example, on one occasion a candidate admitted that he had offered to reduce the session fee to a difficult patient; Anna Freud reassured him, saying: 'Do not worry, years and years ago we offered cups of tea to patients to keep them in analysis.' But in her presence, as I was able to confirm years later, it was easy to realize that behind that appearance of fragility and *bonhomie* there was a granitic solidity of character which allowed her to be quite ruthless toward her opponents, and even caustic toward those who disagreed with her without good reasons. Those seminars were an invaluable preparation for taking on patients under supervision. My choice of a supervisor again reflected my uncertainty. For my first control case I turned to Eva Rosenfeld who, some time after a second analysis with Melanie Klein, had become interested once more in Anna Freud's ideas, having worked closely with her in Vienna at the beginning of her career as a teacher.

The central point of Eva Rosenfeld's technique was that in the beginning of a psychoanalysis one should avoid transference interpretations, and the analyst's intervention was required only when the transference had become a resistance. When the latter finally became manifest, it was so violent that my very first psychoanalytic patient and I myself were left totally shattered. We emerged from it reasonably well, but to this day it is not altogether clear to me how that happened.

My second supervision was with Sylvia Payne, who had firmly aligned herself on Melanie Klein's side, having had previous scientific contacts with Sachs and Abraham. With Sylvia Payne's help, at long last I felt ready to tackle Melanie Klein's seminars. I was by that time in the third year of training. Until that time there had been many occasions, during the Wednesday scientific meetings, when I could appreciate Melanie Klein's clarity and acumen, which would be much in evidence in the discussion of clinical details. Whilst feeling a very considerable degree of respect and admiration, I also felt somewhat intimidated, as I had more than once heard her commenting unfavourably on various lecturers.

At a distance of many years, it is difficult to describe the doubts and confusion arising in the mind of a candidate, on hearing this formidable and, equally, extremely courteous woman, whisper in a very audible manner that everything she had heard in the course of a meeting had nothing whatever to do with psychoanalysis.

As far as I was concerned, and ignoring some justifiable and understandable anxieties, I found her seminars infinitely pleasant and informative. I still remember now how her slightly melancholic facial expression would give way to a smile of satisfaction when she could suddenly see the opportunity of demonstrating to us the origins of a patient's anxiety.

Thus, she would show us the importance of concentrating on the here and now and on what the patient was saying or doing, as this was the one and only method of discovering the truth. Once more I was confronted by this truth which preoccupies all of us so much. But what truth was the object of our concern? Was it the truth pertaining to a patient's psychic life; or the truth of the analytic process; or of psychoanalysis itself? At this stage of my analytic education when I was present at a scientific discussion, often bitterly contested, I was left in a state of considerable perplexity as I felt that truth was about to escape me altogether.

In a confidential paper presented by Strachey as a preliminary to the 'Controversial discussions' of 1943, for the purpose of considering the repercussions caused by various opposing currents in the theoretical approach to psychoanalytic education, he put forward the hypothesis that 'the problem which has been confided to us is ultimately a *political and administrative problem* and not a scientific one.' He noted how 'political adaptability is not at all compatible with respect for scientific truth; furthermore, the rigidity put to the service of the practical application of a conviction was the evidence of the truth of the conviction.' Strachey continued: 'There are people inclined to say of their opponents, "His views are wrong, so his technique must be wrong" . . . If one presses the matter a little and asks how the speaker *knows* that his opponent's views are wrong, the result is sometimes a trifle circular: "Oh, he uses a wrong technique, so his views *must* be wrong" ' (Strachey, 1943, p. 4). This was the atmosphere that prevailed in the British Psycho-Analytical Society, many years after the '*états majeurs*' of Melanie Klein and Anna Freud had taken the field, one against the other, with the moderating assistance of a large number of non-partisan analysts. In reality, then, neither the various discussions nor the political compromise had resolved anything from the scientific point of view. The two grand ladies of psychoanalysis were still implacable enemies.

I shall quote again from Strachey's document:

The members of the British Society, for various reasons, having arrived at what seems to them the truth about certain phenomena, have decided that they wish to disseminate their conclusions as widely as possible, and the business of the Education Committee was to consider how best to put that decision into effect . . . It is quite likely, that upon our decision the whole future of psychoanalysis in this country [Great Britain] will depend. For if we decide unwisely, one of two equally bad consequences may in the extreme case follow. On the one hand, the dissemination of psychoanalysis may become extremely restricted . . . Or on the other hand, we may effect a very wide dissemination of views, and yet, if those views bear only a faint resemblance to those of psychoanalysis or are actually opposed to them, our policy will be no less of a failure. (p. 5)

Strachey's position was to become the basis for the famous compromise that was to cause widespread repercussions, especially if we consider the idiosyncratic development of American psychoanalysis. Strachey was quite correct in opposing the transformation of psychoanalysis into a closed system of limited truths, incapable of any amplification or modification. This would have been quite contrary to Freud's views that psychoanalysis was not a rigid and closed philosophical system, and that it had to rely for its advancement on the help of experience, even incomplete, but was always ready to correct and modify its theories. This attitude is perhaps more difficult to accept than it may appear at first sight. However, reading Freud's texts was to be used in the following years, and even today, as the basis for introducing novelties in the theoretical and technical fields, with the appearance of veracity.

But I wish to refer more extensively to those theoretical discussions of 1943. Very little could be written on the subject, as some of the participants were still alive and until recent times some of them objected even to the private publication of the proceedings in the *Bulletin of the British Psycho-Analytical Society*. It has been no secret, however, that the scientific gaps between the opposing factions, as revealed by the debates, had become insurmountable. For example, papers were presented by Susan Isaacs, Paula Heimann, and Melanie Klein herself. Some people have been surprised by the fact that the three fundamental papers, which were to form the basis for the discussions, were all Kleinian, but after all it was essentially their theories which were subjected to careful scrutiny.

'The nature and function of phantasy' presented by Isaacs (1948) provoked a debate of immense interest and brought out criticisms of a fundamental nature. Anna Freud centred her attack on those points which had appeared to her to be incompatible with current theories. She noted, for instance, how an attempt was made to preserve old concepts whilst the new formulations actually denied them. In her view, the theories concerning the first year of life were disrupted. She also deprecated the abolition of the so-called fixation points. It was therefore inevitable that the orthodox

Freudians were deeply offended by theoretical concepts which according to their orientation seemed to reduce the concept of regression to zero. Amongst the critics, Friedlander objected particularly to the fact that the whole concept of the libido seemed to be attached to these early fantasies, without following the biological phase of development as described by Freud, and how it is observed in young children. There was therefore a suspicion that regression was no longer regarded as necessary as there was nothing primary to regress to.

These arguments were fiercely contested by Michael Balint, though he too had been disturbed by the theories concerning the role of hate, frustration and aggressivity in the first years of life, as outlined by Klein. At the end of the discussion of Isaacs's paper, Anna Freud formally requested that the minutes of the meeting should reflect the fact that in the absence of any counterarguments being offered to Isaacs's views, 'it was not indicative that we are satisfied with her replies and her points of view' (A. Freud, 1943, p. 154).

Segal (1979) devotes a whole chapter to these discussions in her book *Klein* and comments that: 'The discussions did not bring, as Jones had hoped, a better mutual understanding. On the contrary, they seemed to have led to a still sharper polarization of views and sometimes degenerated into acrimony' (p. 109). This account, accurate as far as Klein and her school's position goes, is lacking in other respects: the reader, for instance, is not aware that the discussions of Isaacs's paper cover 117 pages of typescript.

Gillespie (1980), who was present throughout the debates, has taken a firm stand against this account, because according to him Segal did not have access to confidential reports, which had preceded the meetings, a serious drawback in his view. Gillespie adds that these discussions were provoked not only because Jones, a Klein supporter, wished to put to the test the scientific value of her doctrine (as suggested by Segal). According to him there were 'two main issues, both of a political nature rather than a scientific one, concerning the tenure of office and the fact that in practice the affairs of the Society had been entirely in the hands of Ernest Jones and Edward Glover'. The other issue 'had to do not so much with the scientific status of the Klein school, as with their alleged attempt to corner the training system and so eventually to achieve the control of the Society' (p. 86).

Gillespie insists that Segal, whilst giving an excellent account of the contributions of Klein, Isaacs and Heimann

. . . ignores the important fact that there was another side to the discussions, contributed notably by Glover and Anna Freud, but also Balint, Brierley, Burlingham, Fairbairn, Friedlander, Foulkes, H. and W. Hoffer, Jones, Rivière, M. and W. Schmideberg, Sharpe, the Stephens and Winnicott. Thus what fails to appear in Segal's account is that the outcome of the controversy was the emergence not only of a limited number of what came to be known as Kleinian analysts, but also of a much larger number of analysts who were neither committed to the full Kleinian theory and technique, nor prepared to jettison it in the manner favoured by Glover and the Viennese school . . . In fact, the most constructive contributions to the discussion came from these non-partisan analysts. (p. 87)

It would therefore seem that those who wish to obtain a clear picture of what actually took place forty years ago should refer to Segal's volume as well as Gillespie's review.

I have stressed the events of those distant years because Anna Freud and Melanie Klein were the central figures in them. The first one represented, and was to remain until the end of her life, the principal supporter of the theories and techniques of the founder of psychoanalysis. Klein, on the other hand, was to revolutionize the whole of psychoanalysis with her innovations, but as an outsider.

It has been said that those disagreements which led to the formation of three groups of analysts, at loggerheads on scientific grounds, could be understood to have been based on the simple choice between a father or mother figure, with others preferring not to take sides with either parties in the dispute. This explanation appears to be somewhat naive, if we realize that the essential disagreement between the two leaders revolved around issues related to the psychoanalysis of children. The theoretical and technical differences were, and remain, insurmountable, with inevitable repercussions in the theoretical approach to adult psychoanalysis. Nevertheless, it must be conceded that there are signs suggesting that some of the original gaps can now be filled, especially if they can resolve some of the more intractable semantic problems. There could therefore be some basis for Flournoy's suggestion that we have left behind the quarrel between Freud and Klein and that 'the conflict between Kleinians and Freudians which periodically threatens the psychoanalytic movement . . . is beginning to look a bit like a *comédie d'arrière-garde* [literally a rearguard comedy]' (Flournoy, 1980, p. 912). After all, those who have grown up with the classical methods of defence can also become accustomed to projective identification and splitting, which are generally regarded by the majority of analysts as essential to the better and full understanding of the analytic process.

I am interested on the other hand, at this point, to examine whether the scientific position of a group is enhanced by the cohesiveness generated by having developed around a charismatic figure. For instance, in London there was a plethora of analysts whose charisma had won them countless numbers of adherents, but few of them had attracted as many devoted followers as the two leaders at the centre of this discussion.

When Anna Freud retired from active participation in the life of the British Society to devote herself to the founding and development of the Hampstead Child Psychotherapy Clinic, there followed a movement from hot to cold war. Only after Klein's death did analytic training in London take a definite turn towards an ecumenical approach. Nevertheless, the faithfulness and obedience to the various groups and devotion to the respective leaders hardly changed. The Independents were the only ones to claim the absence of any obligation amongst themselves, and to this day they are proud of not having a leader. In my opinion this attitude was influenced by Winnicott's hostility to the idea of a group led by anybody, and in this sense he ended up by acting as a leader.

It could perhaps be argued that the London experience is a unique phenomenon in the history of psychoanalysis, but I doubt it. It is of course unlikely that the British compromise, with its three distinctive groups, would be reproduced elsewhere. The observation of some analytical societies which have come into being in North and South America and in Europe reveals the presence of transcultural factors which will be accounted for by the scientific orientation of various psychoanalytic groups and the charismatic force of their leaders. Observing the behaviour and attitudes of those who are members of these groups, without exception, will lead us to conclude that we are dealing with a transference phenomenon to the group and to the leader, and this is all the more obvious when the leader is someone of the calibre of a Klein, a Bion, a Winnicott, or Anna Freud.

We shall also note how these transference phenomena, which are also characterized by profound idealization, have escaped a resolution. Scientific and political positions are often maintained and defended by rigidity and, at times, unusual blindness. Even when the transference to the training analyst has been resolved, the transference towards the group and/or its originator appears to be without resolution. For this reason, several generations of analysts have in fact preserved a profound attachment to Freud, the founder of the science which keeps us united in the international field.

As is always the case in all good families, even when we are about to tear each other apart we do not hesitate to unite against external attacks, and this, in my view, is due to the transference towards a particular leader, or indeed towards Freud himself.

'We are all Freudians', as Winnicott told me at the beginning of my career. That sentence, thrown away so casually, was to become the founding stone on which I was to build my identity as a psychoanalyst, which is inevitably based on an unresolved transference towards psychoanalysis.

An interesting examination of this phenomenon is to be found in the writings of a Lacanian analyst, François Roustang. In a book which contains a number of notable assertions, brilliant and fascinating, this author writes:

> If the Lacanians can read Freud as a text-to-be-analysed and not as a text of truth, it is because Lacan has done the work for them . . . when they resolve their transference on to Freud, they are protected by an unanalysed transference on to Lacan, who plays the role of guarantor and interpreter of the truth. *In advance*, and for the future, they put their trust in Lacan. Their relationship to Freud has been assimilated into deferred action. Nothing, however, has changed. Another transference is in the same, blind spot, the transference on to Lacan. Those who understand his writings are content to repeat his words, or to embroider upon his theory. Those who do not understand his writings, assume that Lacan understands them and that if they are very studious, they will one day also understand. Under no circumstances do they question Lacan's sayings or presuppositions. In group discussions, for example, a quotation from Lacan acts as a concluding point or verdict, as the last word, which no one dares to criticize, analyse, or assess from a subjective point of view. No one even questions the status of the quotation, taken from a formula, and spoken by someone who is not the author, and who in any case changes its meaning completely. (Roustang, 1982, p. 21, author's italics)

What Lacan has done is mirrored in Klein's writings, where Freud is quoted scrupulously and precisely, even if indiscriminately (and, for that matter, amongst those who declare themselves to be Bion's followers). Perhaps here is the reason for the fact that so many members of the Kleinian schools, all over the world, do not read Freud all that much, just as some orthodox Freudians think they can go on existing without bothering to read Klein, Winnicott, Bion and – why not – even Lacan.

It is difficult to offer a satisfactory explanation for these missing resolutions of transference to leaders who may be more or less close to one, and, in some instances, no longer alive. It has occurred to me that it is perhaps impossible to analyse the transference to Freud or Klein, using the method which they themselves had developed. Nevertheless the absence of any self-criticism or the presence of an intractable idealization will make us suspect that some analyses tend to ignore the need to analyse either of these factors. It is probable that we are dealing here with an anxiety in the analyst, who fears to destroy or sabotage his or her faith in the method.

With regard to the transference to a group, it is likely that sharing ideas with a leader is fair compensation for a lack of personal originality. However, what Freud says about 'group psychology' is very relevant in this context, and particularly his comments about the artificial groups of the Church and the Army, which are linked amongst themselves by the prestige of the leader or an ideal. At the end of chapter 5, Freud writes: 'If another group tie takes the place of the religious one . . . then there will be the same intolerance towards outsiders as in the age of the wars of religion: and if differences between scientific opinions could ever attain similar significance for groups, the same result would again be repeated with this new motivation' (Freud, 1921, p. 99).

We shall also recall the role attributed by Freud to idealization resulting from identificatory processes, concluding that: 'A primary group of this kind is a number of individuals who have put one and the same object in the place of their ego ideal and have subsequently identified themselves with one another in their ego' (1921, p. 116). Some will say that Freud's 'Group Psychology' has been overtaken by new understandings. In that case the one and only alternative to be considered is that the behaviour of scientific groups, formed around charismatic figures, should be examined in the light of projective identification.

The disappearance of leaders in our profession is always associated with a sense of loss which is only compensated for by the fact that their contributions will survive in the history and practice of psychoanalysis. Anna Freud and Melanie Klein, as personalities, were different in the extreme, just as were their respective positions in the world of psychoanalysis. The first one continued to participate in international meetings, even when she had ceased to be active in the British Society, being held in respect and veneration for over half a century. The other, instead, had to fight for her existence and her true recognition in the international field. Yet, some believe that the limitations placed on the presentation of her ideas at international congresses until quite recently ended in promoting her popularity.

Each one of us will remember them in a more or less personal way. I remember Anna Freud's assertiveness when, during a conference on psychoanalytic training, she was asked when it would be advisable to terminate a training analysis. Her reply came firmly and unhesitatingly: 'When we are sure that our patient would not turn to drugs in case he runs into some difficulty.' It is also not easy to forget her criticisms of the International Psychoanalytical Association for insisting too much on the formalities of psychoanalytic education instead of relying on the efficacy of psychoanalysis.

Klein, too, pushed the faith in the efficacy of the method to an extreme degree. As Flournoy writes, 'the Kleinian analysand will be a Kleinian or not. This is the malaise of exclusivity or exclusion' (1980, p. 916). This author goes on to underline how this must be regarded as an important addition to the elitism of psychoanalytic societies.

But someone like James Gammill will remember her in a different manner:

One day, during a supervision, Melanie Klein said: 'Thank God, you did not interpret the concept of envy in this material as there was really nothing about it. For the whole week, several people have brought me material in which they had interpreted the envy, often without giving me any proof. At times I do not know if my scientific work will be destroyed by my most fierce partisans, or by my worst enemies. It has happened to me that someone has broken a relationship with me because of a new concept, as they insist on believing that this new concept is supposed to account for everything.' (Gammill, 1982, p. 13, my translation)

Perhaps Klein was thinking of Paula Heimann, who did break off her longstanding relationship with her on account of their dissonant ideas about countertransference and envy. It was almost ironical that Paula Heimann, whose desertion of the Kleinian group was as clamorous as it was unexpected, should have died so soon after the death of her dear friend Anna and just at the time of the centenary celebrations of another old ex-friend and collaborator. It almost seemed as if there had been a flare-up of the rivalry which had attracted many analysts' interest, coupled with admiration for both.

This is where my reminiscences and reflections end, with the hope that I have succeeded in communicating my feelings of gratitude for these two exceptional ladies.

In the course of the years, my interest in searching for truth has fluctuated considerably. At times the desire for *knowing* obfuscated its importance. Nevertheless, I believe that 'à nous la vérité' is just as important, in so far as it seems inconceivable to renounce the freedom of choice in thoughts and actions, especially when a large part of a lifetime has been spent searching, if not hunting, for truth and knowing.

2 THE ORPHEUS MYTH AS REFLECTED IN PROBLEMS OF AMBIVALENCE AND REPARATION IN THE OEDIPAL SITUATION*

I   ORPHEUS OBSERVED

MANY YEARS AGO I had a patient who was identified with Orpheus. The identification with the Poet-Hero of classical antiquity came to light suddenly and unexpectedly at the end of the fourth year of a psychoanalysis which my patient, whom I shall call Mr A, had requested on account of deep depression, inability to use his intellectual resources and a tendency to find himself rejected by men and women.

Mr A believed, with some justification, that all his problems were due to the fact that, owing to the war, he had been separated from his parents for long periods from the age of two and a half onwards. His state of mind during those early years could be reconstructed in the analysis when, during the first three years, Mr A would often phone the analyst late at night, 'just to hear [his] voice'. In due course this was understood as an attempt to resuscitate the analyst who was felt as having died during the unbearable twenty-three hours' separation. The only improvement at the time of the session I wish to report was shown by the abandonment of a search for a homosexual solution to his problems and the development of a well defined heterosexual disposition. Just as he was beginning to feel more secure in his dealings with women, Mr A suffered one more rejection as a result of his unwillingness to commit himself. The young woman with whom he had been in love for some time had finally married someone else. Mr A came to his session after attending the wedding ceremony, looking depressed but unusually willing to talk about his feelings, claiming that this

* This paper was first read to the '1952 Club', a private psychoanalytic club in London, in 1964.

—18—

time he had really lost everything. Admitting that he felt extremely jealous of the newly wedded couple, he insisted he was fully justified in feeling sadistic and murderous.

At the start of the next session, Mr A announced in an unemotional way that although he had felt deeply depressed he did not think that the loss was irreparable. Just as he was leaving to come to the session, he had caught himself whistling some music from Gluck's *Orpheus* and had felt self-conscious in case a friend who was still in the house would guess what was on his mind. He added that he had spent several days playing the third act of the opera and explained that he was particularly fond of the well known aria in which Orpheus sings: 'Is she dead? Is she dead? I have lost her forever. I myself have brought her death. Remorse will haunt me forever. What can remain for Orpheus?' After a pause he remarked with considerable satisfaction that Orpheus was in no way to blame for the failure of his mission, and Eurydice was wholly responsible for her first and second death. Relying on my recollection of the story, I ventured to say that he seemed to want to defend Orpheus but I, like his friend, knew what he was thinking. He had been so angry with his ex-girlfriend that he felt that, like Eurydice, she was dead. I reminded him how often he had felt as if I had died during a separation. Mr A shook his head, obviously unimpressed by my interpretation, although he volunteered the information that he did feel as if he were Orpheus. In a triumphant tone of voice, he added that I seemed to have forgotten that in the opera Orpheus gets his wife back in the end. In acknowledging my poor recollection of such an important detail, I showed my patient how he had made full use of the manic denial provided by the libretto writer to assuage his own guilt for feeling so aggressive towards the woman he had once loved and lost.[1]

The material elicited in this session was sufficiently unusual to make me want to record it at once but in the event it became the focus for the analytic work over the next few weeks. There were some complications in so far as Mr A was at various times also identified with Eurydice, a discovery that made him all the more aware of his fantasy of having a dead woman inside him (the endlessly attacked primary object). Thus we could account not only for his feelings of deadness but also for his insistence that all those around him should somehow 'rescue him from himself'. Eventually as the depth of his identification with the Hero became apparent, Mr A displayed a newly found readiness to engage in the exploration of his inner world.

My notes of that phase of the analysis show how I was led to think that my patient's earlier lamentations, the flaunting of his depression and the proclamation of his suffering, closely resembled Orpheus' alleged behaviour following the loss of his wife. But our work unmistakably showed the persistence of a total lack of interest in making any kind of reparation. The idea was so alien to Mr A that he constantly met my remarks on the subject with scorn, cynicism and persecutory feelings. Needless to say, the reparative failure was reflected in the transference when the patient insisted that my absences and the presence of so many patients exonerated him from any responsibility towards me. With the gradual development of insight into this difficult area of Mr A's psychic life, the analysis was brought to a satisfactory conclusion.

(As a 1988 postscript, I shall record that Mr A has long been married with a family, whilst he is professionally engaged in very creative work.)

I had little cause to think about the possible deeper meaning of the legend until several months later when my attention was again drawn to it by another patient.

Mr B had a brilliant mind and an anal character. His early life had been marred by a series of traumatic experiences which had left him scarred, mistrustful and persecuted. His mother's pregnancy when he was just over two years old 'had hit [him] between the eyes'. When some years later, and still a child, he needed some eye operations, he felt he was waiting for his execution. To make things worse, a sibling had died in an accident which prompted my patient to think that he had not acted sufficiently promptly to save him.

Over and above all these misfortunes, B's jealousy of his mother had caused utter havoc to his psychic life. In the transference any separation was experienced as a betrayal and at times he would return from an interruption fully convinced that I had died. That he succeeded in resuscitating me was shown by his insistence that his presence was essential to my staying alive, insisting that he was my iron lung, or the reverse.

When Mr B had entered analysis, he was sexually impotent, owing to a preponderance of oral and anal sadistic components in his sexuality. In spite of this, he had married and some years later his wife had become pregnant, although there had been no penetration. When I suggested that his unconscious had got the better of him and that he had given a child to his wife as a kind of reparative act, B ridiculed my interpretation. Intensive work in the area of his conflicts about reparation did bring some normality to his sexual performance, followed by the birth of a second child. One aspect of my patient's conflicts seemed to be related to a mistrust of the love object, based on the belief that restoring it to full health (life) was of little use to him as he would have to share it with someone else. Did he not have to share me with all the other patients, he would ask again and again? Was it not true that they were all stealing *his* breast?

Mr B's involvement with Orpheus emerged in the course of one of his daily sessions during the fifth year of analysis, when he arrived looking rather depressed and preoccupied. He began by suggesting that I went to see a film, *Black Orpheus*, which was being shown again in London. He then proceeded to give me a confused account of a man (Death) pursuing, for no reason at all, a young woman (Eurydice), intending to kill her whilst a black man (Orpheus) is unsuccessfully attempting to prevent it. As an after-thought, it occurred to him that Orpheus was responsible for the woman's death. During the flight, Eurydice had found refuge in a place which was in total darkness. Orpheus, hearing her screams and not being able to see her, succeeds in turning lights on. In so doing a cable on which Eurydice was hanging becomes live, causing her instant death. Soon after, Orpheus is killed by his fiancée who was jealous of Eurydice. Mr B thought the girl's revenge was unnecessary and unfair. Later in the session, it transpired that my patient was more identified with the girl he had criticized than the Hero. In the working through, though, Mr B admitted that for years he had felt as if he were being pursued by the Furies, fearing that he, too, would end up being torn from limb to limb. It was obvious that, as he was watching the film, Mr B had rapidly identified himself with the aggressor but, on the other hand, had also been deeply moved by Orpheus' attempt to save the woman he loved. He could now reluctantly recognize that the failure of the rescue had made him aware of his own ambivalence and guilt about his persistent refusal to make any reparation towards the damaged internal object (mother). Furthermore, later work revealed that as the film unfolded, he was witnessing a primal scene central to his masturbatory fantasies.

I did see *Black Orpheus* but there was little to add to what Mr B had told me, except that I did appreciate its haunting quality.[2] The experience itself, though, provided me with the stimulus to begin an investigation of the myth which was to occupy me for a considerable time.

II   EARLY AND LATER VERSIONS OF THE MYTH

Orpheus was the son of the Thracian king, Oeagrus, and the Muse, Cal-liope. Apollo had presented him with a lyre and the Muses had taught him to play and sing. He learnt the art so well that wild beasts were enchanted and even trees and rocks followed the sound of his music. After joining the Argonauts and helping them to overcome many difficulties, he returned to Thrace and soon married Eurydice. Not long after, his bride, as she was walking through some woods, met Aristaeus the Shepherd, who attempted to rape her. As she fled, she trod on a serpent and died of its bite. Orpheus, unable to bear the loss, decided to descend into Tartarus, hoping to fetch her back. He so charmed the ferryman, Charon, and Cerberus with his music, and so soothed the savage heart of Hades, that he was allowed to take his wife back to the upper world. But there was one condition: that he was not to look back behind him until she was safely under the light of the sun. It was only when he reached sunlight that he turned to see whether she was still behind him, and so lost her forever (according to Hyginus, Euripides, Pausanias, etc.) (Graves, 1960). Some say that he tried to follow her but he was not allowed to enter Hades again. The Hero was inconsolable and began to wander around, carrying his grief with him. From there on accounts vary a great deal and the story becomes complicated as soon as Orpheus becomes involved with the development of religious mysteries, later known as Orphism.[3] It is said that when Dionysus came to Thrace, the Hero did not honour him. He not only told his followers that Apollo was better than Dionysus, but he also preached sacrificial murder. Finally, Dionysus set the Maenads (Bacchantes) on him whilst Orpheus was officiating in a temple where their husbands were assembled. The Maenads murdered them all and the Hero himself was torn limb from limb. His head, thrown into the river Hebrus, floated to the sea, still singing, till it reached Lesbos. The Muses collected his remains and buried them at the foot of Mount Olympus.[4] Our difficulty, however, is in understanding the intervention of the Maenads. Ovid (1955) gives a somewhat different account in the *Metamorphoses*, noting a series of bad omens from the wedding day, right up to the woman's death. He writes:

Anxious in case his wife's strength be failing, and eager to see, the lover looked behind him and straight away Eurydice slipped back into the depths. Orpheus stretched out his arms, straining to clasp her and he clasped: but the hapless man touched nothing but yielding air. Eurydice, dying now a second time, uttered no complaint against her husband. What was there to complain of but that she had been loved? (p. 246–7)

This is the first recorded attempt to defend the Hero's behaviour, linking it with an expectation of forgiveness by the wife, and perhaps women in general. Ovid continues:

> Three times the sun had reached the watery sign of Pisces, that brings a year to a close. Throughout this time, Orpheus had shrunk from loving any woman, either because of his unhappy experience, or because he had pledged himself to do so. In spite of this, there were many who were fired with a desire to marry the Poet: many were indignant to find themselves repulsed. Orpheus, instead, preferred to centre his affections on boys of tender years, and to enjoy the brief spring and early flowering of their youth: he was the first to introduce this custom amongst the people of Thrace. (p. 247)

Slowly, our Hero's psychiatric history is beginning to unfold as he moves towards his tragic end. With his songs he continued to draw the trees and rocks to follow him when suddenly the Ciconian women caught sight of him.

> Looking down from the crest of the hill, these maddened creatures with animal skins slung across their breasts, cried out: 'See, here is the man who scorns us, and one of them flung her spear at the Poet . . . From that moment, the women's rash attack increased in violence till all restraint was lost and maniac fury had been under way . . . The birds, the host of wild creatures, the flinty rocks and the woods all wept for Orpheus . . . His ghost passed beneath the earth; he recognized all the places he had seen before and searching through the blessed, found his Eurydice and clasped her into his eager arms. There they stroll together, side by side; or sometimes Orpheus follows her, while the wife goes before, sometimes he leads the way and looks back, as he can do safely now, at his Eurydice. (Ovid, pp. 268–70)[5]

III   ORPHEUS AND EURYDICE IN THEIR MANY DISGUISES

Apart from Gluck's *Orpheus* which was first performed in 1762 and thoroughly revised twelve years later as *Orphée*, the legend has been the object of great interest to many composers including Monteverdi, Haydn, Offenbach and Milhaud. In the eighteenth century no less than sixteen operas were produced around this theme but the nineteenth century was no less interested. The only artistic work of note during the latter period is Offenbach's *Orpheus in the Underworld* which was first performed in 1858. The work is a satire of the Second Empire and a burlesque of the legend as treated by Gluck. Orpheus behaves as a truly reluctant hero, showing little desire to rescue his wife from Death, whilst Eurydice is represented as a flighty woman, madly in love with the Shepherd, Aristaeus. When she dies her husband would be quite content to leave it at that but the Gods urge him to descend into Hades. Under pressure also from the *'opinion publique'*, he cries out: *'Mais avant d'être époux, je suis orphéoniste.'* (Before being a husband, I am for Orpheus.) Nevertheless, and in spite of this narcissistic outburst, he does what the Gods tell him to do, perhaps only because they go with him. Needless to say, on the way back he turns around to look at his wife and promptly loses her. Again the Gods come to his help but this time Jupiter, after restoring the woman's life, turns her into a Bacchante.

The most recent version of the myth that has come to my notice is to be found in the film *Black Orpheus*, already mentioned, but over the last sixty years some leading writers have given us their own versions.

Jean Cocteau has taken up the story in his drawings, stage and film work and it is common knowledge that throughout his life he was fascinated by the Poet-Hero. *Orphée,* first produced as a play in 1926, was made into a film in 1949. This is a meditation on death which, in Cocteau's view is intimately connected with poetry. The poet must pay for the privilege of poetic creation; Orphée pays in terms of suffering. His gift makes his inarticulate, bourgeois wife jealous, and stirs up the hatred of rival cliques and the hostility of the public. On the other hand, he seems to be more interested in his dealings with Death (a beautiful Princess) than his pregnant wife and, later, his newly born son. Cocteau is only too well aware of the narcissistic elements in the Hero's character, hence the film is loaded with allusions through the use of mirrors and water reflections. The mirrors, in fact, appear to be an ambiguous symbolism referring at one and the same time to the author's narcissism and his dealings with death.[6]

Tennessee Williams first wrote his *Orpheus Descending* in 1955, later to be turned into a film, *The Fugitive Kind*. This is a play in the Greek manner where Fate and inevitability drive the restless, guitar-playing protagonist to his death. The real interest in the play lies in the author's concern in developing the direct oedipal situation at the cost of neglecting all other issues, thus showing considerable insight into at least one of the deeper meanings of the story.

Jean Anouilh's *Eurydice*, instead, is a *pièce noire* written in 1941, in which we are confronted by the author's cynicism permeating the study of a young actress who meets her death in a car accident. At the end of the play, which follows the myth very closely, Orpheus accepts reunion with his lover in death but only after Monsieur Henri (Death) points out to him that in all probability, had Eurydice lived, she would have been unfaithful to him.[7] (Compare the case of Mr B.)

IV   PSYCHOANALYTIC STUDIES OF THE MYTH

Freud briefly mentions Orpheus in *Totem and Taboo*, when he follows the lead of the anthropologist, Reinach, who had written an essay on the Hero's death, linking it with the doctrine of original sin, which is of Orphic origin. The background of this doctrine is that mankind, being descended from the Titans, is burdened by the guilt of the murder of Dionysus. 'The tumultuous mobbing, the killing and the tearing to pieces by the Titans reminds us clearly of the totemic sacrifices . . . as for that matter do many other ancient myths, including for instance, that of the death of Orpheus himself. Nevertheless there is a disturbing difference in the fact of the murder having been committed on a youthful god' (Freud, 1913b, pp. 153–5).

Jung (1940) follows very similar lines when discussing the question of redemption, expressing the view that the eternal son returns to father through suffering crucifixion. He finally quotes the Orpheus legend as being a foretaste of the later one.

The only thorough study comes from the French psychoanalyst, Bougard (1934). His review of the historical, mythological and anthropological background is masterly. Accepting Reinach's view, this author states that there is more to be understood in the myth: as in almost all instances, the ancient Heroes are looking for a maternal image, often emerging all-powerful from a night of cohabitation with the mother. Having established the oedipal roots of the legend, Bougard turns his attention to the ferocity which underlines the Hero's death. He suggests that self-castration was the unconscious desire of all Orphic adepts in their superhuman effort to deflect their mother-fixated libido; in this way they imitated Orpheus who turned away from the Thracian women to remain faithful to the image of Eurydice. He writes: 'Truly, this descent to the bosom of the earth is an effort to return to the maternal bosom, the terrible mother; the counter-figure of the feeding mother will be the deep cause of the death.' Bougard brings a good deal of clinical evidence in support of this contention, finally linking it with Orpheus' homosexuality which in the end will draw the anger of the women on to him. Orpheus becomes the first and foremost chaste Hero of antiquity, his story being 'an affective process which aims at regaining the integral beatitude of infancy . . . It has its origin in the dissociation of childhood, tenderness and guilt over adult eroticism' (Bougard, 1934, p. 356).

Jones (1931) alludes to the myth in *On the Nightmare*, suggesting that it is deeply concerned with issues of pathological mourning. In his view 'the story is an example of love being concerned with the reunion of parted lovers, even when parting has been brought about by death' (p. 100). He further concludes that behind the wish for reunion, there may be a sense of guilt on the part of the living. In line with this stress on the romantic quality of the manifest content of the legend, it could be argued that it served the purpose of concealing its latent and more distressing aspects.

Marie Bonaparte (1954) makes an interesting contribution in suggesting that Orpheus lost Eurydice because it is wrong to love incestuously. A patient's dream had led her to think of the myth and also of the taboos on looking, which are undoubtedly an important element in the story. The author's contention is that we lose what we love because we love it ill; an interesting observation which seems to rely more on intuition than objective clinical or anthropological findings.

Ekstein (1966) examines the myth from the point of view of a specific transference paradigm. The patient had made a number of homicidal and suicidal attempts but had improved when she became intensely interested in the film *Black Orpheus*. Ekstein is only concerned with the girl's identification with Eurydice within the context and framework of the therapy. He also examines the therapist's problems in extricating himself from being pushed into a rescuer's role by the patient's demand to be rescued from death and his own desire to rescue his patients.

V   AMBIVALENCE, REPARATIVE FAILURE AND THE OEDIPAL SITUATION

In this section I propose to enlarge upon the clinical presentations of a group of patients who are unusually young and promising subjects for psychoanalysis. They are often in their twenties and although intellectually well endowed, they are dissatisfied with their achievements and their inability to sustain relationships. Their basic personality is schizoid with a tendency to use splitting and projection as the main line of defence against a world which is often experienced as persecutory. In men sexual impotence, or its fear, is common. In women there is an inability to reach orgasm associated with indecision about marriage and maternity. In both sexes latent homosexuality can be shown after some years of analysis as being responsible for difficulties in personal relationships which are also much affected by excessive demands for attention and jealousy. This often leads to friends and lovers turning away from these patients, who seem to be in an almost permanent state of pining for lost love objects, feeling vindictive and angry. Some of them do get married quite early but it is not unusual for a partner to present mirror images of their problems.

In the early history of these patients there is evidence of traumas, mostly represented by the birth of a sibling, separation from parents, operations and hospitalizations. Severe periods of depressions are brought into the open as soon as the analysis gets under way, when difficulties will be experienced as a result of the patient's refusal to acknowledge any sense of guilt or any need to make reparations towards the damaged internal objects. The persistent depressions, the stagnation of the patient's creativity and work problems, inevitably lead to an interminable analysis. As a result of it, earlier and primitive elements of the patient's instinctual life and pathology will come under scrutiny, at times keeping at bay the examination of unresolved and disturbing aspects of the oedipal situation. There will, however, be clues in the transference and countertransference provided by a sudden relapse after good progress in the wake of one more disappointment in a relationship which is loaded with oedipal overtones.

Behind a façade of co-operation and keenness to be analysed, punctuality and protestation of good feelings and even affection for the analyst, there lies a deep lack of trust. The slightest inattention provokes accusations of indifference, neglect, etc. Periods of separation, always difficult from the start, continue to be badly tolerated with well concealed rage reactions in response to the perception of the analyst as a real object or to the coming into contact with other patients. As the analysand's ambivalence and jealousy within the oedipal situation come into focus, it becomes apparent that any anxiety about the analyst's health and welfare has little depth. Complete indifference is closer to the truth as is the patient's unwillingness to do anything helpful to the therapist, such as agreeing to a reasonable increase of the fees, a change of time, etc. Many patients are unwilling to pay appropriate fees only because they feel the money will not be used exclusively by the analysts; on the other hand they indulge in the fantasy of giving expensive presents in the knowledge that they are not permissible.

We owe it to Melanie Klein that nowadays we are constantly alerted to the importance of the processes of restitution and reparation in fostering mental health and the sublimatory capacity of the individual. In one early paper (1935), she suggests that every injury inflicted in fantasy by a child on his parents, particularly in their coitus which has become sadistic as a result of his own wishes, must be made good. But her most revealing statement is about the dread of harbouring dying or dead objects (especially the parents) inside one and that this is followed by an identification with objects in this condition (Klein, 1935, p. 265). In describing the manic defence, later in the same paper, Klein mentions that the reparative drive is acquired in the previous (depressive) position but now (in the manic defence) the reparation takes place 'in accordance with the phantastic character of the whole position which is nearly always of a quite unpractical and unrealizable nature . . . the objects in the manic defence were killed but since the subject was omnipotent, he supposed he could also immediately call them to life again . . . the resuscitation corresponds to the reparation made to the object' (p. 278).

Klein could have been describing Orpheus' predicament and, for that matter, that of my patient, Mr B, as well. It will also be apparent, though, that her comments are invaluable in conceptualizing the psychopathology of the patients I have outlined above. Klein's comment concerning the possibility that an excess of guilt leads to a reparative failure through a reluctance to admit to any guilt at all is an important contribution to the understanding of the deep resistance we encounter in the analyses of these patients. (Compare the case of Mr A.)

In keeping with Klein's description, those who are unable to make reparation because of unresolved oedipal problems seem to be capable of a love which is exceedingly greedy and destructive. The precocity and the capacity to feel intensely in early infancy was their undoing, further aggravated by the tendency to develop sadistic fantasies within the context of profound jealousy, hence the mistrust of the primary object. There is no doubt that real or imaginary abandonment or separation are acknowledged and experienced as the death of the object. My observations in analytic reconstructions lead me to think that the object is callously left to die by part of the self or alternatively is actively killed and revived, a process which is endlessly repeated. Some relief of guilt is achieved by exposure to the possibility of being rejected but analysis will invariably show that the rejections are brought about by indifferent or sadistic behaviour, in itself a source of erotic excitement.

VI   THE ORPHEUS MYTH AND
REPARATIVE FAILURE IN THE
OEDIPAL SITUATION

Psychoanalysts are familiar with the idea that a myth can throw light on clinical material or a work of art, and the reverse is also true. The reworking of a myth may suddenly illuminate one of its aspects which has escaped our notice but this can only be somewhat limited. As Malinowski has shown, 'It is easier to write down the story than to observe the diffuse, complex ways in which it enters into life, or to study its function by the observation of the vast social and cultural realities into which it enters. And this is the reason why we have so many texts and why we know so little about the very nature of the myth' (Malinowski, 1926, p. 39). This view, however, should not deter us from attempting to bring together what we have ascertained so far about the legend and the clinical material reported in this paper.

The general trend of the story as it has reached us over thousands of years suggests that the Hero turns around, in spite of Hades' injunction not to do so, to reassure himself that his wife is still there. His behaviour is capable of being accounted for on the grounds of (1) impatience; (2) greedy love; (3) ambivalence, due to jealousy which interferes with the conscious wish to bring Eurydice back to life; or (4) hate prevailing over love. As a result of his failure to restore life to his wife (the internalized damaged mother), Orpheus becomes a murderer who will later suffer punishment at the hands of the women (the Maenads standing for the revengeful internalized persecutory maternal image).

The ambiguity implicit in the Hero's behaviour did not escape my patients. The introduction of the story into their psychoanalysis indicated and underlined the fact that 'death' entered vividly into their fantasy life (cf. the appearance of mysterious figures referred to as 'Death' in some of the cited artistic works). In the case of both Mr A and Mr B and of other patients with similar psychopathology, the oedipal hostility is shifted from the father to the mother to a limit where they no longer know whether their problem is due to an excess or lack of love. One patient, for instance, remarked how in his case 'this situation leads to killing by love or loving to kill.' The story in itself is rich in oedipal overtones provided by the killing of the woman by the serpent symbolizing the sadistic intercourse and Aristaeus representing the threatening male sexuality of the oedipal father.[8]

But what is the role of Eurydice, the woman who died twice? We have seen how writers and artists have freely added their own fantasies to the basic story suggesting that she was at fault. Not only is she at times described as an untrustworthy and flighty female but also as seductive and as impatient as her husband. We cannot, on the other hand, fail to comment on the fact that the writers who have offered us a new script appear to be more than disillusioned with the female sex in general. Neither can we ignore the suggestion already put forward in antiquity that the ambivalence displayed by the Hero towards the woman is attributable to his homosexuality. How can we account, though, for the wide appeal of such a sad story? It is, of course, easy to see that Orpheus and his lyre are symbols of the capacity of music to replace words when we are confronted by unthinkable grief and a vast range of emotions. This fact did not escape eighteenth-century music lovers but it did not sufficiently impress Cocteau who was more concerned with narcissistic problems and creativity. In the last resort everything seems to point to ambivalence and reparative failure as the central feature of the legend. Within the oedipal situation its popularity could well be due to the fact that as Eurydice has already been killed 'by accident', there is little chance of feeling guilty when watching her second death. There is also considerable relief in observing someone else failing in the attempt to rescue a damaged love object and we can indeed enjoy the manic defence when it is offered to us, as we noted in some of the works that have been cited.

I doubt that psychoanalysts ever think of Orpheus' journey into Tartarus in the course of their daily work. Yet, it is almost inevitable that at times we become involved in a patient's desire to be rescued or that we are urged to be responsible for rescuing his or her damaged internal objects. The pleadings of a patient who is consciously or unconsciously identified with the Poet-Hero, be it that he caused the death of his wife-mother through excessive love or hate, are irresistible, especially when he appears to have no peace. It is no coincidence, perhaps, that a fellow poet, Dante, should have placed Orpheus in Limbo with 'many a soul of mighty worth, only so afflicted that they live desiring without hope' (*Inferno*, Canto IV).

NOTES

1   The story as told by the Italian, Ranieri da Calzabigi (Gluck, 1762), depicts Orpheus' despair and how he is approached by Cupid who wishes to console him by giving him the Gods' permission to descend into Hades. On the way back to the outer world and life, Eurydice, as soon as she appreciates that she is alive again, longs for her husband's embraces and cannot understand his refusal even to look at

her. She finally accuses him of infidelity and threatens to go back. Orpheus, no longer able to resist her entreaties, turns to look at her and loses her. Cupid once more comes to their rescue, restoring her life, singing: 'Never again dare doubt my power.' (Stage instructions indicate that Cupid is to act as a real *Deus ex machina*.) The opera was first produced at the court of the Emperor Francis of Lorraine in Vienna, on the occasion of his birthday. We can perhaps assume that the composer and his libretto writer did not wish to sadden such an occasion with a true rendering of the story. We must, however, underline the distortion which makes the woman's second death entirely her responsibility. It would seem that the Hero's alleged impatience and eagerness to repossess his lost bride made little sense to Calzabigi, considering that it was associated with the open disregard of the divine command not to look back. This, of course, does not entirely exonerate the writer from a well founded accusation of male chauvinism. In his defence we can only assume that he was aware of some old texts which did represent Eurydice as a less than cautious woman who was even alleged to have provoked the sexual assault by the shepherd Aristaeus.

It is relevant to note that the role of Orpheus was written for male castrato voice but it was not sung by a female contralto until 1859 when Berlioz revised the score. The ambiguity of a female singer taking the role of a male was no doubt of considerable significance to my patient, Mr A, who was so taken by the special version of the myth. As Eurydice sings, 'Jealousy tore my heart asunder, cruel mistrust in my bosom did reign', A felt absolved of any sense of guilt towards his unfaithful love objects.

2   *Black Orpheus*, a film directed by Marcel Camus, was first shown in 1958. Based on a Brazilian book, it combines an atmosphere of carnival with the tragic overtones of the myth. Orpheus, a black Brazilian bus conductor from a shanty town, sheds his uniform and takes his guitar, preparing himself for the festivities. Although he is already engaged to a local girl, he falls passionately in love with a stranger from a village, Eurydice, who is pursued by a mysterious figure (Death). After a night of love, whilst still dancing together in the street, Eurydice is forced to run away from 'Death'. It is night-time, and in the course of the flight, the woman reaches a tram terminal where all electric current has been turned off. Orpheus is there too and as he hears her screams, not being able to see her, he suddenly switches the current on. Eurydice who was hanging from an electric cable dies painfully and instantly. The film reaches its climax with Orpheus being killed by his enraged fiancée.

3   Orphism was a popular mystery religion in the early Christian era centred on a belief in redemption. It was a transformation of the older Dionysian religion which originated from Thrace and retained a great many orgiastic-mystic elements. The 'Descent into Hades', a manual which contains all the essential rites of Orphic

initiation, is based on the old myth of Orpheus descending into Hades to rescue Eurydice (Walker, 1983). However, the woman now becomes a much more ambiguous figure, in so far as she is regarded as having been one of Demeter's matriarchal Furies, who in Greek writings becomes a daughter of Zeus, whilst in some writings she is even identified with Persephone, the Death Goddess, often represented holding a serpent (cf. Hays, 1963). Around the Mediterranean area, Orphism and the Christian religion developed side by side for centuries until Orpheus was finally identified with Christ.

4   Pausanias, amongst others quoted by Graves (1960), gives a different account of how Orpheus died. According to him, his death was a revenge by Zeus for having divulged divine secrets. On careful reflection, it is even difficult to accept that Dionysus was angry with him, in so far as there is enough evidence to suggest that the Hero was the principal in Dionysian rites, in which case we can expect him to suffer the same fate as his God, who was also torn to pieces. (Proclus, commentary on Plato's *Politicus*, cited by Graves.)

5   Unravelling a myth is similar to the work of the picture restorer who is confronted by the presence of totally unexpected hidden layers. One element of surprise came from the discovery that Eurydice's death and her husband's failure to bring her back into the sunlight figure only in late myth. It is believed that this could have been mistakenly deduced from pictures showing the Hero's descent into Tartarus to plead successfully, it would seem, for special privileges for all ghosts initiated into the Orphic mysteries. There were also other paintings showing Dionysus descending into Tartarus in search of his mother, Semele. This is not all, as there seems to be a superimposition of attributes pertaining to the Moon Goddess, whose titles were Eurynome (Wide Ruler), and Eurybia, amongst many, including Eurydice (Wide Justice), described as the serpent, grasping ruler of the underworld. Male sacrifices were offered to her, their deaths being caused by viper's venom. Thus it was Eurydice's victims that died of snake bite, not she herself (Graves, pp. 111 ff.). Here we see the confluence of several stories and we can only speculate on the significance of the Heroine assuming the name and, perhaps indirectly, the attributes of a dangerous Goddess. It should be noted that Virgil was the first to mention a snake in relation to the sudden death of the Hero's wife (quoted by Bougard, 1934).

6   Jean Matter (1951) has written extensively about the narcissism as being central to Cocteau's films. Narcissus in love with himself can only be in love with death because to contemplate oneself is fatally linked with thoughts of death. The mirror leads to death by an inevitable incline. Matter concludes that Orphée (Narcisse) has a horror of the idea of reproducing himself in another being and is incapable of getting out of himself. It is understandable that the birth of a son could

inspire Orphée with nothing but hate (p. 250). In the film, the expected birth is symbolized by a woollen sock which the Hero kicks with rage. Unfortunately the analytical insight of this writer seems to fall short of the understanding of the complexities of feelings and impulses, envious and murderous at times, aroused in a child by the sight of a pregnant mother (cf. case of Mr B).

7   The young actress in Anouilh's play has many lovers and a heart of gold. She meets Orpheus and for the first time she experiences love. She runs away with him but later, in response to blackmailing pressures from a former lover, she leaves him. In the process of literally running away from an impossible situation, she meets her death in a car accident. 'Death' in the guise of Monsieur Henri, a young man who has followed the couple around from the beginning of the play, suggests to Orpheus that he could have her back. He readily agrees, although he has learnt of the woman's sinful life. The two lovers meet at night at a railway station but he is not to look at her until dawn. Orpheus, eaten up with jealousy, presses her to tell him the truth regarding her previous love life. He is not satisfied with her replies and he insists that only looking into her eyes would reveal to him whether she really loves him. She pleads with him to let her live but he turns around and loses her once more.

8   Aristaeus has a prominent role in *The Mask of Orpheus*, a three-act opera first produced in London in 1986. The composer, H. Birtwistle and the libretto writer, P. Zinovieff, have created a reworking of the story, brilliant in musical and visual effects. In the synopsis of the libretto we are told that the logic of the work is derived from what is guessed about Orphism, relying on 'the Aristotelian view that Orpheus did not exist as an individual but as a collective inheritance' (Birtwistle, 1986, p. 2). They follow his development in his transformation from a man into a God, whilst tracing the evolution of the birth of music to its destruction. The first act leads us into the wedding feast which is overshadowed by many bad omens. Soon after, Eurydice wanders into the fields to meet her friends, the Wood Nymphs, but she soon gets bored sitting by the river on her own. Aristaeus, the bee-keeper, sees her and falls in love and from there on they contrive to meet every day. They walk through the woods and the Nymphs watch in jealousy whilst Aristaeus enchants her with his talking about bees and the cultivation of grapes. One day he makes love to her but afterwards Eurydice becomes frightened, guilty and runs away, with Aristaeus following her to reassure her that no one will know of her deception. Suddenly she stumbles and as she falls, a rattlesnake comes out of the water and stings her. Unable to revive her, Aristaeus later tells Orpheus of Eurydice's death. The Wood Nymphs punish him by killing his bees and destroying his grapes. Orpheus is stunned and uncomprehending of the failure of his music to bring back his wife. During the funeral he retires to a cave where he falls asleep and dreams of his descent to Hades, but the dream soon turns into a nightmare. As the sun shines onto his eyes, he wakes to the realization that the figure of Eurydice he saw in the dream

is no longer following him and is slipping out of his grasp. What follows is a conglomeration of the different accounts of Orpheus' subsequent life and violent death as it has been handed down to us through several generations. In the 'Exodus' we find that Aristaeus was able to propitiate by sacrifices the Nymphs who allow him to return to the cultivation of his bees and grapes.

3 A RE-EVALUATION OF ACTING OUT IN RELATION TO WORKING THROUGH*

IT SEEMS LOGICAL that any discussion on acting out, in order to be meaningful, would have to be related to the concept of 'working through'. There are few aspects of our daily analytical work which are more challenging than acting out and more directly pointing to the necessity and arduousness of working through the patient's resistances, as Freud (1914) has warned us. The problem is not only that the tendency to act out needs constant attention by the analyst but also that disturbing episodes of acting out may well occur in the course of working through anxieties and conflicts under apparently quite satisfactory circumstances. I am referring to those optimal conditions where analyst and patient work well together and, of course, where the analyst has in no way contributed to force the patient to act out as a result of his own incompetence or because of the persistence of unresolved conflicts in himself. However, it would be fair to say that there are many instances when the analyst may unwittingly play a part. The experienced analyst is not only disappointed at seeing years of insightful working through wasted but may even come to the conclusion that the patient's resistances are intractable to the point of abandoning analysis.

The trainee analyst's difficulties are even more complex. The patient with acting out propensities at the onset of treatment makes him feel out of his depth. He may go so far as not to regard some aspects of the patient's behaviour as acting out, since he feels this might be unfair to the patient and, in any case, lacks the skill to see through the patient's rationalizations. Acting out as it occurs in a transference setting inevitably creates counter-transference reactions. This fact has been noted and taught to students of

* This paper was first published in 1966 in the *International Journal of Psycho-Analysis* 47: 274–82.

psychoanalysis for a number of years. In spite of this, in the course of discussions with colleagues, seminars, and in scientific writings, it is possible to see that, for many, acting out is, more than anything else, a threat to the order of things. There are exceptions. Khan (1964a) writes, 'Perhaps in no other area of analytic research has our attitude to the patient undergone such dynamic re-orientation as in the toleration of acting out . . . In the treatment of borderline cases with a schizoid repressive ego structure acting out is in some ways our chief clinical ally' (p. 67).

James (1964), writing on the problems of acting out and its counter-transference in the treatment of pre-adolescents, states: 'These factors have a positive aspect provided both acting out and its management are taken as unconscious communication and not only as the resistance to abstinent technique which they also are' (p. 499).

A CRITICAL REVIEW OF THE LITERATURE ON ACTING OUT

In reviewing the literature, the reader soon becomes aware that analysts deal with acting out in a personal and individual way, as one might expect, but also in accordance with their theoretical assumptions, and of these there are many.

In all theoretical formulations Freud's clear and concise opinion expressed in his (1914) paper on technique still occupies a central place. There he singles out those cases where 'we may say that the patient does not *remember* anything of what he has forgotten and repressed but *acts* it out. He reproduces it not as a memory but as an action. He *repeats* it without, of course, knowing that he is repeating it' (p. 150, author's italics). Later on he adds, 'and he repeats it under conditions of resistance'. Freud's affective response to this momentous discovery was to urge the patient to remember, but it is worth noting that his original observation of the phenomenon was made in relation to his patient, Dora, breaking off treatment prematurely in 1905.

Glover's (1926) contribution is notable because whilst denying the existence of a simple fixation point, he postulated a specific developmental disturbance in the ego. Many years later, Fenichel (1945b), with admirable clarity, wrote, 'This is an acting which unconsciously relieves inner tension and brings partial discharge to ward off impulses, no matter whether these impulses express directly instinctual demands or are reactions to original instinctual demands, that is to say, guilt' (p. 197).

But we had to wait until 1950 for the outstanding contribution by

Greenacre on 'General problems of acting out'. In that paper she drew our attention to the belief in the magic of action and a distortion in the relation of action to speech and verbalized thought which is often present in patients who tend to act out. But what really stands out, in my opinion, is the terse statement, 'Acting out is a form of remembering' (p. 456), especially if it is taken in conjunction with her observations concerning the patient's difficulty in verbalizing. Quite understandably many writers have brought confirmation of Greenacre's views. Since then much has been added to our knowledge of the personality, character, and ego structure of patients who repeatedly act out in the course of analysis irrespective of the analyst's skill and understanding. We know that these patients are usually intolerant individuals who seem quite unable to wait – we know that some have suffered trauma in early infancy – that the disturbance has often occurred in the second year, and that oral drives are almost invariably present (Kanzer, 1957; Khan, 1962; Rexford, 1963). It is indeed quite startling to come across a statement by H. Deutsch made in the course of a discussion on acting out (1963) when she said, 'I do not think that vicissitudes of the oral stage are always the reason for increased tendencies to act out – I also doubt that the primitive intolerance to frustration is always the culprit responsible for acting out' (p. 237). To that I would add that, perhaps, faulty verbalization and faulty remembering are not always responsible for acting out.

In this respect I should mention the few papers where a wider meaning was attributed to the faulty remembering: as it occurs in the case described by Silverberg (1955) where the acting out, besides implying memory, was a persistent effort to rectify the helplessness of the original traumatic experience; and in Khan's 'silent patient' (1963a) whose silence was a mode of acting out and served the function of recollecting, integrating and working through the pathogenic early relationship to the mother. Winnicott (1949) has also reported on a case where acting out appeared to have a special function. He writes: 'In acting out, the patient informed herself of the bit of psychic reality which was difficult to get at, at the moment, but of which the patient so acutely needed to become aware' (p. 249).

I do not wish it to be thought that I underestimate or that I ignore the importance that possible faults in the verbalization and manner of recalling may be present in some cases. All analysts are familiar with the patient who re-experiences each traumatic event of his past life first of all through some dramatic acting out, inside and outside the consulting room. It is also true that these patients have severe difficulties which can be traced back quite early in the analysis to disturbances of the pre-verbal phase of development.

In such a case the impulse to act out is usually violent and excessive.

Is it not possible, though, that this situation, especially as described by Greenacre, applies only to certain groups of individuals with a schizoid personality and a severe tendency towards splitting processes, denial and unreality feelings, plus the history of trauma in infancy? But my main concern here is to bring to attention the possible consequences of placing too much reliance on limited psychological concepts to understand a multiformity of situations. Furthermore, it is not surprising to find that the inexperienced analyst will respond with feelings of irritation and exasperation towards the patient who acts out, especially if he, the analyst, believes that everything would be all right if only the patient would remember and talk instead of acting. A similar situation would result from any approach which lays too much stress on the indeed obvious aggressive and destructive aspects of much acting out. This seems to detract considerably from the many valuable views put forward by the Kleinian school on this subject, where the emphasis is definitely on the hostility. Melanie Klein, in writing about 'The origins of transference' (1952), states,

> The patient turns away from the analyst as he attempted to turn away from his primal objects. He tries to split the relation to him, keeping him either as a good or as a bad figure. He deflects some of the feelings and attitudes experienced towards the analyst onto other people in his current life, and this is part of acting out. (p. 55)

All analysts appreciate the fact that much emotional material leaks out of the transference situation in this way but there is still a good deal to be accounted for. Years later, Klein (1957) added the view that 'acting out, in so far as it is used to avoid integration, becomes a defence against anxieties aroused by accepting the envious part of the self' (p. 219). Klein's hypothesis is taken further to its logical conclusion by Rosenfeld who writes (1964),

> It depends on the extent of the hostility with which the patient turned away from his very earliest object, namely the mother's breast, whether the patient is capable of co-operating in the analysis with only partial acting out or whether he is constantly driven to act out excessively . . . If there has been little hostility in the patient's turning away from the breast, we shall encounter in the analysis only partial acting out, pro-

vided that the transference is fully understood and interpreted . . .
(p. 203)

Rosenfeld goes on to say: 'On the other hand, the patient's need of excessive
acting out is in my opinion always related to an excessively aggressive
turning away from the earliest object' (p. 203). Those analysts who believe
in the almost universal component of oral drives in acting out would
recognize the validity of these remarks. Rosenfeld's observations are without doubt correct with regard to certain episodes of acting out in psychotic
patients. On the other hand, the theoretical implication that all acting out as
it occurs in the analysis of neurotics has deep unconscious roots, as Klein
and Rosenfeld describe, is questionable and restrictive.

No review of the literature would be complete without reference to the
fact that direct intervention or prohibition, as originally recommended by
Freud, is generally speaking no longer considered advisable and yet it is
possible to come across the following sentence as late as 1962: 'Acting out
within the therapeutic situation requires constant vigilance and scrutiny as
to the extent it can and should be permitted to take its course . . . acting out
in the service of resistance has to be interpreted or otherwise rendered
innocuous' (Blos 1962, p. 157).

The first suggestion, that interpretation should be used, requires no
comment; but the second one, in my opinion, has no place or use in any
form of psychological treatment, unless the patient is a danger to himself or
others. Greenacre (1963) is also critical of analysts who say that patients
who act out must be stopped somehow. But her position is less clear when
in the next paragraph she states:

There are patients with a habitual repetition of specifically patterned
acting out, who continue with such episodes even after they have gained
some insight into the conflict and become aware of the peculiar excitement which often initiates such a burst of acting out . . . [The patterns
express] hostility of a deeply ambivalent nature. It is necessary to indicate to the analysand that the analysis cannot possibly continue as long as
this kind of indulgence is accepted by the patient. In this way the
expression of hostility can be forced into the analysis. (p. 231)

In my experience the type of situation described by Greenacre is one in
which the patient cannot use the insight he has acquired. Direct interven-

tion could well make analysis impossible or may limit further understanding.

My aim in this paper is to explore the possibility that acting out, especially where it occurs in the course of repeated working through, has special functions for patient and therapist which can be used to further the analytical process.

ACTING OUT AND ANTI-SOCIAL BEHAVIOUR

Generally, psychoanalysts appear to recognize two forms of acting out. The first one occurs as part of a chronic personality disorder which is seldom accepted for psychoanalytical treatment. The second form is usually considered to be a manifestation of the patient's resistance. But are we justified in regarding all cases of acting out as resistance? I suggest that we immediately run into difficulties where such episodes occur well within the transference relationship. Take the case of the analysand, Mr A who, in an early phase of his analysis, calls at the consulting room at the usual time, overlooking the fact that it is a national holiday. What is the motivation and where is the resistance? Is the patient acting out his impulses in relation to the primal scene and should one interpret the anti-social aspect of the wish to interrupt the analyst's holiday (i.e. intercourse)? Or is he remembering his deep anxiety in relation to separation in infancy (no doubt accompanied by much hostility) and is he not making a simple statement that he cannot bear the thought and feeling of not having direct access to the analyst at all times? I suggest there is little evidence of resistance here; but I shall return to this later.

The difficulty in defining when acting out is a part of resistance is all the more clear if we accept the inevitable fact that the term is currently and widely used to refer to events which occur outside the pure analytical situation.

My observations are based on material from analytical cases but also non-analytical ones, largely derived from work with delinquents, as it is my belief that much can be learnt from widening our experience. The connection between delinquency and acting out is well known and has been widely investigated, much information being obtained from it (Winnicott, 1956).

For some years I have been struck by the similarity of the behaviour and symptomatology occurring in cases of social maladjustment and analysands who act out. It has occurred to me that the analyst's attitude is sometimes not unlike that of the family where one of the members is showing signs of anti-social behaviour. They respond by being either over-indulgent, or punishing, or both. We also know that when the environment does not understand the inner significance of anti-social behaviour, such behaviour is likely to become aggravated. This applies, too, when the analyst ceases to be in communication with his patient. In both instances, one aspect of the acting out is clearly a signal that help is required. In extreme cases the environment may finally react with rejection or indeed with a tremendous urge to 'do something about it' although no one knows quite what is really wanted. This is not unlike the situation which confronts the analyst. He is then strongly tempted to abandon interpretive technique or to stick to his own favoured theoretical formulations. However, the comparison can be taken a little further.

In working with delinquents and patients who display anti-social tendencies, I have come to understand that acting out incidents, often presenting as the main symptomatology, fall within three fairly well defined groups. Eventually this very schematic classification seemed to me useful in distinguishing between the different types of acting out as they occur in analysis. In presenting material and in our daily clinical work, the grouping of observed phenomena helps one to bear in mind the fact that there may be several aspects to one problem.

In the first group, acting out is an expression of the individual's fantasy life and appears to be personal (i.e. it has a mark of originality) and at first its motivation is unconscious. It often defies understanding: for instance, as in cases of housebreaking, arson, etc., or in the case of an eighteen-year-old boy who used to roam the streets at night cutting telephone cords in public call boxes. He felt very guilty about his nightly activities and was greatly relieved when he got himself arrested for some other offence.

The equivalent situation in the analytical patient occurs when he tends to act out repeatedly in a variety of media and it is only with great difficulty that on each occasion analysis succeeds in disclosing a new motivation. It is in the course of full psychoanalytical exploration that one realizes that in this group part-objects reign supreme, presenting us with all the technical difficulties due to their interchangeability and the ruthlessness which belongs to the earlier phases of development. In consequence we shall also encounter the most primitive fantasies and the most primitive mental processes such as projective identifications, and so on. An example of this is to be found in the case of a young man, a brilliant scholar, who once wrote an obscure paper which caused quite a stir. Exhaustive analytical work showed that he literally intended to confuse his audience as a means of getting rid of his own confusion. When the same thing happened again some time later, the motivation was quite different as his obscurity now was a wish not to be understood and it was linked with fantasy which had been reactivated by the transference.

In the second group, it is much more clear both to the person who acts out and the observer that the activity is a means of relieving an unbearable tension but is mainly directed at finding a fresh solution to inner conflicts and anxiety. Again it often occurs on a background of splitting processes, denial, and poor sense of reality, but what is striking is that after a while it is more and more difficult to speak of unconscious motivation as one acting out incident follows upon another. Many sexual offenders fall within this category and also the very common cases of compulsive taking and driving away. The latter may appear to be quite trivial on the surface but it is with the greatest ease and without deep exploration that one uncovers the oedipal origins of this behaviour disorder. Characteristically our analytical patients engage in promiscuous relationships, have accidents, and respond with rage whenever they meet up with situations likely to arouse their envy, jealousy, or rivalry. In this group it is the Oedipus complex which dominates the scene. With these patients we are hard put not to become involved in their attempts to externalize their internal problems, but their relatives, friends and work associates may find it quite impossible not to join in. Another characteristic of this group is that it may take a very long time before a two-person transference relationship develops in a feeling way. When this has been achieved, it is quite predictable that an outbreak of acting out will follow; this seems to be particularly common in the treatment of homosexuality.

Lastly, there is a type of acting out which is seen in almost identical form in psychiatric and analytical practice. Its essential quality is that it is a form of communication, concise, secretive, elusive if the person at the receiving end is not in tune. In my experience, these people are particularly likely to bring this crude mode of communication into the first psychiatric interview. It is essentially part of testing out processes, often a harmless and safe expression of greed. At times it has all the qualities of sexual seductiveness and it is most difficult for the therapist to deal with it unless he employs his own personal understanding in terms of transference. Similarly the patient in analysis may reveal himself from the very beginning of treatment through a whole series of minor acts which all have an anti-social flavour. At the very first interview he may fail to disclose his financial position or will soon after display a tendency to steal time at the end of the session; sessions may be cancelled, bills are forgotten, etc. In my opinion this kind of statement from the patient should be welcomed as it gives the analyst the opportunity of showing to him quite early in the treatment that he is trying to solve his problems by means of anti-social acts and that there may be feelings where he believes there are none. I do not believe there is anything deeply unconscious about these activities, as can be shown by the facility with which they are dealt with, often in the course of a single interview; if there are any unconscious factors these will inevitably reappear in later stages of the analysis and will probably be the central focus of the working through processes.

That early acting out becomes a useful pointer of what is to come was well brought out in the case of Mr B, a twenty-seven-year-old man who, shortly after entering analysis, began to act out in a way which placed him in a position of being deprived in relation to the analyst through missing some sessions. Very quickly, and without much help from the analyst, the series of incidents were related to the violently traumatic experience of being separated from his parents from the age of eighteen months onwards for periods of up to twelve months. This patient's acting out was his way of giving me his personal history. The incidents were helpful in disclosing the failure of repression in his early life and there were times when I felt he was quite conscious of what he was doing. However, it was apparent that from the outset of his analysis he was engaged in a determined effort to alter his previous experiences. It was also useful in so far as it indicated where the lines of main resistance would develop in later stages of the analysis.

Such was also the turn of events in the case already described of Mr A, who called during a holiday, where for years all feelings in relation to analytical 'breaks' were radically dealt with by splitting, denial, reversal, etc., and where the only evidence of 'feeling' was to be seen in the original incident.

ACTING OUT IN RELATION TO WORKING THROUGH

I shall not attempt to re-define working through and its functions according to our modern views but will assume that it is generally accepted that affective insight belongs to it and that it usually involves a re-awakening of anxieties and guilt. Problems of undoing, reparation and integration of guilt are essential components of the 'working through' process. In consequence, we should not be too surprised if, in an attempt to reject the impact of feeling such guilt, the analysand may act out. In so far as it is also his attempt to find once more his own solution outside the analytical relationship and often in defiance of such insight as he may have acquired, it is a resistance but it would appear to be a very special kind of resistance. Whilst direct communication at the verbal level is interrupted, the analyst's and the patient's attention has been mobilized by the outbreak of acting out. What is outstanding is the expression of the patient's wish to communicate in a way other than verbal – and there are many occasions when all the analyst can do is to acknowledge the fact that such a situation is in existence. But, in my opinion, all this does not necessarily suggest a disturbance at a pre-verbal stage of development. Even when this can be postulated on account of the nature of the illness, it does not follow that the patient may not act out for other reasons. A young married woman, once an asthmatic, broke down during her analyst's vacation and was seen as an emergency. The crisis was ushered in by a sudden outburst of temper in the course of which she broke some china. She later explained that after the analyst had left she had felt better than expected. She was grateful but soon discovered for the first time that she 'really' missed her analyst, became angry at the thought of her dependency on someone who was absent and she felt she might go mad. She tried to get her husband to understand how she felt but he insisted there was nothing to worry about. She then thought of acting as if she were mad, telling herself, 'Perhaps that would make him understand.' As a result of the previous analytical work, this woman had good insight into the nature of the deep anxieties released by separation from her analyst but could make no use of it. The harmless 'hysterical' behaviour was only a minor part of her cry for help which had to be answered in her own terms. In fact she rejected three appointments with the 'stand-in' analyst but accepted the fourth which she assumed would be in the course of his lunch hour. This case is of particular interest as the acting out was meant to have a different meaning for each person involved in this woman's life. Besides a desire to tell her husband of her predicament and need for help, she was warning her analyst that she was not ready to be left on her own. Also the 'stand-in' analyst had to prove that he was a worthy substitute for her lost analyst.

In this respect the patient's behaviour is similar to that of the individual who turns to delinquency or anti-social acts, as Winnicott (1956) would say, in hope. In writing about the anti-social child, Winnicott says, 'The child is looking for something somewhere and, failing to find it, seeks it elsewhere, when hopeful . . . the child is seeking that amount of environmental stability which will stand the strain resulting from impulsive behaviour' (p. 310).

Such remarks would be quite appropriate to many episodes of acting out occurring in the course of psychoanalytical treatment when adequate working through of problems of love, hate, greed, etc., have caused a fresh outbreak of conflicts and guilt, as well as a search for punishment unrelated to the original situation which has aroused it. Like the true delinquent who believes that he succeeds in feeling no guilt while satisfying urgent internal needs, the analysand may also believe that acting out outside the transference relationship will have a similar result – all this, of course, at the cost of discarding once coveted interpretations. On the other hand, analysts are apt to forget that interpretations are meagre satisfactions to our patients who long for action from them. Such longing, as we all know, is the last to die out and at the moment of achieving insight, which may well mean giving up such desire once and for all, the patient will hope for one last try even if it means involving him in hostility and destructiveness. We should also remember that, for many patients, the environment has often lent itself in a variety of ways to such a possibility. As analysts we are all familiar with the turning of loving feelings into hostility; an angry analyst is preferable to an indifferent one and patients soon learn to detect the analyst's disapproval of certain activities which at first sight suggest failure of the analytical process. In consequence, I would go as far as suggesting that some acting out, or the occurrence of minor delinquent activity so to speak, can be expected in the course of analysis. The complete absence of any such incidents should arouse the analyst's suspicion in two respects. Either the patient is not reporting fully to the analyst or else affective insight is not being achieved. The third possibility, that the patient is not aware of his acting out, and, therefore, does not report it, does not apply to the type of acting out I am discussing, which occurs in later phases of the analysis and almost invariably, in my experience, at a conscious level. Characteristically, many patients will say, 'I can see myself doing it', and in saying this they do not refer only to the conscious manifestations of the acting out.

Presumably the lack of true unconscious motivation and the anti-social aspects of the analysand's behaviour add to the countertransference reaction and to the occurrence of direct intervention by the analyst. I am well aware that we are often confronted with serious problems of responsibility in relation to the patient and society. For instance, in the case of Mr C, a thirty-four-year-old man, each moment of affective insight in his treatment was for a very long time punctuated by a motor car accident. A physical illness in childhood had left him with a disability for which he had finally compensated by taking up competitive car racing. After a serious accident he had given this up but to stop driving altogether would have meant to feel once more helpless and castrated. Luckily his accidents were, to some extent, 'well staged' and never involved other people. Both analyst and patient were aware that he was repeating and remembering a past experience, specially the feeling of lying ill and helpless. The anti-social aspect of this behaviour was also only too clear to them but was almost secondary in importance to the omnipotent fantasy of living through danger, which had to remain at the centre of the interpretative analytical work. It is of some interest that after eighteen months' accident-free analytical work this patient dreamt he was in a car accident and he freely expressed his dislike of this new development, adding that he was much more frightened of having to tackle the Pandora box of his unconscious in his sleep than tackling some real driving hazards. Again we see that acting out for this man affords him the means of escaping from the inner world where there are memories and fantasies of all kinds into a world of reality which he thought he could control.

This last example is to be seen as an indication that I agree with those workers who have noted that patients who tend to act out believe in the magic of action. In my experience, omnipotent fantasies are practically always a component of this syndrome. We may also remind ourselves that omnipotence is felt by many to be a central part of the psychopathology of the delinquent. In analysis it often becomes a source of collusion between analyst and patient. It is also likely to mobilize and reactivate in the analyst a need for therapeutic omnipotence. A clash may follow and perhaps it is in these instances that prohibitions are issued or else the same interpretation is offered again and again. To borrow from Greenacre's (1956) strong language, 'In the most degraded form these repeated interpretations appear much like the slogan of an individual propagandist' (p. 441). The analysand, of course, may contribute greatly in fostering feelings of omnipotence by attributing omnipotent powers to the analyst. However, it is not uncommon for him at times to act out, again quite consciously, in order to test out the omnipotence of the interpretations which he has received, only to prove – or shall we say, to discover – their uselessness. An alternative situation is that both analyst and patient can only stand by and watch things happen in a state of helplessness and impotence.

Undoubtedly the most serious technical problems are encountered in those cases where the belief in omnipotence at the service of denying impotence is fed by the feeling of being in control of the environment and being capable of provoking pre-set reactions in people. Acting out for these patients is the oxygen of their psychic life. It would also be true to say that in the majority of cases it is clearly a transference leakage onto the outside world. One of its redeeming features is that, in the later stages of analysis, it is brought back well within the transference relationship. This situation is an ideal one, even if somewhat uncomfortable at times, from the point of view of the analyst who will then be able to make full use of it. However, this view is not shared by a certain group of patients who retain the capacity for the somatic discharge of affective experiences. When the avenue of acting out outside the analytical situation is no longer open to them they are faced with the inescapable implication of the lack of such an outlet and may now find a fresh solution in developing a psychosomatic illness.

This situation is all the more apparent in the course of regressive phases in the treatment of severe neuroses where affective insight is always fraught with danger. Mr D, who first came to treatment with a desire to rid himself of active homosexual tendencies, had gone through such a phase. In the transference he had at last experienced real feelings of love for his analyst and for the first time in many years, had felt really better. On the day following the session when this material had been worked through, he came in remarking that after feeling so much better he was now feeling very ill again on account of a flare-up of a respiratory condition. He rejected interpretations which attempted to link up this session with the previous one and his feelings in relation to his analyst. Instead he said that he was uncertain about his desire to discuss his illness or something else which was preoccupying him. This concerned a woman acquaintance whose near-psychotic sexual behaviour was causing embarrassment to many people and he himself had found it necessary to behave in a rejecting manner towards her. It was possible then to show this patient how he was identified with this sexual woman and, in so far as he no longer found it satisfying to act out his homosexual impulses outside the analytical situation, he now felt tempted to bring them into the open in relation to the analyst. His illness was to him a more suitable alternative as well as an expression of his depression related to expected rejection. The early oral aspects of his physical symptoms were clear to both analyst and patient as they had been dealt with in his analysis over a matter of years, but it did not seem to be as important as showing the patient how he was dealing with his internal conflict.

This case was similar to the one described by Morrison (1963) in which the patient, instead of acting a love fantasy towards the analyst, was pushed back into a state of depression and reacted with a respiratory illness of some severity. Morrison suggests that recurrent respiratory, skin, and other infection can be associated with poor vascular supply to the skin and mucous membranes, due to mood changes or depression. She stresses the fact that there are symptoms which express a mood or emotional state and are probably mediated through the autonomic nervous system and related to the endocrines.

The mechanisms involved here are complex. One useful view is that if the organism should meet a stimulus beyond its power to master, regression to an earlier stage of development will occur, but the total organism does not regress – only parts of it, and then only in various degrees (Margolin, 1954). But in such instances, when the psychosomatic illness displaces an impulse to act out, it also underlines the self-punishing aspect of acting out as such.

A review of the numerous occurrences of psychosomatic illness in the course of prolonged analysis has led me to the conclusion that to act out may well appear to the patient as a life-saving measure. From a technical point of view it would seem that there is every indication for tolerating acting out in the course of analysis and for allowing for its gradual decrease. The occurrence of psychosomatic illness in its place should cause no undue alarm as long as the link with the missed acting out is made at the time. Tolerance of course should not be equated with permissiveness and in my experience so long as the transference is carefully interpreted it will in no way give support to the patient's fight against insight, even when it becomes a central feature of the analytical relationship, as Greenacre has indicated. There is of course little doubt that when the process of working through is impeded or arrested by the patient's acting out behaviour this is evidence of a resistance, but in my opinion the latter is no longer directed against the recovery of a memory. Those cases which I have been able to observe over a long period have led me to believe that the apparent loss of insight or the refusal to behave in harmony with it is more in the nature of an inability to use it. The relationship to the analyst becomes particularly meaningful at this juncture as the patient appears to regard him as the keeper or the carrier of his (the patient's) insight. It is indeed deeply reassuring to him to be able to return to the safety of the analytical relationship after some destructive behaviour activity to find evidence that none of the past work or understanding has really been lost. His insight is still there, carefully safeguarded by the analyst's sanity and neutrality, an important fact even if it originates from excessive idealization and splitting processes.

But what is insight? Perhaps it may well be that we do not pay sufficient attention to the possibility that insight may have different meanings for each one of our patients (Silverberg, 1955). The case material presented in this paper supports this contention as well as indicating that there can be no one single explanation of acting out. In the last resort the basic function of working through should be to gain insight about insight. On the other hand, the nature of the problem of inducing the patient to give up his acting out tendencies may also be predominantly one of integration. Rycroft's observations may be relevant here. In his paper, 'Beyond the reality principle' (1962), he put forward the suggestion that, 'The aim of psycho-analytic treatment is not primarily to make the unconscious conscious, nor to widen or strengthen the ego, but to re-establish the connexion between dissociated psychic functions' (p. 393).

If we recognize this we may perhaps feel less disappointed if we see that our interpretations, no matter how careful and correct, may sometimes fall to the ground. In my view acting out can be turned into a useful therapeutic guide in so far as it indicates the level of affective insight achieved by the patient as well as the state of the transference and countertransference.

4 THE ASSESSMENT OF ANALYSABILITY
A Major Hazard in Selection for Psychoanalysis*

THIS PAPER is based on observations derived from my work as an evaluator of applicants for psychoanalytic training and as a consultant with the responsibility of selecting patients for psychoanalysis to be treated either privately or by students in training. Selection under such different conditions and for such a variety of purposes is made more difficult by the lack of well-defined criteria of indications and contra-indications for psychoanalysis. In the course of a week's work a psychoanalytical consultant may be called upon to evaluate the chances of breakdown, severe enough to require hospitalization, in a patient who has been recommended for psychoanalysis. Such event, if foreseeable, is no bar in the case of private treatment, but it would certainly be a contra-indication for a supervised analysis, although the reasons for depriving a student of the opportunity to gain experience in a special aspect of his future work are not altogether clear. More understandably in the case of an applicant for training the expectation of a psychotic breakdown inevitably leads to rejection. In these examples, rationalization plays a part in decision-making. But the situation becomes rather confusing when we consider specific symptoms such as the sexual perversions. Although most psychoanalysts do not hesitate to undertake their treatment in their private practices, sexual perversions are generally regarded as being unsuitable for supervised analyses, whilst they are the basis for automatic disqualification in the case of applicants for training in some countries at least. This wide range of outlook in relation to a symptom or the possible course of an analysis can only be accounted for by

* This paper was first published in 1972 in the *International Journal of Psycho-Analysis* 53: 352–61.

the variability of our assessing capacity and predicting ability, together with the possible over- or under-estimation of analytical skills. This is a puzzling state of affairs, considering that we are dealing with a systematic form of psychotherapy, which has stood the test of time in spite of its limitations and the numerous attempts to modify and distort it by its admirers and imitators, to say nothing of the sustained attacks of its denigrators.

In this paper an attempt is made to examine the various issues arising from the tridimensional perspective of selection, which has just been outlined. The situation is not made easier by the existence of traditionally held beliefs, personal attitudes, or bias. It is suggested here that this state of affairs could be responsible for the communication of confusion and uncertainty as well as over-optimism or excessive pessimism not only to those who are still in training but also to colleagues in other fields, who turn to us for advice and guidance.

In the early days of his career, the aspirant analyst is little concerned with the suitability of his patients for psychoanalysis. As a candidate, and perhaps even as a junior analyst, he relies on his seniors to select patients for him. This passive acceptance is not entirely accounted for by the real need to build up a private practice, or excessive deference to senior members of the profession. It is more likely to be related to the uncritical and enthusiastic belief of the inexperienced that so long as a patient is intelligent and not psychotic he is likely to be suitable for psychoanalytical treatment. In any case, until recently, the London curriculum did not include any lectures or seminars on the subject of indications and contra-indications for psychoanalysis, in itself a significant fact. It was also not unusual for an analysis to begin after the briefest interview, at which only the practical arrangements were discussed. Freud stated his views on the subject clearly: 'I have made it my habit to take the patient on, at first, provisionally, for a period of one or two weeks . . . the most lengthy discussions and questioning in ordinary consultations would offer no substitute' (1913a, p. 123).

Since then the approach to selection has changed very considerably, as shown by the complex arrangements currently in force at the London Clinic of Psycho-Analysis, where the assessment of suitability for treatment is carried out through several stages, leading up to depth interviews by consultants, often followed by extensive discussions in a conference setting. There are those who are scornful of these determined attempts to assess patients thoroughly prior to analysis. They are equally sceptical or doubtful about the extensive and cumbersome selection procedures adopted by training committees in response to demands for better standards of practice.

Those who have the interests of psychoanalysis at heart and who believe in its therapeutic potential will pay little attention to these criticisms as they are often linked with warnings that psychoanalysis is at the crossroads. Such being the case, there would seem to be all the more reason for devoting a great deal of energy and resources to the establishment of appropriate criteria for the application of a valuable method of treatment which is now being challenged from several quarters. Claims of rapid and painless cures offered by organic psychiatrists and psychotherapists, often accompanied by ludicrous promises of instant analysis and breakthroughs, will fail to impress the psychoanalyst, but it is neither possible nor advisable to ignore the remarkable changes and evolution which have taken place in the treatment of the mentally ill. Yet in psychoanalytical circles there is a tendency to ignore the fact that in certain appropriate cases mental suffering can be alleviated and psychotherapy facilitated by a large variety of means, not always available twenty or possibly ten years ago. Even if we paid no attention to the competition coming from esoteric cults and other approaches such as touch therapy, hypnosis, sensitivity training, existentialism, etc., it is the duty of the modern psychoanalytic consultant to make positive recommendations for individual psychotherapy, group or community therapy and for active resocialization when indicated rather than thinking of such therapeutic interventions as *faute de mieux*, i.e. once psychoanalysis has been ruled out. On the other hand, we have only ourselves to blame if our medical colleagues have come to regard our specialization as an end of the road arrangement, when everything else has failed. Leaving such considerations aside, how many analysts can deny that now and again they have doubts about the suitability of a patient for analysis after some months or even years of treatment? In this context it is interesting to note that when we have become convinced that there has been an error of judgement at the time of the original assessment interview, it is only rarely that we can say that the patient in question is totally unsuitable for treatment by psychoanalytical methods. However, it is not unusual to find that a careful appraisal of failures and of the cases which have shown poor response to treatment would reveal only one common denominator: a symptom or a life situation which has proved unanalysable.

But suitable for analysis is not synonymous with analysable. It is suggested here that the interchangeable use of the two adjectives has added to our confusion in establishing adequate criteria for indications and contraindications for psychoanalysis, when important aspects of the theory, technique and philosophy of the analytical process itself must be taken into consideration. As it is impossible to cover adequately the subject of selection in a single paper, I have chosen to discuss the problems and difficulty of assessing analysability in relation to those factors which, in my opinion, have contributed greatly to the clouding of the issues involved. The factors to be discussed under separate headings are: (1) the widening scope of psychoanalysis; (2) assessment of suitability on the basis of diagnosis; (3) assessment of suitability on the basis of presenting symptoms; (4) the overestimation and neglect of the diagnostic interview; (5) our divergent views on analysability; (6) the role of the evaluator.

THE WIDENING SCOPE OF PSYCHOANALYSIS

In his paper 'On psychotherapy' Freud (1905b) wrote on the 'Conditions under which the method is indicated or contra-indicated'. He dealt with the subject quite briefly, stating that

> One should look beyond the patient's illness and form an estimate of his whole personality; those patients who do not possess a reasonable degree of education and a fairly reliable character should be refused. It must not be forgotten that there are healthy people as well as unhealthy ones in life, who are good for nothing and that there is a temptation to ascribe to their illness everything that incapacitates them if they show any sign of neurosis. (1905b, p. 263)

He makes it clear that the method must be reserved for the neuroses and there is a mention of the unsuitability of 'those who are not driven to seek treatment by their own suffering' (p. 263). When Freud takes up this topic again in discussing technique he has little to add (Freud, 1913a).

The period marked by the limited indications for psychoanalysis did not last very long, and the symposium on the evaluation of therapeutic results (Greenacre, 1948) seems to crystallize the emerging state of confusion which existed in the minds of analysts. In reply to an inquiry from Oberndorf, several analysts gave answers which showed not the slightest degree of agreement. There were reports of cases who had not responded to treatment in spite of expectation, whilst other reports now pointed to the possibility of using the method for cases where, hitherto, it had not been considered to be legitimate to do so, i.e. schizophrenic and manic-depressive psychosis, psychopathic personality, organic psychosis and a large number of cases which had been misdiagnosed. A few years later Scott

(1951) writes that many more could benefit from psychoanalysis than expected, and he indicates that it was possible to judge at the initial interview the degree of the original disturbance of development which was of greater significance than the seeming severity of the symptoms. It is possible that this rather optimistic view was responsible for the enormous waiting list at the London Clinic in the immediate post-war period, when it stood in the region of 400.

This trend is developed further in the important papers by Stone and Anna Freud on 'The widening scope of indications for psychoanalysis'. Stone (1954) quite emphatically states that 'practically every nosological category can be treated psychoanalytically under good conditions, although they vary extremely in availability and prognosis.' However, he goes on to say: 'none of us would doubt that a true, although severe, hysteria in a young individual in a good life situation with a reasonably competent analyst has an infinitely better prognosis than a mild schizophrenic, even with an analyst of great experience' (p. 591). Anna Freud (1954), after admitting to having contributed to the expansion of psychoanalytical goals in her work with children, seems more concerned with the possibility and consequences of deviations and parameters arising from it, a point not to be forgotten. She does not agree with Stone that psychoanalysis should not be used for mild, incipient and reactive illness. She regrets that experienced analysts have concentrated on the treatment of serious disturbances, leaving the treatment of hysteric, phobic and compulsive disorders to the beginners. She claims that had we concentrated on intensifying and improving our technique in the original field by now 'we would find the treatment of common neuroses child's play' (p. 610). A challenging statement, hard to refute but likely to arouse uncomfortable doubts in many of us.

The stage was set for the snowball expansion of the therapeutic application of psychoanalysis of the next decade, but it is not clear what was responsible for the increase in its momentum, because it must have been apparent to all that the technique, quite soon, was sadly lagging behind the theory. In such a climate it is understandable that the problems of assessing analysability prior to undertaking the treatment should not be foremost in the mind of its practitioners. But this optimism did not apply to another area of the analyst's work. Since World War II schemes for the selection of applicants for training have been developed in every psychoanalytical Society, and the trend has been towards restricting recruitment and carefully sifting the 'unsuitable' subjects. In so far as it would be dishonest and collusive to deny that therapy is the aim in the so-called training analysis, here is a clear admission and acknowledgement of the limitations of the method. It is debatable whether the widening scope of psychoanalysis has reached its peak. At the Copenhagen Congress in 1967, the chairman of the Symposium on Indications and Contra-indications of Psychoanalysis (Guttman, 1968) asked the question, 'is the sky the limit with psycho-analysis as a therapy?' and one of the speakers (Kuiper, 1968) answered this question by putting forward the notion of a narrowing scope of psychoanalysis. An acceptance of this principle is also implicit in any scheme which aims at optimal selection, even in the case of institutions where the reality factor of the demand exceeding the supply has to be taken into consideration.

How this is achieved in practice is of interest to our further discussion.

ASSESSING SUITABILITY ON THE BASIS OF DIAGNOSIS

An experienced analyst once said of the woman he had been analysing for several years: 'I wish I could carry out a psychiatric interview with her. I would soon know the diagnosis.' Looking at it from another angle, there are many psychoanalytic consultants who wish they could analyse some of the patients they have assessed in order to satisfy their diagnostic curiosity. It is difficult to trace historically when and how the psychoanalyst's dislike of and contempt for diagnostic labels really originated. Some of the earlier writers did tend to discuss suitability in terms of diagnostic categories. Glover (1954) lists the following in order of favourable indications: hysteria, compulsion neurosis, pregenital conversion states, neurotic disturbance, character disturbance, perversions, addictions, impulsiveness and psych-oses. It will not escape the reader that some of these conditions can be regarded more as symptoms than disease entities. But this paper is of considerable value because in pointing out that alcoholism, for instance, may be associated with a large variety of neurotic and psychotic conditions, Glover makes a compelling case for the need to reach the correct diagnosis in the preliminary stages.

But although psychoanalysts have tended to disregard diagnoses, for a very long time it was taken for granted that any patient suffering from hysteria would be suitable for a candidate's first case, and any obsessional neurosis, more or less compulsive, for a candidate's second case. However, training institutes all over the world have been having second thoughts during the past few years, well supported by Knapp et al.'s paper (1960) which is an outstanding contribution to the subject of the present discussion. The authors list a great number of conditions which appeared to be contra-indicated for candidates, notably patients over thirty-five, psychosomatic states, delinquents, psychotic trends, adverse life situations, schizoid borderline psychotics, too long a course of previous treatment, high level of anxiety and tension and in some cases patients older than candidates. With regard to hysteria, they are in favour of treatment by candidates, but depending on experience. Some of these first cases had been very good and some very bad. But the final blow against regarding hysteria as suitable for control cases was delivered by Zetzel (1968) in her masterly description of the 'so-called good hysteric'. Her subdivision of hysterics into four groups is well worth bearing in mind, together with her remarks concerning the most disturbed, 'who should not be referred for traditional analysis without careful assessment, which should include their total life situation and its potential for progressive alterations. All these patients present serious problems during the terminal phases of the analysis' (p. 259). The relevance of Zetzel's remarks lies in the fact that she is discussing analysability and its outcome. The hysterical patients described by her have a tendency towards becoming unanalysable as soon as they face up to the synthesis which is part and parcel of the satisfactory termination of the treatment. They are easily recognizable and have little chance of being missed at assessment interviews, when they may impress the diagnostician by their suitability for a psychodynamic approach in every other way.

ASSESSING SUITABILITY ON THE BASIS OF THE PRESENT SYMPTOMS

If the diagnosis can be an encumbrance, selection for psychoanalysis on the basis of the presenting symptomatology is misleading for the evaluator and is likely to have an adverse effect on the treatment. But the symptoms may be the only guiding line and all that a patient brings to the initial interview. Most consultants are unwilling to make any attempt to go behind a symptom for obvious reasons. But once a patient has been found to be suitable for analytical treatment in terms of his conscious motivations, life situation, availability, etc., it is inevitable that the final judgement will be made on the analysability of the presenting symptoms. Subjective feelings in the assessor become important. He will recall similar cases which he has treated or cases he has observed as they were treated by others. The psychoanalytic literature is rich in contributions by authors who have described the treatment and favourable resolution of a particular symptom and such papers, if at all relevant, will be recalled by the assessor, whilst at other times his theoretical views will prove to be a decisive factor. The following examples should clarify the situation I am describing. Homosexuality is frequently the basis of a request for treatment, and there are perhaps few symptoms which can produce greater divergence of views amongst evaluators. Some patients are rejected on account of the diagnostician forming a pessimistic view of the subject's capacity to comply with the somewhat outmoded rule of abstinence. On the other hand, a homosexual may be accepted on the grounds of the analyst's omnipotent belief in the analysability of all paranoid anxieties.

Another example comes from the sphere of marital problems when only one partner seeks help on account of sexual difficulties which should respond to psychoanalysis. Not infrequently the disturbance turns out to be unanalysable until the other partner is also receiving treatment.

THE OVER-ESTIMATION AND NEGLECT OF THE DIAGNOSTIC INTERVIEW

Depth interviews are aimed at: (a) the collection of data relevant to the patient's past and present history, life situation, finances, availability, etc; (b) evaluation of the patient in terms of his ego functions; (c) evaluation of conscious and unconscious factors which lie behind the present symptoms; such evaluation is based on objective findings or pure surmise on the basis of the consultant's experience in psychopathology; (d) evaluation of the individual's capacity to deal and cope with the analytical process, i.e. the subject's analysability in relation to a, b, and c.

The total picture drawn from these observations is eventually expressed in terms of 'suitable or unsuitable' for psychoanalysis. This is not the place to look into the widely differing techniques employed in diagnostic and assessment interviews. Suffice it to say that reports range from those based on the mainly psychiatric approach, i.e. biographical notes and symptomatology, to those purporting to be miniature analyses. Major areas of disagreement occur in the way evaluators deal with the interaction between the interviewer and interviewee, and the transference manifestations which occur at all first interviews. To draw too many conclusions on the basis of these findings can be exceedingly misleading, because none of the observed phenomena has anything to do with the transference neurosis which is to come. It could be said though that some interviewers are far too cautious in rejecting any opportunity offered by the patient to test out the latter's capacity for synthesis and abstraction. So long as interpretation is confined to the linking up of statements or events in a patient's history, it is difficult to understand why it should be regarded with any sense of alarm.

Some analysts are frankly sceptical of the findings obtained at an assessment interview and tend to ignore them altogether. In recent times it has become increasingly common for evaluators to end their reports with a prediction concerning the outcome of the treatment. It is to be hoped that this practice will promote interest in delineating the problems of analysability likely to be encountered before the treatment is brought to a satisfactory conclusion.

OUR DIVERGENT VIEWS ON ANALYSABILITY

Although a large variety of symptoms, conditions and situations, as well as personality and character traits, have been examined quite thoroughly by several authors, no clear definition of analysability emerges (Nacht and Lebovici, 1955; Knapp *et al.*, 1960; Waldhorn, 1960; Aarons, 1962).

In the context of this paper, the term 'analysable' is taken to refer to the possibility that in the course of analysis a given condition, life situation, symptom, etc., is capable of being understood by the analyst and patient alike. Furthermore, it is taken for granted that such understanding as may have been achieved will lead to increased insight on the part of the analyst with regard to the patient's personality and character accompanied by psychodynamic changes in the latter.

The conclusion that a symptom or an event in the present or past life situation of a patient is not analysable is reached with the utmost difficulty and only after considerable self-scrutiny on the part of the therapist, who is often reluctant to express an opinion, even after a long period of analysis. We are all familiar with the patient who turns up very punctually bringing his dreams and free associations day after day. We admire his courage in tackling numerous problems which are meticulously analysed. The analyst's notes will frequently contain the remark 'We have turned a corner' or 'A crucial bit of analysis has just been worked through.' But has it? A lengthy analysis can eventually be very successful, but it should not be taken for granted that it is indicative of analysability whilst it is still going on. In any case, the mystery of the patients who persist with analysis against all odds in the face of poor treatment has puzzled the psychiatric and psychoanalytic professions for a very long time.

The preceding remarks are meant to underline the simple fact that, in general, therapists consider it unsafe to express definite views on analysability whilst treatment is in progress, and that they can expect little help from their analysands, who seldom give it up in the realization that their problems cannot be reached by the method they have relied on for several months or years. It is not surprising if we found that the evaluators are even less prepared to state categorically that someone they have known for less than two hours is analysable. In case discussions they will disagree about this issue or will concentrate on other equally important elements in the interview. This is particularly in evidence in the selection of applicants for training. No one would doubt that there is every indication for psychoanalysis for someone who wishes to work as a psychotherapist, and indeed the applicant who reaches the interview stage will impress the selector by virtue of his motivation, reality situation, presence and extent of psychopathology, ego structure, including self-awareness, capacity for worthwhile object relations, and finally the guarantee to bring the analysis to a satisfactory conclusion. In spite of all these qualities being present in the successful applicant there is a 25 per cent wastage in the student population in the USA (Bak, 1970). In the United Kingdom in the last ten years, there has been a 15 per cent wastage through students discontinuing training, but in at least another 25 per cent there was evidence of marked difficulty in the analysability of certain character and personality areas during training. It is likely that similar figures are applicable to patients treated in private practice or institutions.

Quite understandably, evaluators are preoccupied with the assessment of the subject's ego structure, its function, defence and capacity for modification, all of which are observable at the time of the initial interviews. Tolerance of anxiety, adaptability, reality testing, object relationships, motivations and insight will never fail to mobilize the attentions and reactions of the interviewer, and due weight will be given to these functions in the final assessment of analysability.

In reviewing a series of positive recommendations, covering all aspects of selection, the writer has retained an overall impression that evaluators are not infrequently influenced by the subject's capacity to survive the most remarkable, and often repeated, traumatic experiences. The obvious resilience of the ego is taken almost as a guarantee that treatment will succeed, a fact which can be quite misleading, as shown by the following case.

A young man of good intelligence, a member of the upper class, was faced with a long prison term as a result of his fraudulent activities. He was one of several children born from his parents' numerous marriages. He lived in several homes in various parts of Europe and went to a number of boarding schools, where progress was slow but punishments were frequent as a result of his dreamy and detached attitude to his surroundings. As a child he was exposed to severe parental strife, father's rigidity and mother's alcoholism. When he was ten his mother fell down a flight of stairs in the course of a drunken bout and was killed. There had been a minor disagreement between the mother and the child just before the accident, which occurred before his return to boarding school. The patient had been married for a short while and there was evidence of development towards maturity. The assessor and the therapist were in full agreement that analysis had a fair chance of success. But it was stipulated that the patient would be treated whilst in hospital. For the first few months he showed enthusiasm for the new venture and co-operated in every possible way. But as soon as his early emotional experiences came into focus, he promptly committed a serious offence which got him away from treatment and back to the safety of prison and non-awareness. The diagnosis of neurosis in the patient could not be doubted, but his treatment revealed that the emotional disturbance related to his multiple traumatic experiences was not to be reached by analysis.

Doubts and difficulties in ascertaining the elusive quality of ego strength are probably underlying the recommendation that a person undergoing analysis should be healthy or that a patient should have a relatively mature, strong, and unmodified ego for the treatment to be successful (Szasz, 1957). Whether such a person is more easily analysable is debatable, but it is difficult not to agree with Fairbairn (1958), who 'cannot imagine how anyone should seek analysis under such conditions unless the id and superego constitute problems sufficiently serious to compromise the ego to a significant extent' (p. 374).

More recently Namnum (1968) has pointed out that the will to be analysed is part of autonomous ego function and reminds us of the capacity of the ego to utilize its own regression. Symptoms and anxieties which are ego-dystonic are more likely to be influenced by analysis, whilst the transference neurosis which is ego-syntonic cannot be analysed or not experienced. However, predictions concerning the type and quality of the transference are particularly hazardous and at times they are nothing short of pure guesswork. In spite of our continuous progress in the understanding and technical handling of the transference psychosis, this is often an unexpected and unwelcome complication which can lead to the interruption of the analytical work or even the failure of the psychoanalytic process. When this unfavourable development has occurred the original diagnosis of 'neurosis' is altered to 'borderline condition'. A careful reappraisal of the original interview will usually reveal that signs pointing to the possible eruption of psychotic manifestations in the transference were missed or else were glossed over by the excessive optimism of the interviewer. Prediction hazards are also to be expected in the assessment of the treatment alliance. It is not unusual to come across the analysand who has shown the greatest degree of insight, co-operation and keenness during the preliminary stages, but as soon as things begin to move he reveals a hard core of basic distrust which will prove to be a serious stumbling block to the analysis. In a review of the literature on the treatment alliance, Sandler and his co-workers (1970a) wrote: 'the assessment of the capacity for treatment has not yet been the subject of systematic study' (p. 555). They suggest that increasing weight should be placed on the assessment not only of his (the patient's) insight into his illness, but also of his capacity to form a treatment alliance with his physician. The wisdom of this advice will not be missed by the diagnosticians, but its practical applications may present considerable difficulties. In the state of our present knowledge the chances of assessing with accuracy the meaning of health or cure for a patient who is still totally unaware of his impulses are minimal.

A brief examination of the most important factors related to the improvement and wellbeing following successful therapy may be appropriate in this context. It is generally agreed that regaining and reintegrating lost parts of the self is an essential part of the therapeutic process and that knowledge replaces omnipotence, enabling one to deal with one's own feelings and the external world in a more realistic way (Segal, 1962). But it is precisely when we try to assess the probability of a reduction in splitting processes that we run into danger of serious miscalculation. The functional ability to neutralize aggressive energy or integrate it, thus enabling the individual to develop his creativity satisfactorily, is difficult to achieve and certainly not easily predicted. Analysis in its primitive significance means 'to take to pieces': a relatively easy task both for the therapist and for most patients, but the capacity for (re)synthesis in a most meaningful way may be the privilege of the few and a real challenge to the most skilled therapist, as shown by the following case history.

Mrs X, a fifty-eight-year-old widow, sought help on account of deep depression following the end of a love affair which had been unsatisfactory in more than one way. There was also evidence of unresolved mourning for the husband who had been in analysis at one time with the psychoanalyst she was now consulting. She herself had received psychoanalytical treatment on and off for nineteen years, by a much respected analyst, who was no longer available. Mrs X showed no resentment about this, whilst unexpectedly displaying a strong positive transference for the prospective therapist, with an almost total amnesia for the anger she had felt immediately after the death of her husband. She also showed a complete lack of insight into the fact that her unhappy love affair had developed during the closing stages of her analysis and its termination had been followed by the breakdown of the relationship. She was also unaware of intense idealization of her analyst. There seemed to be some indication for a limited period of therapy which in effect lasted less than a year. Attention was focused on the patient's incessant demand for more interpretations and her refusal to apply whatever insight she had to herself. On the other hand, she was quite ready to offer interpretations to all those who came in contact with her. It soon transpired that throughout her life she had been surrounded by 'lame ducks' and that she had been responsible for several of them obtaining psychoanalytic treatment. As it happened, one of her more disturbed friends, a manic-depressive, suffered a very serious relapse and had invaded her home, making heavy demands on Mrs X, who was quickly discovering that she had not been able to use her good analysis on account of her persistent tendency to split, project and idealize. Her sick friend clearly represented a split-off, psychotic part of herself and to have her living with her was experienced as a violent and dangerous attack. One morning, as Mrs X was trying to leave her house, her friend pursued her and tried to prevent her from getting into her car. She eventually drove away furiously but she had come very close indeed to causing a serious injury to her persecutor. The analysis of this incident was not only painful but it also met with increased resistance and a strong desire to revert to the old defensive mechanism of splitting. There were several interesting features in this case and of no little relevance was the fact that a great deal of integration appeared to be possible, in a manner which is not infrequently encountered in the course of a second analysis. But our knowledge of the working of the latter is too imperfect to allow for any conclusions to be drawn.

The case which has just been outlined illustrates to some extent that the position in relation to 'insight' is, to say the least, complex. Real insight is achieved in stages, over a period of time, but it is effective only when it is an affective process. It will also be associated with an awareness of derivatives of unconscious conflict which have been carefully worked through (Zilboorg, 1952). The acquisition of insight is likely to confront some patients with the unfamiliar and unsavoury task of having to take decisions and the consultant will have to assess whether the conflicts arising from it are analysable. For a minority, the thought of being free from symptoms and inhibitions is associated with fears of murderous impulses, suicide or madness. These fears and the reaction formation surrounding them cannot escape the diagnostician's attention and their presence can be taken as an indication that problems of analysability will be encountered. Denying a patient the possibility of relief from suffering is no easy matter but, on the other hand, it would be difficult to give unqualified acceptance to the proposition that 'when there is doubt concerning analysability our bias should be in favour of analysis on the grounds that if properly conducted it will do the patient no harm and at least it will be of research value' (Anna Freud, 1954, p. 619). Nevertheless, it is true to say that most psychoanalytic consultants when doubtful about making a positive recommendation for analysis tend to remind themselves of the fact that it is not unusual for some individuals to become analysable in the course of time. This and other factors are often taken into account, as shown in the following brief account of a successful analysis, which appeared unpromising at first.

A forty-year-old professional man, engaged in very creative work, entered psychotherapy on account of bouts of profound depression, feelings of unreality and a tendency towards psychosomatic manifestations. Analysis was out of the question by reason of other commitments and, furthermore, over a long period of observation he showed little capacity for understanding unconscious processes as well as an almost total inability to grasp the meaning of the transference. However, he made up his mind to have a course of psychoanalysis and turned up, quite punctually, a year later as arranged. His treatment was undertaken essentially because he was a valuable and gifted person in distress and the seriousness of intent promised well in terms of suitability. In a moment of profound reflection, this eminently analysable patient asked the question, 'Where does analysis take place?' He wondered whether it took place in the past or the present; or perhaps in the conscious or unconscious part of his mind; yet again at times it felt as if it was all happening in his real world but he could not possibly ignore his fantasy life.

If we were to answer this man's question directly, we might say that analysis takes place in the transference but his remarks, which accurately reflected events in his therapy, do evoke a feeling that for the treatment to succeed, it must also take place in a non-conflictual sphere of the ego. How different this man was from those patients whose analysability we doubt, because they are forever entrenched in their present or past life or in a developmental area to the exclusion of all others.

The accurate forecast of the patient's behaviour before therapy has begun is a challenge to the diagnostician, who nevertheless has the means of eliciting evidence of the prospective analysand's capacity to move freely within his psyche. But he will be able to do this only if he is prepared to move freely within the interview situation, so that he can induce fluid responses in the interviewee. The silent and inactive evaluator, who clings faithfully to the psychoanalytic model of behaviour, will obtain only a partial if not distorted picture of what he is meant to observe.

THE ROLE OF THE EVALUATOR

In the previous sections of this paper frequent reference has been made to the role of the evaluator, who occupies an important position in all psychoanalytic communities, usually with few rewards. His failures are more readily remembered than his successes, and in both instances experience plays its part. A lack of it is probably responsible for the sustained flow of unsuitable cases being referred to the London Clinic of Psycho-Analysis by psychoanalysts over the years, and will account for some unsatisfactory referrals in private practice. On the other hand, although the ability to predict is very considerable in the more experienced, they miss out in assessing the patient's capacity to communicate and to relinquish gratifications of infantile fixations and in the evaluation of paranoid mechanisms. But they will assess accurately the capacity to tolerate the analytic situation (Knapp *et al.*, 1960; Levin, 1960).

Any attempt to account for mistakes and errors of judgement in selection should always call in question the role of the assessor in the interview situation, in the light of his reactions to the patient as an individual, his present symptoms, and his current and past life situations. A host of subjective impressions and feelings are evoked in the interviewer which could be conveniently designated as his 'total response' in order to avoid using the term countertransference, which has its own special connotation. However, when conclusions are drawn and final decisions made, the consultant's personal attitudes and theoretical beliefs in relation to the set of problems presented by the patient are just as significant as his reactions to the latter. It should also be noted here that interpersonal reactions occurring in the course of an initial interview should be well differentiated from other phenomena ascribable to projective-identification mechanisms.

The first interviewer's total response, which cannot ignore external pressures from relatives and referring agencies, has a far-reaching effect on the course of the analysis. For instance, the immediate identification with the patient should make one aware of possible transference and countertransference complications in a subsequent analysis if undertaken by the interviewer. The least that could be expected to arise from such identification is that the assessor might be influenced in the choice of therapist, a source of complication which has not escaped other contributors (Levin, 1960), but it could also result in taking the wrong view of the patient's analysability.

As in the case of the countertransference, the evaluator's total response will prove an invaluable asset if it is subjected to thorough scrutiny during the next few days following the selection interview.

The part played by intuition in the total response is not to be dismissed lightly in spite of our insistence that in presenting our findings we adhere to scientifically observed facts. But the assessor is not always entirely free to use his intuitive gifts because his own personal theoretical, technical and philosophical position will act as a restraint. It could happen that the consultant has arrived at the conclusion that a patient would present few problems if he were referred to a particular analyst, with a special background. The purist in our midst will probably feel duty bound to pay little or no attention to such a clearly intuitive thought, whereas another consultant will act on it in the knowledge that the age, sex and background of the analyst, and not least his theoretical position, can have a profound effect on the earlier stages of the treatment.

The selector's path is not an easy one and there are many hidden hazards, which cannot always be avoided. It would be unwise to underestimate the limitations of our abilities to assess what is analysable and what is not. Selection is a challenge still to be met by psychoanalysts. In the meantime we shall go on working, knowing that there are no ideal patients waiting to be assessed by omniscient assessors for treatment by omnipotent therapists.

SOME SUGGESTIONS FOR FURTHER INVESTIGATION AND STUDY

This paper does not set out to be a guide to selection or to the assessment of analysability. It deals with extremes, but possibly this is the only available method of treating an intractable subject. Although no ready solution is at hand, it may be appropriate to consider what can be done to remedy the current situation, where selection procedures are somewhat out of step with clinical practice.

In the first instance we must strive for a clearer definition of what we are selecting for. The position is a difficult one, particularly when we find ourselves caught up in the dichotomy of psychoanalysis as therapy and research work. We cannot ignore the fact that most people who seek analysis (including applicants for training) expect relief from their symptoms. Few would disagree with the view that research does come into our work, but for the majority of psychoanalysts who are engaged in the day-to-day treatment of the mentally ill, it is only a secondary consideration. When research is our primary concern, we should say so and adjust our aims and methods accordingly.

Education committees should become more acutely aware that the issue of analysability can become clouded when undue weight is given to the qualities required of a future practitioner of psychoanalysis. 'Halo' effects are common features of admission interviews.

The possibility of avoiding *undesirable* 'matching' between analysands and analysts suggests itself as being worth further exploration. Clinics where patients are treated by students in training could well provide the ideal setting for this type of investigation. The selectors would feel happier to know that a case with a specific problem does not fall into the hands of a student who has a similar one.

Our attitude to the loss of a supervised case by a trainee is a source of major complications, in so far as the selector cannot help being over-preoccupied with the staying power of the patient. The student's performance is distorted by his fear of premature loss of the case and the stigma attached to it. As a result of it, good analysability prospects go by the board, quite apart from the possible unhealthy development of clinging habits in relation to patients.

The implications related to the transfer of treatment from one analyst to another is not fully understood, although it is common knowledge that a second analysis is often very successful. It might perhaps be advisable to encourage such a step when it is obvious that a previously analysable case is running aground. If we were to do this without too much embarrassment, we might learn a good deal about analysability.

All cases where analysis has become interminable should come under close scrutiny as they frequently contain evidence of unanalysability. This topic was taken up again by Bak (1970), who goes as far as recommending the resumption of the 'trial period'.

In my opinion, it is not necessary to put the clock back in that sense. Equally we need not fear that much harm will come from narrowing the scope of psychoanalysis so that it can operate within its natural limits and not least within the limitations of those who practise it. It is also probable that we would encourage further the expansion of psychoanalysis and promote greater support amongst our medical and psychiatric colleagues.

POSTSCRIPT (1988)

At a distance of sixteen years some afterthoughts seem appropriate considering the accumulation of literature on a topic which is still beset by contrasting opinions, owing to the insurmountable difficulties of comparing data based on subjective experiences and variable technical approaches. A comprehensive review of the literature has been published by Bachrach (1983) but here I shall confine myself to comment on a few relevant studies.

Sashin et al. (1975) set out to study the possibility of predicting the outcome of psychoanalysis on the basis of data obtained in preliminary evaluations. The patients were treated by candidates but no attempt was made to evaluate possible influences of analyst-factors or analyst–patient match factors. The investigation ensured a high level of participation by senior analyst evaluators at all stages, including strict arrangements about supervisions, etc. The project relied on 105 items obtained from the literature and other experienced personnel at the Boston Psychoanalytic Institute. It was intended that the items would cover almost all the evidence elicited at the preliminary interviews. There were 130 outcomes obtained from the analysts who had treated the patients which fell into three categories: (1) those who completed analysis by mutual agreement; (2) those who prematurely terminated analysis against the advice of the analyst; (3) those whose analyses became interminable. The investigation showed that the predictors were of no use because they showed no variations among the patients or because they were left blank or were rated too low. The only items that proved of value in this disappointing study were those that referred to family pathology in the patient's background.

Erle (1979) has reported on a study of forty consecutive patients selected by experienced analysts as first and second supervised analytic cases at the Treatment Center of the New York Psychoanalytic Institute. Forty-two per cent were found to be involved in a psychoanalytic process; 60 per cent were rated as having had therapeutic benefit. It is worth nothing that twenty patients were in treatment between one and three years only. What is even more significant is that of nine patients treated for less than two years, 12 per cent had substantial benefit, whilst of ten patients who were in therapy for more than five years, 100 per cent had substantial benefit. The collection of data and analysis of the findings are impressive but the author does not avoid the well known confusion between suitability and analysability when she states: 'Suitability for analysis is a crucial term. It would be defined only in terms of the analytic process established; such issues as therapeutic benefit must be clearly separated' (p. 215).

No one would argue against the second part of the sentence but it must be obvious that suitability must be isolated from the analytic process which is the basic pointer to analysability. If a person is in psychoanalysis and is able to withstand the rigours of the setting for several years and if he has made use of the transference enabling him to understand the past in the present, such a person must be suitable for analysis. Is it possible that any analyst would tolerate the absence of the analytic process for years and years? When we speak of interminable analysis we do not think the patient is unsuitable but interminability alerts us to the presence of some area which is impervious to analysis. I am thinking here of a paranoid core of the character which makes its appearance quite late; or some deep anxieties about integration-disintegration which only become manifest in the last stages of some analyses. But Erle is well aware of 'the significant limitations when applied to the assessment of analytic treatments, particularly in retrospect' (p. 222).

Some of these points were confirmed in a later paper by Erle and Goldberg (1984) when they found a similar number of unanalysable cases (59 per cent) and a high number of therapeutic benefits (over 60 per cent) in patients who were in analysis with experienced analysts. The authors acknowledge the fact that an analytic process may still be in evidence although a case may end up with a limited resolution.

Weber et al. (1985) have also carried out an interesting survey which included 295 psychoanalyses and 286 psychotherapies conducted and terminated by candidates at Columbia Psychoanalytic Research Center. There were 159 candidates involved in the project but eventually only 34 patients and 16 analysts were selected for final study. The criteria of analysability were based on the patient's: (1) capacity to bring dreams, fantasies and affects; (2) better use of resources; (3) use of insight gained through the transference. Overall analysability was present in 64 per cent of the cases with close association to therapeutic benefits. Only two-fifths of the patients were considered to have been analysed at termination. In terms of therapeutic benefits, the majority of patients were reported as clinically improved with 91 per cent of analyses continuing after graduation. Weber *et al.* conclude that there was no consistent pattern of relationship between the assessors' expectations and the measure of therapeutic benefit and analysability. In the case of privately terminated analyses, patients' reality situations, diagnosis and history of object relations failed to show a consistent relationship. We should note that by modern standards, these were rather short analyses, seldom lasting over four years. What can we say, in fact, when in some instances cases were said to have completed the analysis in two years?

This is one of the elements that invalidate the findings of Kantrowitz (1987). Her study, which was begun in 1972 at the Boston Psychoanalytic Institute, had as its goal the determination of suitability for analysis. The research was based on four variables: (1) reality testing; (2) level and quality; (3) affect availability; (4) motivation for treatment. The expectation was that with a high score of these variables, the response to analysis would be more positive. Only twenty-two patients were considered, a figure hardly of statistical significance, also considering that they were all in therapy with candidates. Great importance was attributed to the administration of a battery of tests, which has long been discounted as being of much value in assessing suitability. (See Wallerstein's (1987) discussion of this paper.) It would seem that only 40 per cent (nine out of twenty-two) of patients had an established or partially resolved transference neurosis, whilst another 60 per cent had not. The author recognizes that the study did not show whether the patients had a pathology unyielding to analysis, or that there could have been some other interfering factors in the analyst–patient relationship.

Similar limitations in terms of statistical significance could apply to Wallerstein's masterly report of a thirty years' research project carried out at the Menninger Foundation (Wallerstein, 1986). Subjects were selected from the Menninger's waiting list. Twenty-two patients were chosen for analysis and twenty for psychotherapy, with an equal number of men and women. The ages ranged from seventeen to fifty. The sample was an unusual one, in so far as over half the patients were hospitalized at least once, at some time during the course of therapy, a fact that would immediately suggest a very severe disturbance with a doubtful prognosis. Furthermore, all analysts treating patients were inexperienced.

Although the preliminary assessment was carried out by skilled personnel, serious pathology escaped detection. Psychoanalysis was found to be ineffective in a group which included alcoholics, severe sexual dysfunction and drug addiction; concurrently psychotherapy, turned out to be of better value to the patients. Wallerstein deals at length with the principle that if nothing will help, why not try psychoanalysis, and underlines the value of supportive psychotherapy, but as a reviewer of this work has pointed out, 'it is possible that with less sick patients, supportive psychotherapy would not have led to the same positive changes.' The writer goes on to ask, 'does the value of psychotherapy hinge on demonstrating the limitations of psychoanalysis?' (Richards, 1988, p. 143).

In my view, this very brief survey indicates to what an extent analysability and suitability for therapy continue to be a major area of controversy. In so far as the above reports come from the USA, where the practice of psychoanalysis is, of necessity, more homogeneous than in other parts of the world, we are struck by the degree of difficulty in making predictions which match results. Such discrepancy of points of views and assessments would be even worse if the studies came from countries outside the USA, where there are major variations concerning the analyst's functioning, the appraisal of object relations and technique applicable to patients and candidates during their training.

Regretfully, little new light emerged from a dialogue and open discussion on analysability in relation to early psychopathology at the Helsinki Psychoanalytic Congress of 1981. The American position was presented by Hans Lowald (only an abstract from the Congress proceedings has survived and I am transcribing it here), who suggested that analysability varies with the depth and range of the analyst's countertransference potential and with his capacity and ability to express, modulate and muster his initiative and responses, predominantly through verbal communication and interpretation. The other dialogue participant, Zimmerman, from Brazil, focused his arguments on the assessment of analysability from two complementary points of view: the dynamic (with the data obtained at the preliminary interview) and the genetic (with data obtained from early childhood by means of psychoanalytic treatment). As the analysis goes deeper, doubts may arise in all respects. Zimmerman singles out some early psychopathological experiences: traumas, deprivations, bad relationships with important objects (a psychotic parent, for instance) which determine analysability, its limitations, or even impossibility (Zimmerman, 1982).

Although the reports I have quoted would appear to be inconclusive, I must draw attention to the useful inclusion of data concerning the therapeutic value of psychoanalysis, irrespective of analysability. This accounts for the continued support for a method which has been the object of persistent attacks and criticism by those who have had little extensive, first-hand experience of it.

In conclusion, I must admit to some disappointment that my expectations and hopes expressed in my original paper have not been fulfilled. There have, in fact, been few attempts in Europe and Latin America to carry out extensive surveys translatable into reliable statistics. At the London Clinic of Psycho-Analysis, where only some thirty analyses are offered in response to several hundred enquiries a year, discussions have been in progress for some time for the purpose of finding a way of evaluating outcomes without interfering with the analytic process. Several years ago, with the help of four senior colleagues I, too, attempted to assess the progress of psychoanalysts after graduation, matching the data against the admission interviews. The project was abandoned when it was apparent that there could be a breach of confidentiality, especially if we added some searching interviews with each subject of the study.

In the light of my added experience, I am now less inclined to recommend a narrowing scope of psychoanalysis, although I have often observed, in various circumstances, the sudden discovery of a psychotic nucleus which will defy analysis, making it interminable. This is indirect confirmation that we should have serious doubts about the suitability of psychotic states, even when the psychoanalytic approach has been modified. I am aware, though, that analysis can act as a true lifeline, the only means of survival for some psychotic patients.

On the other hand, I am impressed by the favourable outcome achieved in borderline, and particularly psychosomatic, states. The supposition that social, psychological and physiological factors combine in the causation of severe illness, is finding confirmation in the laboratory. The observation that stress can be immunosuppressive has led to the creation of the new field of research known as 'psychoneuroimmunology' which studies the mechanisms in which experiences via the central nervous system transduction can alter resistance to disease (Solomon, 1987). Psychotherapy has much to contribute here. Psychoanalysis will continue to be plagued by its poor results which attract more attention than its successes. On the basis of my own experience and that derived from observations of supervised analyses and verbal reports from senior colleagues, I have come to recognize that many unsatisfactory outcomes are often due to a combination of factors arising from both analyst *and* patient.

What is it then, that will cause one analysand to be less accessible to analysis than another? Is it an intolerance to the setting which is so clearly responsible for much therapeutic benefit in many cases? Is it a failure on the part of the analyst to adhere strictly to the setting which can be so supportive of his/her interpretations? Is the cause to be found in some incorrect handling of the transference and countertransference? We are all aware of the importance of analysing the past in the present within the transference relationship but that in itself will not be enough if sustained interventions are not accompanied by changed feelings and behaviour. It is the simultaneous link between emotional responses in analyst and patient and their verbalizations that will be of the utmost therapeutic value. Furthermore, what is happening must make sense to both partners and the analyst's behaviour should not contradict what he is saying to the patient (Loch, 1988). I am also very much in agreement with this author's belief that both patient and analyst must be united in the wish to know (in my view not synonymous with therapeutic alliance) and that at times the analyst cannot convince/seduce the analysand into grasping the truth of the statement that a better understanding of himself is likely to lead to better life and well-being.

As psychoanalysts, we must come to terms with the fact that some patients will choose unquiet and unhappy living, a perverse choice it may be, possibly because the meaning of mental health is far too daunting for them.

In bringing my views on analysability up to date, I have once more underlined some of the challenges which are still there. In psychoanalysis we have something positive to meet them.

5 THE TRAINING ANALYST AND THE DIFFICULTIES ASSOCIATED WITH PSYCHOANALYTIC TRAINING*

TRAINING IN PSYCHOANALYSIS has been at the centre of debates ever since the International Psychoanalytical Association created a Training Commission in 1925 to control the spreading of 'wild analysis' and the troubles caused by self-appointed teachers. The Commission did not last more than a few years, owing to the difficulty in establishing any kind of uniformity of training within the increasing number of psychoanalytic groups.

For the last twenty-five years, psychoanalytic educators have met at two-yearly intervals under the sponsorship of their Association to discuss their work. In 1973 I was invited to chair a conference on the difficulties experienced by training analysts in their capacities as therapists and educators. In that capacity, I entered into a correspondence with senior colleagues from all over the world. The response indicated not only an interest in the topic but considerable anguish aroused by the dual role forced on the training analyst, as well as a need to confide in someone. In addressing the two hundred delegates who attended the conference in Paris, I used many of those statements made to me in confidence, as well as points raised in the course of open discussions by many speakers of different nationalities over the years.

Learning is a painful experience at all, and at the best of, times. It is the more so when someone is also learning to be a patient. Teaching does not come very easily, and when it is carried out in the evening by part-time,

* This is an expanded version of a paper published in 1974 as 'The training analyst and the difficulties in the psychoanalytic training situation' in the *International Journal of Psycho-Analysis* 55: 71–7.

amateur, and even inexperienced, men and women, whose main interest lies in treating others, problems arise which can be overrated or underrated. Such is the nature of the syncretic position in which training analysts and candidate-patients have to function, whether they like it or not, and irrespective of the measures they take towards limiting it, alleviating it or eliminating it. Ambiguity may, in fact, be a more emotional and accurate word than syncretic to describe this situation. The majority opinion believes there is something to worry about if any one person or any group thinks that he or they have solved the dichotomy of the analysing functions of the training analyst and his responsibility as a member of an Education Committee or its derivatives.

The constant interaction between the analyst and his colleagues and the Training Institute is bound to create problems. The situation regarding the candidate is even more complicated. In order to understand what is to follow, the reader must bear in mind that in training there is an unavoidable contamination of the analytic relationship by the more complex clan or 'extended family' relationship with the Institute as well as with fellow candidates. Thus there is an actual psychoanalytic family situation to be lived out, which causes untold repercussions in the transference.

It is conceded that the personal analysis is the most significant learning experience in psychoanalytic training. It is also generally agreed that the need to report on the candidate is the most outstanding (some would say outrageous) interference in the analytic process.

There are still those who believe it is not the judging that interferes with the analytic situation. What matters most is the candidate's fear of being judged, and the analyst's fear of judging the one thing he is capable of judging, namely analysability. It follows that most difficulties about reporting should be capable of being analysed, even when paranoid anxieties are involved and some will say that such difficulties even foster the analysis.

Firmly entrenched in the opposing camp are those who believe that the analyst is the person who has the least amount of lucidity about his students who are equally blind in their perception of the analyst. Everything must be done to discourage the belief in the existence of the psychoanalytic phallus-breast endowed in the training analyst. The educational role of the training analyst is unlikely to deepen and expand his therapeutic results.

At times analysts are forced to hold apparently irreconcilable views. This is the case when they believe that many proposals and counter-proposals for changes in training practice are basically disguises to change the core of psychoanalytic theory and its application to training and treatment. Yet these analysts would also readily agree that nothing is more likely to interfere with our therapeutic aims than the starting of the official course by the candidate and we must bear it in mind that these aims do not remain unaffected even when there is no selection for training in the early stages. Patients in personal analysis will regard it as a training procedure whether we wish it or not.

Does the answer to these problems lie in a two-track training programme so that the personal analysis is kept entirely separate from the educational arrangements? Are we justified in perpetuating the existence of an elite called 'training analysts' or would it help if we were to regard the term quite simply as a title or label of quality? An aspirant analyst would not necessarily choose the holder of such a title for his personal analysis. He could then be evaluated on his own merit and not on the basis of the analyst.

DIFFICULTIES ARISING FROM THE TRAINING ORGANIZATION

There is little that is more reassuring to the psychoanalyst educator than the observation of a student's personality blossoming and developing in the course of his personal analysis in spite of his exposure to a structured educational process. Institutional training is probably antithetical to analysis; under ideal circumstances it produces a degree of infantilization which could hinder the process of individuation and maturation fostered by the analysis.

A current criticism is that training is becoming increasingly institutionalized. In general we have two types of organizations: in one we find a proliferation of committees, the workload being well spread out. This acts as a guarantee against despotism but it creates problems for the leader who must ensure that communication is not lost or that general rather than personal policies are adopted. In the other type, power is kept in the hands of the few with all attendant complications. This may be inevitable in the smaller Societies, but it is possible even for growing Societies to be slow in following up their expansion with an adaptation of their training arrangements. For this reason there is a great deal to be said for the Education or Training Committee to be ultimately responsible to the Society. Yet it is well known that Training Institutes can be victims of the structure of the Society, whose by-laws are often static in nature.

The separation of the two bodies has at times led to considerable strife and hostility by allowing one body of people to be set against another. In the long run, as I have been able to observe, this leads to the development of a special group transference against other colleagues.

It is true that Society and Training Bodies do not always keep under constant examination those factors based on tradition, history and prejudice which favour regression in candidates and which are probably responsible for the air of immaturity frequently displayed by training analysts as soon as they begin to operate within the Training Institute. The role of splitting processes, especially those involved in paranoid anxieties, and their absorption into the organizational structure and behaviour, has perhaps not been taken sufficiently into account as a factor responsible for the perpetuation of certain difficulties and it may be worth further exploration.

The collective conscience of a group (Organization) is not necessarily of the highest quality, despite the fact that it serves democracy, law and order as well as maintaining standards. That the group conscience may not be the most valuable conscience for psychoanalytic practice is a reality which we have to accept. Psychotic processes can be seen quite readily at work in group psychology, and group countertransference reactions to a student or fellow member are not at all uncommon.

A sound Institute, in order to operate effectively, requires a training analyst to be administrator, selector and also a willing and capable guide to young people. Many teachers succumb to the power struggles. They either become engrossed in them or they opt out whilst others are better able to keep on the sidelines. Psychoanalysts ought to be particularly concerned about the intrapsychic processes responsible for the appearance and endemic prevalence of such situations in their Societies, yet they seem unable to do much about them. It has been suggested that these internal tensions are related to unresolved narcissistic problems of the Institute's members. The question has even been asked whether our narcissism is involved in being a member of the organization and how this narcissism struggles to defend its maintenance.

Pathological developments of power struggles can be modified both by intrapsychic and social means but once more a polarization of views finds analysts well divided on the issue. Some will say the remedy for the training analyst who appears immature in handling conflictual behaviour in his interaction with other analysts, and who is still trying to cope with his narcissism, is to have yet more analysis. This is necessary because his reaction to what appears to him as authoritarian group pressures is only due to intrapsychic problems. On the other side we find those who believe that the trouble is due to the pathological structure of the Institute. More analysis is no solution (especially when it is *you* who should have it). The stress is on examining, analysing the social structure of the Institute and attempting to modify it rather than seeking to resolve it individually through intrapsychic examination. Perhaps this problem does contain both remnants of pathological narcissism and pathological group structures, fostering each other in different degrees.

In spite of the diversionary opinions, most people agree that we should have fewer prima donnas, a phenomenon which is generally seen as due to the corrupting effects of the group around leaders in the Institute. The origin of this phenomenon is probably not a minor factor in the suggestion that the training analysis is either obsolete or an antilogy; that is, a contradiction in terms or ideas. Its abolition might result in a truly therapeutic analysis.

From individual rivalries to group rivalries, power struggles assume a curious amalgam of theoretical and political trends. The effects on both analyst and students through the existence of such groups can be far-reaching. Two opposing groups become the representatives of parents' disagreement, which may produce a real or fantasied state of affairs in the life of a trainee. As transferences are influenced, acting-out opportunities proliferate, whilst the idealization of each group influences the trainee's therapeutic behaviour. It has been suggested that this situation leads to the creation of destructive mental images of analysts which could be called persecutory internal analysts. There must be doubts about the analysability of these processes yet it should be possible to use such material for the purpose of facilitating growth in the analysand.

Although analysts can be very enthusiastic or critical of the organization they work for, most of them would have difficulty in defining the kind of ideal Institute they would like to be associated with. In this respect it would seem that we are apt to forget that our training is very special. Some Institutes have attempted to model it on university teaching in an unsearching manner, as what is done at university may not fit at all with our training needs. The influence of universities on our educators is of great interest in itself. The slow but steady disappearance of the full-time analyst is coupled with his increased involvement with the universities. Subtle changes are taking place almost everywhere and as psychoanalysts invade the medical schools, attempts will be made to use our Institutes for training in other disciplines or practices. This is the thin end of the wedge, which needs careful watching if we wish to preserve the idiosyncratic nature of psychoanalysis, which has stood well the test of time against considerable odds.

Basically, we know we do not want our Institute to be authoritarian nor do we want it to be anti-authoritarian. Those are extreme notions, rigid, political and ideological attitudes that do not permit the development of insights into the dynamics of teaching and learning. As a result of this, insecurity is confused with authoritarianism as much as anti-authoritarianism.

Vital questions are easily side-tracked in Institutes. Discussions on the right to train are perhaps of less importance than deciding on what a trainee needs to learn, how we can help him to learn it and how we know that he has learned.

DIFFICULTIES ARISING FROM
THE TRAINING ANALYST

The argument that organized training is unnecessary is probably based on the belief that the status of 'training analyst' is superfluous to the aims which are essentially therapeutic. We must note in passing that the abolition of organized training could only bring in its wake chaotic conditions, reintroducing the spreading of 'wild training analyses'. However, in analysing a prospective candidate, before or after selection, the analyst carries an added responsibility to the Education Committee and the Society in general. Even in those instances when the analyst is less involved in actual decision-making, we must expect that from time to time he will be wondering about his analysand's aptitude for his declared chosen career. This is an area that will call for close examination of the countertransference, which on the other hand should be distinguished from counter-reactions which are more easily manageable, provided the analyst remains aware that he is dealing with a contaminated situation. When this does not happen, there may be a temptation to introduce new techniques. Attempts to understand the unconscious significance of the analysand's communications, when they are manifestly related to training circumstances, are abandoned. Not infrequently the first major difficulties in these unusual analytical situations are encountered at the first mention of career goals.

Current career goals must be analysed on a realistic basis as well as explored and differentiated. Reality presses for recognition of no progress or of progress, whichever is the case. The analyst's performance in this respect can make a difference to the future but the candidate responds with transference reactions irrespective of the analyst's position or behaviour. The technical problem appears to be then that of keeping the lines open for observation and also of keeping the analyst's responses conflict-free and as reality-orientated as possible. This is what an educator must be in order to avoid recreating the parent–child situations with hypocrisy, tergiversation, etc. The analyst who is not interested in the progress of his patient-candidate-colleague-to-be is out of touch with himself and reality.

The need to differentiate transference from reality has its supporters as much as its technical difficulties. The suggestion that confrontation with reality may destroy fantasy formation is not easily dismissed.

It is under these circumstances that the analyst offers himself as a model, as a 'functioning' analyst to his analysand-patient. The latter's ego is under considerable stress as it is experiencing and observing at the same time. Splits may occur or integration may lag behind progress in other areas. A particular difficulty in identifying with the analyst is at times due to the sexualization of the ego and superego functions which the potential analyst needs to conduct his own analysis and that of his patients. This is often made worse by positive and negative transference manifestations, which can be overlooked by both partners. The mishandling of this complication is known to promote disaffection with analysis and the birth of techniques and questionable theories on the part of the future practitioner.

Turning to those attitudes which may have an adverse effect on the candidate-patient, mention must be made of the following: the therapist's wish to produce the 'perfect analyst'; his need to be important; his quest for disciples; his fear of criticism by colleagues leading to the holding back of the candidate's progress and even interminable analysis; his compulsion to foster unconscious identification. This last trait can be conducive of abnormal loyalty in the candidate with a malignant sharing of the analyst's fate. We should note that the candidate's fantasy of turning his analyst into the idealized parent he never had is well matched by the analyst's fantasy of turning his analysand into the ideal child he never had. A narcissistic collusion, of major if not intractable force, will be the natural outcome of this pathological event.

Certain qualities such as shyness or exhibitionistic tendencies are well-known reflections of narcissistic residues in the training analyst which make him vulnerable. The need to rescue sick candidates is probably another aspect of the same problem, coupled with an urge to become an optimal figure for the analysand.

The persistence of narcissistic traits in the analyst and awkwardness in dealing with a narcissistic transference neurosis in the candidate has indeed led some people to think that this particular pathology can affect psychoanalysts' functions from one generation to another.

There are other difficulties. Alongside the tendency to minimize the Institute's training demands that threaten the analytic process, there is the even worse sin of responding to the candidates' involvement with training by forgetting the therapeutic aims. The reason for this attitude is often a desire to avoid internal tensions and accusations of restrictive practices. At the other end of this spectrum there is the analyst whose entire practice is devoted to the treatment of would-be, or accepted, candidates. The countertransference problem of relying on such clients for one's living is worth some speculation.

Lastly, we must consider our attitudes towards our ageing and ailing colleagues in whom feelings of insecurity at times make their appearance in a subtle way. The first sign is often that of an elderly colleague who takes up younger analysts' causes *ad absurdum*. We know well enough what it means but how to deal with it is a different matter. Far more important, however, is the problem created by a colleague who is sick and does not know it, or worse still, the sudden occurrence of acting out in a training analyst of previously impeccable character. In this event, the intervention of one or two trusted friends can be more effective than the authoritarian approach of an ethical committee. On the other hand, almost all psychoanalytic groups have at one time or another had the unenviable task of coping with a colleague who has achieved the status of educator in spite of his tendency to be somewhat erratic in behaviour, at times amounting to acting out. It is not always clear whether we are dealing here with an occupational hazard and if so whether it is something that should have been, or could not be, dealt with in the individual's personal analysis.

DIFFICULTIES ARISING FROM
THE CANDIDATES

When we consider the difficulties directly attributable to the candidate we cannot easily distinguish them from their interactions with the analyst and Organization unless the psychopathology is particularly severe. For instance, there will always be the candidate who will be seeking instant analysis, or indeed, a good breast, preferably *à la carte* and without the need to suck it, who will find analysts ready to offer it, under the benign auspices of a failing Organization. There will always be the very sick and disturbed candidate, the brilliant professional, who cannot tolerate the blow to his self-esteem (or narcissism) caused by the change from the vertical to the horizontal position. This is the case which will induce the analyst to make all kinds of mistakes and the Organization joins in with early and wrong interventions, finally standing by helplessly waiting for the denouement, which it is hoped will not bring unfavourable publicity to the Society or the psychoanalytic movement.

Is it true that the transference is only a pallid version of emotionally heated transference reactions in other situations? If the answer is in the affirmative, how do we account for the violent reactions and negative responses to the exposure of infantile conflicts, which is so readily experienced as a blow to self-esteem rather than a valuable step on the way towards greater self-confidence? Being a patient whilst aiming at being a therapist touches the deepest core of the narcissistic investment in the self. This situation is more likely to produce a transference resistance than a dilution of the transference. But it is true that transference leakages may occur and that certain areas, surprisingly perhaps, are more likely than others to escape (or resist) analysis; witness unresolved homosexual transferences.

It is perhaps this kind of occurrence that has led some analysts to express the view that in the long run a candidate may become almost incapable of a genuine analytical process and the therapeutic aim has been lost or invaded by and often sacrificed by the analysand's ambition to do well in order to reach graduation quickly. These are extreme views, of course, but in my own experience when that has happened it is promptly followed by a turning away from involvement in psychoanalytic matters and even resignation from membership of the Society.

This brief review cannot ignore three other areas which we believe have a bearing on unfavourable outcomes in the immediate postgraduate phase. The first one relates to the increasing discontent in the student, his complaint of lack of excitement in analysis. As all interest goes out of analysis as such (not immediately apparent in his own analysis) he turns to other therapies. The second area concerns identification. Should the analyst's personality have proved forceful or overwhelming, the student becomes clearly identified with the aggressor. This is likely to lead to a caricature of techniques once the student enters practice. The third outcome is postgraduate breakdown, often due to foreclosure of conflicts and symptoms, mainly because of the analysand's desire to graduate. It would be illusory to deny that many unfavourable developments are a reflection of faulty technique, particularly in the understanding of the transference and countertransference. In assessing results, though, we should not ignore the unsatisfactory state of our selection procedures.

In examining our candidates' position within the Training Organizations we must question the lack of rebelliousness in them, not always attributable to maturity which is missing in so many other respects. It is indeed possible that we have created Organizations that promote an unnaturally passive acceptance in the trainees. It is unlikely, however, that external measures alone will modify the nature and quality of the candidate's experience. Nevertheless it will be vital to attempt to isolate the direct responsibility attributable to the analyst and his way of interrelating with other parties involved in the training situation. It will then become possible to isolate the latter from the human difficulties, foibles and weaknesses of men, which prompt them to misunderstand, misuse or misapply psychoanalytic theory and practice.

The discussion that followed the Chairman's address was dominated by the feeling that to deny the complications arising from the dual role of the training analyst would be unrealistic. It was acknowledged that here was a lively challenge which could be met by disavowal, splitting and projection onto the Society of problems that were internal to the analyst.

Although the training analysis has a basic therapeutic aim, its second function creates far-reaching goals in the mind of the analyst, who tends to feel he is the repository of an analytic ego ideal, often sensed and resented by the candidate.

The emotional pressures on the analyst were discussed at length. Not only does he have to accept comments about his technique and theoretical beliefs from his patients, as well as comparisons of himself and other analysts, but he must also tolerate hearing comments about his analysands from colleagues. Questions were asked whether there was something unrealistic about the expectations an analyst has about a candidate, unlike his feelings about ordinary patients. It was suggested that this could be part of an understandable ambition.

The training analyst's narcissism did not escape examination, as it could be stimulated by the candidate's expectations of an idealistic, unrealistic kind; fantasies of obtaining power; of possessing secrets; of becoming superman, etc. The therapist's unfulfilled wishes, inadequately dealt with in his own analysis, may show up in the form of acting out or in attempts to keep other analysts out of the magic circle of the Education Committee.

Emotional demands, of course, are increased in those training analysts who are too insecure or have insufficient belief in their own judgement.

Thus, there was some support for the possibility that some degree of self-idealization may be healthy but it would require considerable effort to work through the mourning process involved in giving it up. The training analyst, in fact, ought to become more aware of his own relative insignificance. The need to parade good candidates interferes with good analysis and could lead to missing a silent part of the patient who acts out after graduation, either in the direction of rigidity or chaos. This could be aggravated in those cases where the analyst has used the analysand to satisfy or fulfil his own unconscious needs. The strain of having to accept the fact that our candidates are with us forever and that this exposes us to gossip, rumours and the charge of being bad 'therapists' for having produced such awful analysts, was not ignored.

There was much sympathy for the fact that most training analysts are well over forty years of age by the time they are recognized as such; and therefore they will be confronted by problems arising from ageing, male and female menopausal or mid-life crisis in some form or another. The need to help colleagues who get into difficulties under these conditions was much stressed.

In discussing the position of candidates, it was agreed that the combination of a personal analysis with educational aims was responsible for the frequency of re-analysis. Although the failure of the first attempt was often attributed to the training situation, it was recognized that feelings of dissatisfaction and disappointment with what one had hoped to achieve with the first analysis should not be underestimated. Studies of re-analysis showed that the immediate reason for seeking further help was due to excessive idealization that leads the patient back to his former analyst with the desire to acquire his special magic powers; whilst others, denigrating the former therapist and complaining about his pathological character problems, which they felt had impeded their progress, would go to a new analyst in the same search for fantasy power. A third motive was attributable to the fact that mourning processes were not always properly worked through, and that underlying transference problems had been overlooked. Even so, it requires a certain capacity for elaboration and maturity to resolve these difficulties. In this sense a second analysis acquires different aims than the first one.

A suggestion that an applicant's wish to train was to be considered a symptom was less well received. If so, a delegate commented, all of us did not succeed in getting rid of it. A candidate may be in the position of a person who, behind and beyond his professional reality reasons, wants to go through a psychoanalytical experience. This is something that he may not be able to admit to others and to himself and we should always consider it beyond every 'reality' justification. Hidden in this difficulty in admitting it is the basic fear of growing up that is a basic factor in life for everybody. A person may reach a point of wanting to be treated psychoanalytically in a moment of his life process which was difficult for him to predict, but it is invariably a meaningful life situation. During the ensuing analytical process, a candidate can at least reach the position of being capable of identifying with somebody else, and with the analyst first. But the real process of identification which will contribute to form his psychoanalytical identity is lived out after graduation. The process in itself is not always unhindered, in so far as the newly qualified analyst may start to identify with his analyst with the secret aim of becoming a training analyst or quite simply of wanting to be like him. It is at this point that postgraduate breakdowns may occur with the inability to negotiate the correct type of identification, leading to re-analysis.

A further source of trouble for the candidate was found in the concretization of the transference, because of the identification with the original family situation, as noted by the Chairman. A candidate who longs to be an only child, becomes part of an adoptive family and at the same time idealizes the Training Organization. In time this leads to disillusionment and withdrawal from organizational activities. On the other hand, in the more hopeful and better analysed cases, similar fantasies can promote a furtherance of professionalism and the feeling of belonging to the analytic family which continues throughout the professional life.

Although Education Committees were criticized for clinging to power and for creating a situation in which training analysts are kings and nobody listens to non-training analysts, it was nevertheless agreed that these training bodies were a valuable repository for the protection of psychoanalysis against the dangers of dilution and deterioration. Much appreciation was expressed for the attempts on the part of officials to rescue colleagues from impossible situations with psychopathic or unsuitable candidates. Whilst admitting that the difficulties could be minimized but not really overcome, there was unanimous condemnation of the over-cathexis of training which induces a messianic spirit and increasing demands for perfection from all those involved. It is to the credit of the discussants that they were able to express the view that to become a training analyst is the only way to be one of the best, or one of the elite, which could well turn out to be an unhealthy kind of narcissistic triumph, whilst administering a severe narcissistic blow to those who do not achieve a similar status.

As the Conference drew to a close it was clear that nothing could be settled but a great deal was gained from bringing so many issues into the open. The Chairman, on the other hand, was left with a firm view that the neutrality of the training analyst is nothing but a myth.

POSTSCRIPT (1988)

The difficulties arising from the analyst's dual role in a Training Organization are unlikely to be resolved in the foreseeable future. In supporting this contention, I can only mention that on the occasion of the 35th Congress of the International Psychoanalytical Association held in Montreal in 1987, another Conference of Training Analysts was called to discuss 'The conflicting loyalties of the training analyst: to the analysand as a patient and to the field and its future'. The reader who is now more familiar with the intricacies implicit in issues described in the previous sections will not be surprised to hear of a possible conflict of loyalty. The organizers of the Conference will be forgiven for having chosen a title with a somewhat moralizing slant, in view of the fact that psychoanalysts continue to be dangerously close to being disloyal in the impossible situation they find themselves in. Their attempts to deal with it at a conscious or unconscious level are unlikely to be effective whilst they can continue to have far-reaching effects on the transference and countertransference.

The concept of loyalty, however, was understood to have different meanings: love, attachment, affection, submission even. It was said that one could be loyal out of very primitive motives to very primitive objects. There was some concern, though, about the theoretical position of the loyalty concept in view of its superego and ego (that is to say, moral and affective) aspects of the concept.

On this occasion little new emerged in relation to the issue of a therapeutic versus a didactic analysis. It was pointed out that there was a risk of altering the nature of analysis by artificially dividing the patient into a suffering human being who needs help and a professional colleague who needs guidance to improve his skills.

Little new emerged from a discussion of the reporting versus non-reporting issue but some useful comments were forthcoming with regard to the role of selection procedures. It was hoped that refined techniques would reduce the pressure on the training analyst but again there was a body of opinion which was concerned that more stringent selection would cause the deselection of some prospective candidates who might in due course become excellent analysts.

Great concern was once more expressed about the ailing or incompetent training analyst and it was recommended that such a person should be encouraged to seek further analysis and supervision.

I was interested to note that in 1973 it was generally felt that there should be only a minimum contact between analyst and candidate-patient after graduation, whereas in 1987 this was considered to be an added problem; it was as if this gives rise to tensions within the organization through a disruption of social and educational events.

Amongst the worthy conclusions of this Conference, I must record that preventive measures were alleged to be fraught with dangers and were said to take two forms. One is to perfect the training analyst so that he becomes therapeutically omnipotent. This has contributed to the emergence of charismatic leaders who think they can treat and train anyone. The second is to believe that the training programme can be perfected so that it can cope with unsatisfactory analysis.

Looking back over the years and having been in contact with training organizations from all over the world, my views have undergone some considerable changes. I am now wholly against reporting on candidates but I am well aware that conflicts of loyalty are not resolved by the analyst opting out from practical involvements. It must be a foregone conclusion that he should not be the person to decide when a supervision should begin or when the candidate should be graduated. On the other hand, how can an analyst function with the thought that one of his patients has fooled the Education Committee; or how can a future practitioner live with the thought of having done so? Nevertheless, I have been encouraged by the fact that I have found it possible to ease out of training some obviously unsuitable candidates without causing too much injury or disruption and I have also given my support to colleagues in a similar predicament.

With ageing and experience, most training analysts find it easier to tolerate sarcastic comments or seductive behaviour on the part of a candidate-patient-colleague. The envy of an older person is so pathological in itself that it can only be a source of good analytical material. This also applies to all gossip and remarks of all kinds concerning colleagues and the Institute. To act on such comments is unthinkable but it does require some care not to be affected by it.

It is disappointing that in spite of the many opportunities to ventilate the problems described in this paper, there are still some experienced colleagues who are reluctant to admit that there is a remarkable difference between a purely therapeutic analysis and one that is linked with educational and professional attainments. Yet the dramatic changes that occur in the analytic process, once the training has been got out of the way, should provide sufficient proof of its unwelcome interference.

I very much doubt that any real changes will take place in the near future, so long as the demand for training continues to increase. All that we can hope for is that the International Psychoanalytical Association will continue in its relentless efforts to ensure the high standards of training and practice which the public rightly expects from us.

Sources: *Bulletin of the European Psychoanalytical Federation*: Nos 2 and 3, 1973; Archives of the International Psychoanalytical Association; *Report of the 5th Pre-Congress Conference on Training*, 1973, and *Report of the 3rd International Psychoanalytical Association Conference of Training Analysts*, 1987.)

ACKNOWLEDGEMENTS

I wish to record my indebtedness and gratitude to those colleagues who wrote or submitted papers on the occasion of the 1973 Conference. In view of the confidential nature of the majority of these communications, it has been impossible to indicate the origin of the many opinions and viewpoints included. I am especially grateful to Mrs J. McDougall and Dr S. Klein for their reports on the 1973 Conference, and to Dr D. Sachs for his report on the 1987 Conference.

6 OBJECT CHOICE AND BISEXUALITY*

INTRODUCTION

P SYCHOANALYSIS HAS THROWN much light on the factors which
enable some people to retain their homosexuality in a latent state, while
others can successfully satisfy the needs of the male and female parts of their
personality without being compelled to act out their id experiences in a fully
fledged perversion. The capacity of certain individuals to engage in sexual
activities with members of both sexes continues to present a challenge to
our theoretical understanding of human sexuality and of the perversion as
such. In general, theoretical and clinical discussions tend to concentrate our
attention on the homosexual aspect of the dichotomy, neglecting Freud's
reminder that even heterosexuality requires justification (Freud, 1905a,
p. 146).

In this context defence is understood to be directed not only at protecting
the ego against anxiety aroused by instinctual drives, the superego, or
external dangers, but also and preferably at including all the techniques
used by the ego to dominate control and channel forces which might lead to
neurosis or psychosis. In those bisexual cases where homosexuality is
predominant, the heterosexuality may well assume a defensive role, which
does not become apparent until one outlet is suddenly unavailable.

Psychoanalysts are only too familiar with the difficulties of analysing
patients who are tormented by the presence of conscious bisexual fantasies
and impulses that are often enough almost ineradicable. A comparison with
actual bisexuality must be maintained throughout. Masud Khan in his

* This paper was first published in 1975 in the *Revue Française Psychanalyse* 5:
858–67 and in the *International Journal of Psychoanalytic Psychotherapy* 5: 206–17.

paper, 'Ego-orgasm in bisexual love' (1974a), has also drawn attention to the danger of confusing bisexual love, unaccompanied by physical contact, with latent homosexual love. Khan's thesis rests on the dissociation between the male and female elements in the personality of a given person, which, if unresolved, leads to a lack of affective surrender in the heterosexual situation. The dissociated affectivity is acted out in an ego-promiscuous fleeting attachment with objects of the same sex. However, although Khan's conclusions are indirectly relevant to this discussion, it will be readily seen that there is an enormous difference between an intense brief encounter between two men or two women without any physical contact and the man who has intercourse with his male lover shortly after he has had a satisfying experience with his wife.

We do not know how common actual bisexuality is, but we should not be misled by its prevalence in certain circles, since it is quite clear that those who practise it, because it is fashionable, regard it as an ego-dystonic experience. In such cases we are perhaps correct in assuming that a lenient group superego is all that is required to break down shaky defensive barriers. We must, nevertheless, recognize that bisexuality is on the increase generally and as therapists we see more cases than at any other time in the past. It is said to occur in situations of stress, particularly in prisons. Such explanations may amount to rationalizations and should not be accepted too readily. In males, psychopathic disturbances or borderline states are prevalent. In females of predominantly heterosexual disposition, an immature personality will combine with an unresolved and profound ambivalent attachment to the mother. Few bisexual individuals present as having no commitments whatsoever to either sex. Just as it is a serious mistake for the diagnostician to dismiss such cases as being the result of contingency, it is an even worse mistake to try and eradicate either of the possible sexual outlets without having established the possible risk of a severe psychotic illness or even suicide. Psychoanalytic literature contains few references to this subject. Weissman (1962) wrote on the structural considerations in overt male bisexuality, but his interesting paper suffers from a scarcity of material on which his conclusions are based. Furthermore, some of his cases seem to feature almost exclusively that type of bisexual man who is passive in his sexual exploits. We know of course that all homosexuality is basically passive, but it is also true that sexual practices range from passive to active, in accordance with a variety of defensive manoeuvres. Weissman's thesis may be restated as follows: if the overt homosexuality is derived from pre-oedipal identification with the mother and object relations are at a narcissistic level, then the overt bisexuality is basically a homosexual perversion. Strong archaic superego and ego-ideal demands lead to the establishment of overt pseudo-heterosexuality. To explain this, Weissman puts forward an ingenious suggestion: the homosexual achieves the state through the utilization of a fetish, i.e. the woman's body as equated to the phallus. An alternative type of psychopathology occurs when bisexuality is oedipal in origin; Weissman suggests that the superego demands a regressive object choice along with the heterosexual object choice. The acting out of the homosexual component is said to be part of the repetition of the entire oedipal conflict. On the other hand, we could say that the homosexual's ideal image could be restored by supplying a phallus to the woman and then being able to enjoy his lovemaking within a pseudo-heterosexual position. But I think the real problem with this explanation is our knowledge that the fetish is often used to ward off the homosexual acting out which arises from excessive castration anxiety.

There seems to be no end to the complications which arise from any attempt to bring sense and order to a study of the perversions. Treatment is also made all the more difficult because the actively bisexual patient belongs almost invariably to the borderline group, displaying a marked tendency to act out, with a concurrent outstanding dispersal of transference manifestations. The patient in the early stages appears quite satisfied to defend against his heterosexuality with his homosexuality and vice versa. The analyst at first feels nowhere except as a reflection of the patient who is caught up in an impossible choice. In a second stage, the analyst is able to mobilize the patient's feelings in one or other direction; the location of the transference is clearer but nonetheless nebulous in so far as there is utter dependence, quickly alternating with movements to break away from it. In many cases the early appearance of narcissistic transference creates further problems in the understanding and general handling of the situation. Worse things are still to come when the patient establishes a dependent relationship or makes a narcissistic choice of a love object outside the transference. The importance of recognizing the fluctuation between the narcissistic object choice and defences, and the object choice of the attachment type, is a familiar concept to those analysts who have worked extensively with borderline and predominantly narcissistic patients. Eisnitz (1974) has underlined the danger of mistakes in the handling of this delicate area which can cause a repetition of a trauma suffered by the patient in his developing years.

I was able to observe all of this during the supervision of the analysis of a bisexual male who had come for help because his homosexual interest was threatening his marriage. His wife had recently become pregnant and he had been very active in promoting her abortion because his dependence on her was clearly endangered by the appearance of a prospective rival. His male partners were expected to submit to his aggressive demands and, as might have been expected, similar behaviour soon made its appearance in the transference. In the course of time such an attempt was seen to be part of a subtle manoeuvre to cover up deep dependence and attachment to the analyst.

A subsequent review of some cases of bisexuality which had come under my observation during the last few years showed a striking similarity in terms of their psychopathology, transference manifestations, and above all the attempt to retrace the development of their object relations, leading to some degree of separation between the anaclitic and the narcissistic object choice.

The cases to be described are a random sample, the choice being confined to patients who were capable of having sexual contact with both sexes during one period of their lives, which period could spread over months or years. A further factor in the choice was my direct acquaintance with the patients' partners in some instances supported by reliable reports from colleagues who had also become involved with them.

CLINICAL MATERIAL

Mr A was a married man aged forty-four whose family insisted he should have some treatment because it was thought that his homosexual attachments to young boys represented a threat to the safety of his children. He was sent at the age of seven to public school where he was in the care of older brothers who ignored him. He was reduced to an abject state of depression and emotional isolation, disturbed only by much teasing and bullying. A schoolmaster who seduced him was later imprisoned. Mr A married a very young, inexperienced, and helpless woman. During the initial phase of the marriage he made her utterly dependent on him, fulfilling all the functions of both parents for her. He obviously needed her to carry his own dependence because when she matured and later told him of having an affair he became promiscuous with both sexes. His bisexuality came into the open when he seduced the son of his father-in-law's business associate. Until then his dual life had been a well-kept secret, but by that time Mr A and his wife were going their separate ways. She was very active socially, and a very efficient mother, while he was driving himself compulsively as a company director, with his own secret hideout where he entertained large numbers of male and female adolescents of dubious character. He entered analysis as a seriously distraught man who was warding off his deep depression by whatever means at whatever cost, but he broke it off after a year because basically he was too dependent on the analyst and could not tolerate his inability to control him. However brief, the analysis revealed (1) a lack of a good-enough maternal experience in infancy; (2) his passion for boys was of the classical narcissistic type; (3) he loved his father-in-law as the man who protected him, which indeed was the case; (4) his pseudo-heterosexuality was notable for its complete indifference and was probably only a vehicle for creating dependency in women as a relief from his profound feeling of dependence upon and attachment to them. He remained in a curious way attached to and dependent on his wife, who in turn remained loyal to him.

Mrs S was thirty-two when first seen during a serious depressive illness which had been precipitated by an unhappy affair with a woman a great deal older than herself, who eventually could not tolerate her demanding behaviour. During the long association her whole life had orbited around her partner. She had been married for twelve years and had three children. She met her husband as a teenager when they were both travelling on a bus, each carrying a copy of the Bible. She had been very jealous in her late childhood because her mother had two more boys and her father had ignored her throughout. Strong religious influences and uncertainty about her femininity had played an important role in the severe inhibition in her heterosexual development. Improvement was gradual and, when she began to enjoy her sexual life with her husband, I felt my initial optimism to be justified.

Unhappily there had been some omissions in her psychotherapy which were revealed when it was resumed two years later. Seeing her again in a deep depression made me aware that when I had previously terminated her treatment she had been in a manic state. She was now profoundly dependent on me and had been since we had parted. Acute separation anxiety was indeed a very serious complication. Mrs S was again frigid and for the first time she revealed that her husband was not only an obsessive-compulsive character, which I knew, but also was a sexual pervert. Sexual relations at infrequent intervals would extend over several hours with endless preliminaries in the course of which she was required to wear certain articles of clothing, etc. She would also have to parade naked and allow herself to be observed at length. In the course of the next few years I was in no doubt about the early origins of her disturbance. In her childhood she had shared a bed with an aged grandmother and later a maid. This was hardly due to lack of accommodation or social or financial stress. Her depression recurred at intervals, associated with intense homosexual feelings which were carefully evaluated in the transference but at the same time were acted out in a variety of ways at work. As various aspects of the pre-oedipal attachment to the mother were investigated the depression would begin to lift. Heterosexual feelings would follow and with them the manic defence would appear as a clear response to guilty feelings. Her husband was helped into treatment, and later a daughter whose clinging attachment she could not bear was also taken on for psychotherapy. This situation required meetings with a psychiatric social worker and a reasonably sympathetic relationship was established. Slowly the attachment to me was loosened and her treatment was brought to a close, but not before some momentous crises accompanied by suicidal threats. On one particularly dramatic occasion, conscious murderous impulses towards her husband led to an acute confusional state, requiring a few days' hospital treatment, followed by a quick recovery and much insight.

The diagnosis in such a case is a matter of interest, since the possibility of a manic depressive illness had to be considered. The total lack of any response to anti-depressant drugs, on the other hand, and the symptomatology pointed more to a narcissistic disorder. It would also seem that this patient had chosen her partner on a narcissistic basis. This was shown quite clearly in the perverse activity when she was gratified through her identification with him in his admiring and looking at her body. The attachment to the older woman, fully relived for long stretches of time in the transference, amounted to a split in the object choice. This created endless complications in the treatment situation, which cannot be discussed here.

Mr C was a twenty-four-year-old social worker, married, with a child aged two. He had been actively bisexual for two years. When he was first seen his suitability for psychotherapy was in doubt because he claimed never to have been happier since he had gone to live with a twenty-six-year-old man while still seeing his wife. His father had died when he was six. He claimed his mother tried to press feminine things on him throughout his childhood. There had been only some casual sexual play with boys when still at school. As soon as he became engaged he suddenly experienced an intense urge to have intercourse with men. He caught gonorrhoea and passed it on to his fiancée, who reacted by putting intense pressure on him to get married. His promiscuous activities with men began during the sixth month of his wife's pregnancy. After seeing his wife for a few hours each week and having fully satisfying sexual relations with her he would quickly return to his friend and have anal intercourse with him. This acting out was at first claimed by him to be related to his need to reinforce his feelings of masculine supremacy. But it was more than that since heterosexual experiences for him amounted to a total emotional surrender (A. Freud, 1952) which threatened his very existence. In his very complex way of relating, this man projected his femininity upon the wife and was exasperated by her mishandling of her own femininity. He bitterly complained that his wife would not do things for him half as well as his older male partner did. In his relationship to the latter it was clear that there was a re-enacting of a profound attachment to the mother.

In the early stages of treatment an inadequacy in the handling of the psychotherapeutic relationship caused Mr C to act out by bringing his wife to the session. I saw no reason nor could I find a good excuse for not seeing her. She turned out to be a very charming, feminine, slightly overweight young woman who confirmed everything he had said. She quickly admitted to her feeling of having been starved of love by her mother and expected her husband to compensate her. In this joint interview they mirrored each other to perfection, except that she readily confessed that lesbians horrified and repulsed her while she had no objection to male homosexuality. In another interview they both fought bitterly for my attention. He eventually came out with the statement that he often felt he could strangle her. She seemed to be not at all disturbed by this and had little conscious awareness of the danger she was in. Next day he reported that after this very tense interview, he had gone home to his friend, who comforted him and allowed him to lie in his arms while he masturbated himself to sleep. It was also as a result of this interview that I concluded that he had come for help because he urgently needed to remove himself from an impossible heterosexual involvement, but had not the strength to do so. After the final break with his wife had occurred, Mr C felt relief and remarked, 'I no longer see a reflection of myself in her. I have taken my femininity back into myself and I have gone back to X who is much more like the mother I need.' In the same momentary mood of insight he added, 'I suppose like so many other homosexual relationships we shall end up as brothers or perhaps I shall marry again.'

This patient's very real and dangerous impulse to murder his female partner was related to his seeing in her a reflection of his passive feminine self. What is puzzling in this case is that a man who is so completely homosexual in his orientation should be at all capable of having such satisfying sexual experience with a woman. If it is true that the female body is the fetish, I would be inclined to regard such fetish as a transitional object, which would also account for his inability to break away from it.

The case histories which have been described so far concern individuals who display a predominantly homosexual orientation. Severely disturbed patients with poor heterosexual adjustment are always at risk to act out the underlying homosexual impulses while undergoing psychotherapy. Khan (1964b) has shown that psychoanalysis is no guarantee that such acting out will not occur and, in the case he then described at length, the patient was able to make full use of it in furthering the growth and expansion of her personality and femininity. Something of a similar nature occurred during the treatment of a young girl in circumstances which again indicated an attempt to separate the two classical object choices.

Miss D was nineteen years old when she was referred for psychotherapy while a patient in a mental hospital where she had spent the previous three years. When I first met her she presented as a charming and highly intelligent person who could have been either a boy or a girl. Her behaviour disorder had become more acute after an abortion at sixteen. She was utterly confused not only about her sexual identity but also about those of other people, as shown by her Rorschach test. Her psychotherapy had frequently been interrupted. There had been innumerable crises with severe depressive phases, suicidal attempts, abortions, and promiscuity. Progression and regression had occurred in rapid alternation, as we could expect in a case of severe narcissistic disorder associated with a borderline state. The most dangerous complication was her gradual addiction to soft drugs escalating to hard drugs. Her paranoid anxieties were maximal during this phase but well controlled by the addiction. Close contact was maintained throughout this period. However, with the removal of the addiction her homosexuality emerged in full, together with the exacerbation of the paranoid anxieties within the maternal transference. She broke off treatment once more and when she returned some months later she reported that she had had a fairly prolonged lesbian relationship which had left her with a general feeling of disillusionment. Her interest in men had not altered during this phase, and on the whole she had felt 'liberated' and was now more able to enjoy her heterosexual pursuits. However, her more constant male partners had invariably been violent but gifted and capable of engaging in a sado-masochistic relationship. They were in fact indistinguishable from the patient in their existential approach to life and other personality characteristics. They simply could not understand the reasons when Miss D broke away from them, quite suddenly, as if she could no longer bear to see her own reflection in a mirror. In the transference there had been extreme dependence with much ambivalence. The lesbian episode was understood as being related to a splitting off of the libidinal, sexual aspect of the transference but was also seen as the supreme testing out of her fear of being swallowed up or merged with a mother figure.

This was an unusual case where the split transference turned out to be almost an advantage because there were less opportunities for misinterpretation and mistakes. By bringing her partners, and by requesting on occasions that they should be present at her sessions, Miss D also made sure that nothing was missed.

As a corollary to this account I should add that I have observed acting out of homosexual impulses and similar attempts to split the transference in a number of cases of transvestism, notably that of a transvestite whose fear of homosexuality had greatly interfered with his heterosexual adjustment.

DISCUSSION

The patients described had certain features in common which could not be outlined in any detail. Even taking into account the one-sided perspective of their early upbringing, there was fair evidence of deficiencies in parental handling; and at times the parents' behaviour suggested a severe degree of personality disturbance. Some of the mothers seem to have been quite unable to promote a smooth passage from the early stages of closeness and intimacy to separation and final individuation. Typical was the case of Miss D who had been involved in a symbiotic relationship with her mother, who needed prolonged psychotherapy and support in order to facilitate her daughter's own treatment and development. All the patients were highly intelligent but had been precocious, and without distinction exhibited evidence suggestive of an exquisite awareness of early bodily experiences. Bisexuality, however, is by no means confined to the intellectually better endowed. A survey of patients, including others not presented in this paper, points to the occurrence of unbearable separation anxiety, each subject developing his or her own individual way of dealing with it, ranging from denial to transvestism. Splitting processes figured prominently and no one could doubt the capacity of these patients to dissociate the male and female parts of their personality, linked with projective identification and profound disturbance in interpersonal relationships.

If the heterosexuality is viewed separately, the only fair conclusion to be reached is that it has a definite 'pseudo' quality to it. In one case, that of Mr C, the patient reported an ecstatic quality to his sexual experience with his wife, easily traced to a projection of his femininity to her which left him empty and drained. Again, a careful investigation of the homosexuality taken in isolation would reveal little which is not likely to occur in this syndrome with all the variations of its underlying psychopathology. Quite frequently an overall factor which has been stressed by Masud Khan (1964b) is that, as these patients tend to split off their bodily and feeling experiences, the aim of the homosexuality is to mend the split. If we viewed the total situation of these patients' lives and personal relations, and if we had the opportunity of observing their partners from close quarters over a long period, a different picture might emerge. As already indicated, my observations suggest that in the majority of cases of manifest bisexuality the subjects are caught up between the two types of object choices available to them – the attachment and the narcissistic; in some extreme cases they almost set one up against the other.

Writing on the classical theory of object choice, Laplanche and Pontalis (1973) have stated that the two types are purely ideal and liable to alternate or combine. They also remark that it is doubtful whether an antithesis even with ideal types is tenable, a view which I find quite acceptable. Eisnitz, in the paper to which I have already referred, suggests that, in the narcissistic object choice, the cathexis is directed at self-representation and in the attachment type is directed at object representation – a fair account of the situation, as is often seen in clinical practice. However, he goes on to say, 'whereas at any one time either the narcissistic or the attachment elements may predominate, attempts to separate them completely either in therapy or in theory are artificial' (p. 279).

In my opinion, this is precisely what happens in the bisexual who is trying to achieve the impossible: the separation of his original two types of object choice. Prodigal expenditure of libido in self or object through such dissociation accounts not only for the frantic rushing to and from one unreal person to another, but also for much unhappiness and a sense of loss and incompleteness in each relationship and in the self. In the therapeutic situation, havoc is caused in the transference and as I have already hinted this results in enormous difficulty in locating it. There are of course few other instances where we can observe with such clarity the use made of narcissistic defences against regressions within the attachment situation when it becomes too threatening, and we also know only too well how valuable such defences can be in coping with separation anxiety. As it happens, in the transference of bisexual patients we are confronted by the challenging situation that they have a ready-made potential displacement by the very nature of their complaint. In the countertransference the analyst is soon caught up in the problem of not knowing quite what is best for his patient: to be heterosexual, homosexual, or both. Even when the impact of the transference is successful in drawing some of the fire away from the patient's turmoil in his external life, for long periods we operate within a triangular situation. The illusion that we are dealing with two objects can be perpetuated if we do not realize that we are only dealing with one (the original) object. In this writer's opinion, this means that all those instances of protracted and recurrent bisexual behaviour, including the acting out of homosexual impulses in the course of psychotherapy, cannot be understood as being the result of unresolved oedipal conflicts. It is conceded that on first examination these people will impress the therapist as wishing to keep both the male and female partners, i.e., father and mother; or that they are unable to give up either of them, thus creating the appearance of being in the throes of an unbearable oedipal conflict. Careful investigation will show that there is little depth to it. We should also note that their impressive heterosexual exploits on close scrutiny also turn out to be suggestive of pseudo-genitality rather than mature genitality. The occurrence of similar psychopathology in men and women and the predominance of pre-oedipal areas of disturbance in the majority of the cases which I was able to observe at length would support the view which I have just put forward. However, this does not mean that the father plays no part. On the contrary, the bisexual's psychic life is dominated by an intense longing for a 'good' father who will rescue him or her from an impossible predicament. The male often believes that he has found such an ideal object in the masculine partner, only to discover that it was illusory, or that the mate compulsively uses him in some way. In my judgement the establishment of a good, but not idealized, father-transference relationship was essential to progress and development in the cases included in this report – patients whose real fathers were absent or remote figures. (Mr A's father was ineffectual and disinterested; Mrs S complained that her father had ignored her throughout her life; Mr C's father had died when he was six; and Miss D saw her father as a distant, cruel figure.) In understanding the role of the absent father, I have found André Green's remarks in his paper, 'The analyst, symbolization and absence in the analytic setting' (1975), very helpful. He writes, there is no such couple formed by mother and baby without the father. For the child is the figure of the union between mother and father . . . It is true that the father is absent from this relationship [of the mother and child]. But to say that he is absent means that he is neither present nor non-existent but that he has a potential presence. (p. 13)

There is indeed little hope of success in treating a bisexual patient unless this potential presence is fully understood and made more real.

THE ROLE OF PSYCHOTHERAPY IN BISEXUALITY

Bisexuality is a complex state of mind associated with a multiplicity of aetiological factors. Analysts who have had the opportunity of observing a large number of cases agree that those who are so affected have been exposed to direct influences in their environment which have resulted in the formation of an imperfect superego. Investigation of most of such cases will usually show that either a parent, a teacher, or a person in a similar position of authority has actually encouraged or condoned the insurgence or establishment of feelings for, and sexual acts with, persons of both sexes. I would, however, consider this to be only an additional or aggravating factor and arguably responsible for the prevalent attitude of bisexuals in asserting that their behaviour is well within normality. In the cases included in this report the condition was seen to be related to severe narcissistic disorders of character and personality often in the setting of a borderline state. The aetiology would principally be that encountered in these conditions. I would underline here the frequency of an ineffectual or absent father as being of considerable importance. But cold, remote, or possibly mentally disturbed mothers are not uncommon. In my own experience the mothers of bisexuals who have come to my attention were not seductive mothers, as we often meet in the case of homosexuals. A constitutional intolerance, frustration, and limited impulse control are other common features.

Having suggested that actual bisexuality is in general associated with narcissistic and/or borderline states, the issue of treatment becomes relevant. The contrasting views of analysts with regard to the choice of psychoanalysis and other forms of psychotherapy for such conditions is well known. Kernberg (1970) has stated his position very clearly when, in discussing prognostic considerations, he suggests 'that narcissistic personalities, in spite of the fact that their defensive organization is, broadly speaking, similar to that of the borderline personality, benefit very little from expressive, psychoanalytically oriented treatment approaches geared to that category of patients, and that psychoanalysis is the treatment of choice for narcissistic personalities' (p. 72). It might be appropriate to speculate about the possible outcome in three of the cited cases had there been opportunity to offer them psychoanalysis. It would be fair to assume that in the case of Miss D the homosexual acting out might have been averted, but on the other hand it is highly questionable whether any of these patients would have been able to tolerate the rigours of the full psychoanalytic process, a situation also recognized by Kernberg. It is even possible that my patients would not be considered suitable for any form of analytic psychotherapy; yet in my opinion once the treatment is undertaken there must be an all-out effort to trace the early development of object choice, and this can only be done by making full use of the transference. This is contrary to the view expounded in the already cited article by Kernberg, who writes: 'In patients with narcissistic personalities and overt borderline states . . . psychoanalysis is contra-indicated. These patients cannot tolerate the severe regression and reactivation of very early pathogenic conflicts in the transference without psychotic decompensation; a supportive treatment approach seems best for this group' (p. 72). Returning to the subject in a later paper Kernberg (1974) reiterates his belief that those narcissistic personalities who function on an overt borderline level are prone to the development of a transference psychosis. This and the insufficient integration for a more effective social functioning create a contra-indication for analysis and even for the modified psychoanalytic procedures recommended by Kernberg for most patients with borderline personality organization.

In this paper I have tried to show that in addition to employing a number of other instrumental parameters these patients can be approached through the transference in its positive and negative aspects; I hope this will stimulate further discussions as to the numerous issues involved not only in connection with the treatment of bisexuals but also of narcissistic and borderline states. The treatment of bisexuality should not be undertaken lightly and not before there is a full assessment of the patient's motivation for a change and the therapist's willingness to contain a difficult situation over a long period with little to show in the way of apparent improvement. The advantage of working in close contact with the staff of an institution, with the availability of medical, auxiliary, and other administrative support, should not be underestimated, especially when the patients' partners may also need help. Perhaps the answer in dealing with some of the more complex and challenging cases which come our way is flexibility.

7 CLINICAL TYPES OF HOMOSEXUALITY*

INTRODUCTION

IN RECENT YEARS there has become apparent an increasingly marked division in the attitude to homosexuality: at a time when there is a growing tendency for people in all walks of life to regard homosexuality as normal, there remain many who use the term in a derogatory and insulting manner, quite often with an implication of social menace.

With the abolition of the more restrictive of the laws touching on relationships between individuals of the same sex, and the increased permissiveness in contemporary society, it has become apparent that homosexuality remains a condition which may in certain specific instances require treatment.

When treatment is discussed among psychotherapists, opinion is sharply divided: quite apart from doubts and divergent theoretical considerations as to what constitutes homosexuality, views appear to range from unreasonable pessimism to excessive optimism. This state of affairs is particularly unwelcome in a field which demands both co-operation and a multilateral approach to the patient's problem, taking into account that where one form of treatment may fail, another may succeed.

Those who are interested in the more important investigations centred around the hypothesis of a genetic or endocrine basis for homosexuality are referred to the writings of Kallman (1952), Pare (1956), Abe and Moran (1969), and Dewhurst (1969). In general these studies can be said to have

* An earlier version of this paper was read at a meeting of the Royal College of Psychiatrists in London in 1974. It was published in 1979 as 'The differential diagnosis of homosexuality' in the *British Journal of Medical Psychology* 50: 209–16.

thrown serious doubts on the issue of biological bisexuality as a clinical entity. On the other hand *psychological* bisexuality is a reality and is easily recognizable in its origins, as almost everyone from birth onwards is exposed to the influence of both parents and the consequent identifications with them which is to become the foundation of the later development of male and female parts of the personality. For the purpose of this paper we shall assume that the various types of sexual deviations to be discussed cannot be attributed to physical factors, and will therefore exclude all conditions involving abnormal chromosomal dispositions and severe endocrine disorders (Klinefelter's syndrome, hermaphroditism, etc.).

Psychotherapists approach the problem of sexual deviance in a way which differs from that of general psychiatrists and behaviourists, who are inclined to treat it with nihilism or over-optimism. It is difficult to maintain an open mind about each other's work and this is all the more regrettable as co-operation and a multilateral approach to the patient's problem is in the interest of the patient as well as of science. No one could ignore the work of the behaviour therapist in a field where the suffering is intense and where the number of those affected is so great that only a minority can be reached with the more orthodox forms of psychotherapy. Equally, psychoanalysis is capable of giving us a clear understanding of the psychopathology of sexual deviations, although its detractors will be quick in pointing out that each psychoanalyst appears to have his own view, thus giving the appearance of an almost limitless number of clinical conditions. In this paper, an attempt is made to individuate the more recognizable of such clinical types by using both the psychoanalytic and the psychiatric models. In no other field of our daily work is there a greater need for understanding between the two disciplines. The psychoanalyst who attempts the treatment of a 'true' homosexual must be concerned at the possibility of being confronted with a fully fledged psychosis. On the other hand the psychiatrist who undertakes the treatment of a case of impotence may fail to make an impact unless he is prepared to examine the possible underlying homosexual components of the illness.

The alleged aetiology of homosexuality appears to be complex and multifactorial, to a point where it ceases to make sense. Careful investigation never fails to elicit evidence of basic family dispositions impinging on the individual's development throughout infancy, childhood and early adolescence. The interaction between such family dispositions becomes embedded in the character structure of the individual. In many cases we find deprivation, punitive suppression and sexual frustrations. In the background of both female and male subjects, a parent may or may not be absent (Moran and Abe, 1959). The father may be strong or weak; the mother remote or excessively seductive and domineering. The mother may be over-preoccupied with the father or totally indifferent to him. As children, these people may have sustained severe traumas and deprivations, or may have been spoilt. Lack.of love is of as much importance as too much love (Bene, 1965; Craft, 1966). None of the factors mentioned can be taken as indicative of areas of possible psychopathological disturbance and only seldom will be predictive of sexual deviation. There is also no well-defined personality type that goes with this condition although immaturity and narcissistic traits are fairly common, as well as a tendency to deny or project personal emotional difficulties. We must also acknowledge that it is just possible to force oneself, as a result of religious, moral, social or parental attitudes to be either heterosexual or homosexual (Gillespie, 1964b). When such factors are operative, therapeutic intervention is more likely to succeed.

A PSYCHODYNAMIC APPROACH TO THE UNDERSTANDING OF HOMOSEXUALITY

A perversion is a deviation from the normal sexual act, when this is defined as coitus with a person of the opposite sex directed towards the achievement of orgasm by means of genital penetration. In a more comprehensive sense, perversion connotes the whole of the psychosexual behaviour that accompanies atypical means of obtaining sexual pleasure.

The foundation of the psychoanalytic theory of sexual perversions is to be found in Freud's *Three Essays on the Theory of Sexuality*, dating back to 1905, when the child was first described as being polymorphously perverse. At this stage the erogenous zones are interchangeable. Should there be a breakthrough of infantile polymorphous strivings in later life, the defence mechanism of repression would ensure their transformation into neurotic symptoms. In perversion this does not occur. In the homosexual the persistence of the pregenital phases is revealed by a tendency towards compulsive mutual masturbation, oral or anal intercourse, phallic overvaluation and so on. However, the homosexual, like everyone else, will succeed in repressing his aggressive and incestuous feelings which in the circumstances are almost invariably very disturbing. His ego is as a rule well functioning, but is noticeably helpless in rejecting the internal demands for satisfaction of oral and anal wishes. In the case of male homosexuality we find that infantile attraction and fascination for the father's genital, together with a passive attitude towards it, is transferred to all males and so perpetuated. At an unconscious level there will be a strong fixation on the mother, often associated with hatred for her past rejections.

In the girl, turning once more to mother and away from her father, attachment will present itself as a satisfactory solution of the oedipal feelings. The consequence of such a retrograde step will be similar to what happens in the boy; the only important difference being that in her case, this means a *return* to the first love object. As a rule, strong identification with the parent of the opposite sex is indicative of a particularly stormy and unhealthy resolution of the oedipal complex.

There is general agreement that in the more severe cases of deviation the psychopathology is based on a faulty outcome of the early mother–child relationship, when the gratification expected by the deviant adult is exactly that of a child. There is a longing for something similar to a good feeling and nursing experience with a stress on warmth, skin contact and a demand for protection. A longing for a symbiotic relationship is not uncommon. The triangular family situation seems to be of little or no consequence. There may also be cases when the whole relationship is carried out on the exclusive basis of one bodily organ being all that is required to satisfy the subject's needs, even to the extent of the subject treating a person as if he or she were an organ (penis or maternal breast). It is particularly in the true lesbians that the mother–child relationship is sought and re-enacted between partners. There is here a special type of mother fixation where there has been too little gratification combined with intense hatred, leading to over-emphasis of love for the object, and aimed at neutralizing guilt feelings. The hatred of mother is replaced by love of women, just as too much love or hatred for father will drive the lesbian to seek consolation with her own sex.

In some cases the manic defence is very actively involved, causing feelings of guilt and shame to disappear from consciousness. The successful warding off of depression strengthens illusion and the denial of reality, contributing to the creation of a special group morality.

When development and the formation of the character and personality takes place within normal limits, only a small homosexual nucleus will remain to show the evidence of past struggles, conflicts and compromises. This nucleus, which is wholly unconscious through repression, will continue to act throughout life as an internal psychic regulator of profound value and significance.

These are only brief notes on the very complex psychodynamic theory of homosexuality. More detail about the specific psychopathology of certain clinical types will be found in the next section of this paper when further evidence will be offered in support of the view that the homosexual syndrome can be seen as part of a defensive movement directed at lessening anxiety or at creating barriers against the eruption of unbearable conflicts and quite often simply at ensuring survival. In this context, the defence includes all the techniques used by the ego to dominate, control and channel forces which might lead to neurosis or psychosis.

SOME CLINICAL TYPES OF HOMOSEXUALITY AND THEIR SPECIFIC PSYCHOPATHOLOGY

In purely descriptive terms homosexuality can be repressed, sublimated, fantasied or manifest. Each subdivision carries its own specific symptomatology capable of influencing the individual's state of mind, his interpersonal relationships and his role in society.

Repression plays an extremely important role. For instance, repressed homosexual impulses and conflicts may represent the main aetiological factor in sexual impotence and frigidity. When repression is excessive, sublimatory activities will be impaired. When it is ineffective, the deviation may still not be manifest, but derivative patterns of behaviour will appear. Pathological jealousy is a classical example of this, and is well matched by the opposite attitude, i.e. the wish to share or exchange partners.

The relation of the ineffective repression of homosexual impulses to paranoia was first described by Freud (1911) who summed up the situation in the formula: I (a man) love him, he does not love me, I hate him; he (or his substitute) hates me. It is important to emphasize that not only is love turned into hate, but the whole process is latent (unconscious). A criticism of this important psychoanalytic finding disregards its unconscious nature by adducing evidence that a great many persons are paranoid without becoming homosexually oriented (Friedman, Kaplan and Sadock, 1972). These authors also emphasize that the majority of homosexuals do not develop paranoid delusions. It is however the central point of the thesis put forward in this paper that such a deviation of the normal sexual impulse into homosexuality can be and often is used as a defence against neurotic and psychotic processes.

Little needs to be said about those cases where homosexual fantasies have broken into consciousness with much suffering and discomfort, but it should never be assumed that this is an indication of confirmed sexual deviation. On the contrary, such fantasies are often a last line of defence against heterosexuality which appears dangerous owing to its association with strong aggressive impulses and particularly incestuous wishes. The patient's fantasies are a good indication of the effectiveness or failure in all methods of treatment (Marks, Gelder and Bancroft, 1970). Studies which ignore fantasies (Randell, 1959) will give an entirely different exposition of the psychopathology of transsexuals as compared with those studies which have taken them into account (Hoerig and Kerna, 1970), when they will show the importance of the homosexual element.

In manifest homosexuality all defensive barriers against the acting out of perverse impulses have broken down. Accurate diagnosis becomes a matter of the utmost urgency and importance as it will guide us towards appropriate treatment or masterly inactivity, as the case may be. A differential diagnosis rests on the existence of clinical configurations. The innumerable types of deviation met in the literature and in clinical practice, can be divided into three ill-defined, yet clearly recognizable groups.

Group I

In this group, manifest deviant behaviour, often associated with compulsive related day-dreaming aims at preventing the emergence of heterosexuality and is the presenting symptom in a large number of individuals who are basically latent heterosexuals. Some writers refer to these as pseudo-homosexuals, an unsatisfactory term as it implies a falseness in their state of mind which is not reflected by their feelings. Attachment to members of the same sex is linked with the flight from the opposite sex which is perceived as being dangerous, threatening and domineering. Oddly enough, the attempt to deny the very existence of the opposite sex is frequently a sign that one is dealing with latent heterosexuality rather than true deviation. A guideline in differentiating them further from 'true' deviants is guilt, as it is almost always present and particularly in those who seek guidance or help. It is necessary to distinguish the guilt derived from external circumstances, social or moral influences from that derived from unconscious psychopathology, whether it is related to the residual heterosexual conflicts at the root of the deviation, or to the homosexual activity itself.

Freud (1905a) recognized that psychoneuroses could exist side by side with manifest perversions and suggested that heterosexuality had been totally repressed in such cases. The psychopathology will be that of a psychoneurosis; the homosexuality indicating the persistence of a particularly severe oedipal conflict and castration anxiety. The dangers related to the expression of heterosexual impulses are obviously of such a nature that not enough reliance can be placed on the usual neurotic defence mechanisms to ward off fears rooted in the subject's internal world and object relations; the deviation is there to create a citadel which in practice becomes a prison which affords a degree of security.

Anxious, hysterical or obsessional personalities are common in this clinical type. It is particularly the association of homosexuality and obsessional traits which is likely to produce a picture of shallowness of affect, ruthlessness and compulsive behaviour consisting of a constant search for a partner, seldom engaging in sustained or deep relationships. Any attempt at controlling or curtailing the sexual acting out is followed by an outbreak of anxiety and depression. The depth of character and personality disturbance needs to be assessed carefully as it may affect the outcome of the treatment. The presence of serious obsessive-compulsive traits may defeat all therapeutic efforts.

The following case is fairly representative of a clinical picture with a good prognosis encountered in this group:

An intelligent young man with mild obsessional personality traits had become seriously depressed and suicidal whilst still at university, following disappointment in a homosexual love affair. At the age of 3½ he had been separated from his parents who resided abroad, when he was sent to a wartime nursery in England. This was a severe traumatic incident which coloured all his subsequent relationships as all human beings were regarded as unfaithful and untrustworthy. He was totally impotent when he first approached a girl, and soon after he became involved with a male homosexual friend. He felt extremely guilty about his sexual activities and ruminated over them, but he relentlessly went on importuning his friend who eventually showed little interest and no affection for him. He responded well to psychoanalysis and after it was ended he married, had children and had a very successful career. After ten years there has been no recurrence of homosexual interests.

It is worth noting here that once the homosexual attachment could be analysed and understood within the transference relationship, his condition did not differ from that of a classical straightforward psychoneurosis capable of responding well to psychotherapy.

The occurrence of homosexual behaviour as a substitute symptom has been described in the literature (Thorner, 1949) and is of considerable clinical interest when the possibility of removing it is a real one. This writer reports that in the course of treatment, and concurrent with a period of sexual abstinence, a young patient developed a status asthmaticus. This symptom was linked with conflicts over aggression and was quite troublesome until he convinced himself that he was homosexual and acted on that belief. The relationship between sexual deviation and certain psychosomatic states, such as ulcerative colitis, etc., is very obscure. Many observers have reported on the occurrence of haemorrhoids quite suddenly in the midst of a homosexual conflict.

Group II

This group includes all cases of 'true' perversion when the disturbance is deep and the defence against heterosexuality seems almost of secondary importance. Depression is a common presenting symptom with or without periodicity, but conscious guilt is generally absent. Careful investigation will readily show that the homosexuality is employed as a massive defence mechanism aimed at warding off overwhelming separation and psychotic anxieties, a dread of mutilation and even disintegration. Bizarre acting out, marked identification with the opposite sex, promiscuity and a preference for very brief contacts with partners, associated with a tendency to congregate in public lavatories, is sometimes suggestive of a prepsychotic condition or even psychosis. 'True' deviants seek treatment for reasons such as difficulties arising at work or in personal relationships, and occasionally because of some offence which has involved them in court proceedings. They specifically ask that nothing be done to change their sexual orientation. Focal therapy may appear indicated but in practice it is difficult to carry out because of the interaction between the sexual maladjustment and other ego disturbances. It is therefore essential that before undertaking any form of treatment due notice be taken of the value attached by the patient to the deviation in fighting off loneliness, isolation, alienation and aggressiveness. There are three identifiable clinical types:

(*a*) *Narcissistic disorders of character and personality* are very commonly found in homosexuals of both sexes included in this group. The history will often show the presence of psychological disturbance in the parents, severe deprivation and traumatic experiences. There is a tendency to seek partners, younger or of a similar age, but frequently the need to protect and to be protected, to nurse and to be nursed is the primal force in these associations (Freud, 1910). The search for a narcissistic love object may even induce a man to look for a partner who is overtly antagonistic to homosexuality as he may also be (Khan, 1970). Phallic overvaluation is the rule, with loss of self-esteem and a readiness to feel hurt and injured. A double deviation is present when a man is both homosexual and paedophiliac.

(b) *Homosexuality as a defence against severe depressive states* is probably much more common than is generally recognized. The diagnosis is difficult as the presence of reactive depression, which responds to superficial intervention, hides the true nature of the problem. Early traumas, sudden deaths in the family, or separation and divorce of parents in infancy are valuable diagnostic pointers. Some writers see the behaviour of homosexuals who struggle with the threat of severe depression as a solution of the past conflict over weaning, which is felt as not only a narcissistic injury but also a blow to the infantile omnipotence (Bergler, 1951).

In the male, unbearable depressive thoughts and feelings, probably originating in very early infancy, make it impossible for him to have physical contact with any woman as the penis is experienced as a thoroughly bad part of his body (Rosenfeld, 1949). Marked passivity in sexual relations serves the purpose of recovering the lost potency and acquiring something good. At times, the only safeguard against psychotic depression, apathy and despair is to become and act the part of the good mother to the partner (Khan, 1970).

The serious consequence arising from the sudden failure of the homosexual solution aimed at alleviating depressive feelings can be seen in the following case history:

A young woman was referred on account of violent rages in the course of which she was dangerous both to herself and a woman companion. The destructive outbursts of violence had begun after the breakdown of a long-standing lesbian relationship. She had suffered from recurrent depressive attacks for many years and had been very promiscuous. In the course of extended assessment interviews she recognized that she had used her compulsive lesbian activities as the 'cure' for her unbearable depression as she could rely on sliding into a state of mild euphoria after successful sexual exploits. At the time of the referral she longed for the woman who had jilted her to come back and her woman companion (a non-practising lesbian) was gradually becoming the object of her hatred and murderous feelings. Admission to hospital was the only solution.

(c) *Homosexuality as a defence against paranoid anxieties and related states.*

The turning of hatred into love, can be found in early and late psychoanalytic writings (Freud, 1920, 1923; Numberg, 1938). Glover (1938a) has also noted that a perversion will involve the use of libidinization and idealization of the object as a defence against aggression and anxiety, whilst Freeman (1955) has drawn attention to the psychotic quality of the fears and the castration anxiety experienced by the true homosexual in relation to men and women alike. Projection dominates the emotional life of a certain type of homosexual, bringing some relief but much confusion. This defence mechanism implies the throwing out of unwanted or dangerous parts of oneself, which will fill the environment with a host of threatening and persecutory objects to be dealt with by the appeasement implicit in homosexual acts and relationships (Klein, 1932a and 1932b; Rosenfeld, 1949). In certain cases it is clear that behind the phallic preoccupation and castration anxiety there is a marked fear of the loss of individual identity and of total disintegration.

In cases where severe paranoid anxiety is hidden beneath a manifest homosexuality, hostile and greedy oral impulses are directed against authority figures and partners, turning them into retaliatory figures. On the other hand, these will appease by submitting to anal intercourse and reassure themselves by fellatio about the destructiveness of their biting and devouring impulses.

Not infrequently the deviation which presents as a simple neurosis or as a sexual disorder attributable to biological forces, conceals a fully fledged paranoid schizophrenia (Socarides, 1970). Even when paranoid anxieties have erupted into florid schizophrenia, in spite of manifest homosexual activities, the perversion acts as a brake on the threatened acting out of murderous impulses. This was seen very clearly in the following case:

A twenty-four-year-old man had been a compulsive homosexual for as long as he could remember. He would roam around the streets at night looking for a 'victim', someone who could tolerate his castrating anus. He came for treatment because of his uncontrollable rages at work where he would break furniture or get involved in violent fights with fellow workers. At intervals he would experience vivid auditory hallucinations associated with his homosexual 'victims'. During the hallucinatory episodes he would seek hospital care voluntarily as he would no longer trust his homosexual acting out to protect him against killing someone. It is difficult not to believe that this might well have happened in the absence of such an outlet.

Group III

This group includes all those cases of actual bisexual behaviour which occur in situations of stress, prisons and special social and cultural surroundings. Psychiatrists are often under pressure to regard this abnormal behaviour as merely the result of contingency, which is hardly the case. However, in recent times cases of 'false' actual bisexuality have become fairly prevalent amongst some young or even middle-aged persons, who are searching for new experiences; there will be no difficulty in distinguishing these from the genuine cases as the feelings associated with the acting out are wholly ego-dystonic.

Truly bisexual individuals offer a real challenge to the student of sexual disorders. Psychopathic disturbances are prevalent in the male whilst immaturity is a dominant feature in the female. Both sexes will exhibit a profound tendency towards dependency in relation to mother or her substitutes; as a rule, there is a severe dissociation between the female and male parts of the personality, aggravated by very active projections, splitting processes and multiple identifications. Many studies tend to concentrate on the examination of the perversion, taking the heterosexuality for granted in spite of the obvious lack of gratification and serious disturbances present in this particular area. The sudden removal or unavailability of either sexual outlet is known to cause severe depression and even suicide (see my paper on object choice and bisexuality, pp. 88–101 above).

DISCUSSION

The view presented in this paper is that it is not sufficient to regard homosexuality as an adjustive process, as proposed by Sullivan (1955), rather than a problem in itself. In normal conditions, and when repression is adequate, the original homosexual nucleus which originates in the formative years as a result of the interactions with the environment acts as an internal psychic regulator and may even prove to be a source of enrichment to the personality as a whole. In abnormal states of mind it can reinforce shaky neurotic defences, and ensure a more tolerable kind of living. The homosexual solution is a defence which when encountered should be treated with the utmost caution by anyone who attempts to remove it. At all times it should be borne in mind that physical contact with a member of the same sex may be the one and only contact of the subject with a human being. When the perversion is associated with latent psychotic states, there is an overwhelming need for accurate diagnosis, before initiating any kind of treatment which might lead to serious complications or the aggravation of the presenting symptoms. There is considerable danger in attempting to classify clinical types by forcing them into diagnostic categories. Provided, however, that the classification is not applied rigidly, it may prove of value in deciding on the most suitable treatment. For instance, some neurotic patients included in the latent heterosexual group will occasionally show the familiar picture of phobic anxiety or of a compulsive symptom covering up a psychotic illness. Equally, the homosexuality linked with a depressive illness might turn out to be an excellent psychotherapeutic proposition.

In general, all those cases which can be considered as belonging to the latent heterosexual group, should be offered whatever type of psychotherapy is available over an extended period. Behaviour therapy may be indicated as a preliminary step. Careful selection may be rewarded by considerable therapeutic success. The deviation in the true homosexual is very unlikely to be influenced; in this case all forms of psychotherapy regularly prove disappointing. A complete and satisfactory change in this type of homosexual interests and behaviour is unknown to the present writer. It should also be stressed that with the increased knowledge of the problems linked with narcissistic disorders, the psychotherapy of homosexuality associated with such conditions carries a more favourable prognosis than hitherto.

Attempts to treat all kinds of homosexual behaviour indiscriminately must be held responsible for the excessive and unnecessary gloom shared by psychiatrists and the public at large with regard to the likelihood of influencing the course of this syndrome.

Once treatment is requested, the possibility of helping the patient with a host of other problems must be considered. Great care should however be taken in evaluating whether this can be done without disturbing a delicate balance within the sexual sphere. The exquisite nature of homosexual love as described by poets and writers has little in common with the unreal or surrealist relationships which breed isolation and alienation from the mainstream of society, found within certain homosexual groups. Between these two worlds there are vast numbers of men and women who ask for help and guidance. It is hoped that this paper will provoke some interest in their suffering and fate.

8 AFFECTS AND THE PSYCHOANALYTIC SITUATION*

I

IN ANNOUNCING the main topic for the 30th Congress of the International Psychoanalytical Association in 1977, the Programme Committee noted that the problem concerning affects seemed appropriate as a focus for the discussions, since no two theories agree on it. The truth of this statement is affirmed by the most casual reappraisal of the literature as stated in a number of outstanding contributions such as those of Brierley (1951), Rapaport (1953), Rangell (1967) and André Green (1973a). The discrepancy of approach to the problem in various parts of the world is due not entirely to parochialism on the part of some writers, but rather because of the disparities between theory, technique and clinical practice. The major areas of theoretical research are: (1) the drive discharge theory, (2) the debate on the existence of unconscious affects, (3) the relationship to their mental representations and fantasies, (4) the issue concerning the possibility of affects dissociated from the object, (5) the ego as the only seat of anxiety, (6) the problem of narcissistic and schizoid personality disturbances, and (7) the widespread calls for adjustments and modifications of the classical method in the treatment of borderline and narcissistic states, which has generated further complications in the matching of theory with practice. In this paper I shall not concentrate on any one aspect of the theory of the affects or of a specific clinical phenomenon, nor will I attempt to supply any answers. I shall, however, underline certain diagnostic features which are

* This paper was first published in 1977 in the *International Journal of Psycho-Analysis* 58: 171–97.

fundamental to an understanding of the state of *malaise* existing in the relationship between theory and our clinical daily work.

In the course of an address to the British Society, Bion (1976) remarked that 'feelings are the few things which analysts have the luxury of being able to regard as facts.' He added that when analysts embark on theory, they lose their sense of direction 'as they have an inexhaustible fund of ignorance they can draw upon'. As few would dispute so simple yet profound a statement, it is, however, difficult to see how we have reached a situation which was so well summed up by Rangell (1967) when he wrote: 'affects, the original centre, in giving way to subsequent developments have become wrongly, "the forgotten man". In spite of their ubiquity clinically, [the affects] have in a sense been by-passed, or at least minimized out of proportion, and receive a good deal less of systematic attention than they deserve in our total theoretical metapsychological system' (p. 173). Rangell was clearly referring to Freud's (1933) shift of emphasis from representations to the instinctual impulses and to the description of the id as the reservoir of the life and death instincts, later responsible for the developments expressed in the work of Ferenczi and Melanie Klein. The immediate result of this thinking was to link affects with the unconscious fantasies or to regard them as the expression of instincts. The work and experiences described in Balint's and Winnicott's writings have also made us all the more aware of the patient's predicament occasioned by the closeness of bodily feelings to the psychic apparatus. It is prolonged contact with borderline patients that has opened our eyes to the continuous attempts to impinge on the analyst as the object. The understanding of object relations and their implications from the point of view of the countertransference has gained momentum during the last quarter of a century. I am referring to these developments here because it is possible that Rangell's statement may not be easily understood unless it is stressed that his remarks apply to the lack of systematic attention in trying to incorporate the affects in a total metapsychological system.

In our actual clinical work we could hardly overlook the affects as they are often the immediate reason why patients seek treatment, and during analysis the patients continue to note the qualitative and quantitative changes in their affects when assessing their own progress or lack of it.

The success and failure of an analysis could in fact be said to rest on the degree of affective changes which take place during its course. An analysis is most often remembered through the recall of a particular affect which had probably been dominant. Statements such as 'an altogether overwhelming emotional experience'; 'it was very distressing'; 'I could not go through it again'; 'I was depressed all the time' are not infrequently heard from analysands. Analysts will speak of an analysis as having been a 'stimulating' or 'interesting' one, or, when nothing seemed to be happening for months at a time, 'boring'. Neither analysts nor patients are prepared to admit that a treatment was entirely 'intellectual' whereas it may clearly appear to be so to the observer. Some analyses, on the other hand, are stormy from start to finish, and it is surprising how two people are able to keep their interest going in the face of the strain and stress generated over the years; a factor which must have been aggravated by the very considerable length of most contemporary treatments. Considering the large number of patients seen by a psychoanalyst in the course of a day, it is to be expected that he will have to do something in order to somewhat insulate himself. Some therapists are more successful than others in handling the impact on them-selves of their patients' emotional response to the psychoanalytic process, and are therefore able to avoid losing touch with the analysands even when their direct emotional involvement in the relationship is at a low point. The less successful will not infrequently himself become the victim of psychosomatic disorders, and it should be noted here that the defence of intellectualization affords no protection to the analyst against such an eventuality (Sandler, 1972).

I make no apology for focusing on the emotional position of the analyst in the psychoanalytic situation, so vividly described in Gitelson's courageous paper published in 1952. The literature on affects has in fact shown a curious neglect of this aspect of the therapeutic relationship and one has to turn to papers mainly devoted to the countertransference to see it adequately discussed. It was Paula Heimann (1950) who introduced the then revolutionary notion that the countertransference did not simply mean the transference of the analyst towards his patient but that, rather, it was an instrument of research into the patient's Unconscious. She also regarded it as being not only 'part and parcel' of the analytic relationship but also a *creation* of the patient and therefore part of the latter's personality. She did warn, however, against its usage as a screen for the analyst's shortcomings and also deprecated the practice of the analyst's disclosing his feelings to the patient, views which the present writer wishes to endorse very strongly. An example of the consequence of such behaviour in the analytic relationship was observed by me in the course of supervisory work. A student-analyst had explained a recent lapse of his attentiveness to his patient as being due to a feeling state which had affected him. The patient's reaction was to become overanxious and deeply concerned about her therapist's mental health. The opportunity was missed for understanding the impact of the analyst's 'unusual' state on the patient in terms of early life experience of a mother who made heavy demands on her child. Further, the patient was not ready to deal with reality. Such unburdening is much more in keeping with Gitelson's view of the therapist's transference which, he believes, should be brought right out into the open. If this is the case, we can assume that the analyst expects something in return for his admission (confession) and such expectation will be coloured by unresolved infantile wishes and needs on his part.

In theory, by turning to the countertransference, the analyst has the tools (his psychoanalytical concepts and his feelings) to control the affective state of the analytic situation at any given moment. The first few years of my life as a psychoanalyst were profoundly affected by a remark from my supervisor, Dr Sylvia Payne, when she was advising me on the timing of a genetic interpretation. Having made a good case for early intervention, she added as an afterthought, 'In the last resort it really depends on how quickly you wish to decrease the level of anxiety in the patient and how much of it you can take.'

It is fashionable nowadays for analysts to believe they can do just that by giving what they consider is a transference interpretation, which allegedly also includes an examination of the countertransference, by imparting it in terms such as 'you want to make me angry'. This 'you and me' interpretation must fail to elicit an appropriate affective response in so far as it leaves out any clarification of the patient's role at the time. It does not say whether he is in the role of a baby or a child who is experimenting or, say, an adolescent who is deliberately provoking an adult; and it is of course quite meaningless in terms of object relations theory, as it gives no indication who the analyst is at that precise moment. Some analysts, no doubt, would argue that so challenging a remark could lead up to an explanation of the use of the analyst as a particular object. But there is little reason for withholding such knowledge if the analyst has it at his disposal. The vicissitudes of the affects in the analytic situation can, and in my contention are, controlled by the analyst; a point which I shall take up again. His personal attitudes, training and theoretical position will all influence him in his interventions, creating a unique atmosphere. The dissociation of his faculties of thinking and feeling will have far-reaching effects on the course of an analysis. A patient will often respond with increasing persecutory anxiety to an excessively *feeling* approach because it can be experienced as seduction, teasing and, finally, frustrating. A collusive approach at the intellectual level can hide the failure to respond to the patient's attempt to escape from his emotions. This situation could be gleaned from the statement of a drug addict: 'My analyst and I agreed to stop after two years because there was no transference.' In my view that was indicative of a two-way transference block and needed careful elucidation *in* analysis rather than termination of the encounter.

In our work we are constantly exposed to both external and internal experiences. Some, but very limited, protection is afforded by placing oneself out of sight. Our narcissism, however, whether healthy or unhealthy, will always be threatened. The situation is further complicated by the ambiguity in the analytic situation which plays a part not always fully appreciated. For instance, at the outset, we invite the patient to enter into a relationship which offers a mixture of satisfaction and frustrations, and with a demand for utter trust which he can hardly experience towards a total stranger. We stipulate that words shall be the method of communication, knowing full well that most affects cannot be adequately described in words. We assure the analysand that both of us will be able to work better if we are not to stare at each other, yet we know how difficult it is for an infant in the first months of life to take his eyes off his mother. We, further, impose restriction on his movements, thus removing one important element from the triad of cognition, affect and motion, which are intensely and intricately interrelated throughout the individual's development. The time limit imposed on the sessions and their periodicity are 'natural expressions of hate, just as the good interpretations are expressions of love, and symbolical of good food and care', as Winnicott noted as far back as 1945 (p. 147). It should cause little surprise if certain patients may wish from time to time to use every means at their disposal to express their feelings and to create unforeseen situations which can exercise the analyst's emotional responses as well as his technical skills. This is most likely to occur in borderline states and narcissistic character and personality disorders, when the impact on the analyst from the patient's affects, projections and projective identifications will be at its greatest. Problems of management overlap with the difficulty of understanding the patient.

Allowing the fulfilment of wishes for a physical contact with the therapist and the introduction of non-verbal ways of dealing with outbursts of violence are explained as a genuine and honest desire to maintain contact with the analysand. Yet it is difficult to see how it could be claimed that the psychoanalytic process is not thereby affected or prejudiced.

Psychoanalysts tend to rationalize, hence to justify, taking steps which are outside ordinary practice, but they seldom acknowledge that such steps may be gratifying or defensive. There are also those who, as a result of rigidity in their personality, cannot tolerate the behaviour of a patient when it is clearly disruptive and often incompatible with the classical technique. This is often associated with a blunting of the analyst's capacity for affective response, leading to stagnation or the discontinuation of treatment. The use of reassurance, humouring and an avoidance of transference interpretation is less difficult to understand in this context but, in my opinion, is more likely to produce further complications and an interference, possibly total, with the psychoanalytic process.

Before proceeding to the next section, I should explain that my understanding of the term 'affect' is in accordance with that suggested by Laplanche and Pontalis (1973): 'any affective state, whether painful or pleasant, whether vague or well defined and whether it is manifested in the form of a massive discharge or in the form of a general mood, therefore linking it with states of tension'. Affects are linked with ideas or mental representations. A feeling, as an affective presentation, is an internal rather than an overt activity, yet it is seldom out of touch with the external situation. Muscular, glandular and physiological activities can be associated with feelings.

The concept of 'feeling state' as suggested by Joffe and Sandler (1968) is also valuable in differentiating conditions where somatic changes are not in immediate direct evidence.

II

The disruption of the classical method is most likely to occur in the treatment of persons, men or women, who are inarticulate and unable to remember many details of their childhood. They may be highly intelligent and often possess outstanding intellect and exceptional talent. The obvious difficulty in verbalization is almost invariably linked with an incapacity to express valid and genuine feelings and emotions. Love and hate are unavailable to them, love even more than hate. They may complain of depression without displaying it, but we do not believe them to be capable of it. On the other hand, should there be anxiety, this will be of a pervasive, inhibiting, paralysing and primitive quality.

The case material which I wish to present is fairly typical of a situation met in contemporary psychoanalytic work when a patient's affective disturbance has a profound effect on the psychoanalytic process. Negative therapeutic reactions expose the analyst to massive countertransference responses. In this clinical outline, I shall deal only with those aspects relevant to our topic. There were two particular features: a major one being that for months on end the patient would be unable to use the couch; and a minor, but no less irritating, one in her attempt to control omnipotently everything in the external and internal world to such a degree that the analyst was unable to elicit any emotional response from her without feeling tempted to abandon the analytic and therapeutic role.

Clinical material

Mrs A began her analysis at the age of twenty-seven, on account of severe, intractable anxiety associated with poorly described feelings of depression and suicidal thoughts. She also complained, from true incapacity, about being inarticulate. She had given up a lucrative occupation which she had pursued without appropriate training, and which had caused her to feel a fraud. She had been married for some years, but there seemed to be little left in the marriage besides devotion on the husband's part. There was little physical contact, neither partner being greatly concerned about it.

Mrs A had been brought up under unusual circumstances. Her family at first lived in a small village, in total isolation. An older sister and brother excluded her in every way, forcing her to become totally immersed in an ambivalent relationship with her parents. Her father, from all accounts a very disturbed man, had taken over her toilet training from the start and insisted, with her connivance, on 'cleaning her' until she was nearly eleven years old. The mother, preoccupied with supplementing the family income, seemed to be almost unaware, or at least unconcerned, about the father's intrusions into the daughter's life. Mother's father had died the day after Mrs A's birth. After three months of breast feeding, mother had to go away for some weeks, leaving the child in the care of the maternal grandmother. This shattering episode in Mrs A's life was brought into the analysis at the time of the first separation three months after work had begun, when she plunged into a state of total inactivity, blankness, and a whole stream of death fantasies. This incident also marked the disappearance of the early, explosive, erotized transference. On my return I found a patient who had only thoughts and no feelings, and she was soon to discover that she had no more control over her thoughts than her feelings.

After the next separation Mrs A returned, having lost not only her feelings but her thoughts as well. Her blankness, however, had an excruciating as well as exquisitely painful quality to it which, having communicated itself to me, I could then tell her about. When she complained that she was now suffering again, I recalled reading in a story by Chekhov of a doctor telling his patient: 'You must feel the pain, otherwise you are dead.' However, what was causing such intense psychic pain to my patient was still out of our reach; but it was also clear, to both of us, that the anxiety was there to fend off the experience of other affects of a dangerously intense nature. When I tried to put her in touch with her aggression, or rage, easily available in the transference and in her relationships to a number of clearly bad external objects, she would gesture with her hands as if hoping to touch something, saying: 'Where is it? I cannot feel it.' It was at this time that I would become conscious of the rift created by deep splitting and my patient's capacity for dissociation. The occurrence of negative therapeutic reactions would also make heavy demands on my patience and resilience. One serious relapse occurred after an Easter vacation, when she reported having been present at a Jewish Passover celebration. (She, a Protestant, had always been attracted to the Jewish religion as a further escape from her untenable identity.) She had been impressed by a part of the service and had written down her recollection of it on a piece of paper which she handed to me. It read: 'Mouths but they speak not; eyes but they see not; noses but they smell not; hands but they touch not; feet but they walk not; throats but they make no sounds.' This time she had no thoughts, no mind and no body. However, she reported a dream she had had during the vacation in which *she was standing in a street, waiting for a taxi: there were hundreds of them but they were all full. A doctor standing behind her was urging her to get away.* She appreciated the irony in that she had identified me both in the taxis full of people and also in the doctor behind her. She had remembered I existed, but that was no good if there were so many people able to hire me. As she got in touch with the idea of having longed for me during the holidays, she became panicky and no more was possible for that session. The next day she reported having read a book for the first time in years (Mrs A did not read either books or newspapers). To my surprise it was a book which popularized the understanding of somatic illnesses. She was shocked at reading that repressed anger could cause arthritis and that a baby feels so much when left. This had reminded her of the taxi dream. Mrs A's stare during this exchange had become unbearable to me. I was at a loss what to say, having tried in the past every possible approach to get her to use the couch again; I reminded her that in the dream the doctor had been standing behind her, which was how it should be. She then pointed out that the reason why the dream had been so painful was that she could not see me. She was now distinctly irritated and mentioned my persistence in suggesting the use of the couch. She went on to remind me of a 'knocking game' she used to play with her mother when a small infant, in which she would knock with her hand on the side of the cot and her mother would reply with gentle knocks, standing behind her, out of her sight (this was a new detail). She had known about this game all her life but she now had a conviction of remembering the feeling of it. With feeling hitherto unknown to either of us, she asked if I understood that she did not want me to act in the same way as her mother, at least not when I was available to her.

As analysts we often forget that patients do not always attempt to repeat past affective experiences in their analyses; they also try to avoid them. However, persistence in interpreting an obvious resistance had paid well, as it had brought back an early infantile memory of a feeling, linking it with the transference and promoting insight. The feeling had led us to the idea of the disappearance and unavailability of the mother-analyst. This of course does not mean that Mrs A at other times had not used the eye-to-eye opportunity she herself had provided, for indulging in her cannibalistic impulses; or as a substitute for instinctual wishes involving the skin; or for hiding defences and for preventing memories from getting through. Writing down and handing over to me on paper her thoughts and fantasies was a symptomatic action used by Mrs A when under stress. I regarded this as a 'transitional space' valuable in preventing acting out (Khan, 1972). On the other hand, it is possible that I was not sufficiently discouraging because I welcomed such an action from a patient who had been so inarticulate.

This brief account would be incomplete without the mention of Mrs A's love affair with death, which had started when she was four years old. She then played a 'game' in which she would throw herself on the ground and would lie there thinking she was dead until she was disturbed or resuscitated by magical internal means. Her assurances that she would not kill herself had little effect on me until the recovery of this early memory. Afterwards and in the light of all available material, I came to the conclusion that Mrs A, rather than being under the influence of the death instinct, was quite simply anti-life, as she seemed to seek a way of surviving without being or feeling alive. She longed for death, but real death filled her with horror. There must be many meanings attached to the patient's dealings with death and her feeling of deadness which was frequently traced to her mother's similar feeling dating back to the loss of her own father. On the other hand, acting the part of being dead was the ultimate defence against the eruption, into the Conscious, of unconscious affects linked to destructive instinctual drives and impulses (Laplanche, 1975). A clue to such a possibility were the references to be gathered from an affective response dream which I had during a difficult phase in the treatment. In the dream *the shadowy figure of a woman shows me a life-size rag-doll which I pick up and throw across several rooms, until it lands out of sight in a corner. With the female figure I follow the flight of the doll. As we reach it, it suddenly comes to life. I feel anxious, darkness descends. In the next scene I am in my car with a figure again next to me. An electrical wire is on fire and the engine is about to be set alight. A woman appears and offers to repair the car for a fee which seems excessive.* I wake up with a feeling of curiosity and refreshed. I immediately associated the woman who had offered to repair the car to Mrs A, whose conflicts about the lack of reparative drive had dominated the analysis recently. The doll was similar to a puppet which I had as a child, and which was safely out of the way in the attic. The reason for having such a dream did not emerge fully until the Monday session when Mrs A reported having had a dream about loving. As she was reflecting that on Friday she had been upset as she thought I was pushing her too hard, I suddenly recalled that I had been preoccupied with external matters and that I had been somewhat irritable and less than attentive to the patient's relapse into a state of severe anxiety. In the silence that followed, I recalled a third part of the dream in which *balloons containing a bugging device* (day residue) *were floating about my analytic room. As I tried to shoot them down I was aware I should not destroy them.* It may be self-evident that over the weekend I had become conscious of my lapsing from free-floating attention, but what is more relevant is that the dream made me aware that an excess of therapeutic zeal was getting through to the patient, increasing her anxiety and fear of recovery, quite apart from causing me to feel irritable and impatient. I do not propose to go into the personal aspects of the dream material, but I note that having got in touch with my aggressiveness and frustration, a direct response to the negative therapeutic reaction displayed by Mrs A at the time, I was able to recover my analytic curiosity, hence the feeling of well-being on waking.

Comment

My understanding of this woman's predicament was that a fragmentation of the ego (or a regression to unintegrated state; Winnicott, 1945) had taken place in the first few months of her life, causing the kind of disintegration which deals with anxiety that cannot be contained by other means such as projection, denial, negation, projective and introjective identification

(Segal, 1964). The slightest attempt at integration is followed by a fresh outburst of massive anxiety which screens off every emerging feeling state. Unconscious affects in such cases may never see the light of day. My further attempts to understand her illness have led me to a re-examination of Khan's concept of cumulative trauma which I believe is applicable to this case. Khan (1963b) has underlined the effects of a type of maternal stress in which the mother's protective shield is lost and in the analysis such task falls on the therapist, who should not attempt to be a 'mother'. Also, Khan's idea, formulated in his writings included in *The Privacy of the Self* (1974b) concerning affects and threat of annihilation staying hidden and dissociated rather than repressed, appears valid as does his suggestion that when someone has taken himself as an internal object, the fear of annihilation is indeed paralysing. Outstanding in Mrs A was the fact that anxiety linked with psychic pain was equal to anxiety about emptiness and blankness. Concepts such as that of signal anxiety or 'feeling safe' (Sandler, 1972) or splitting processes being responsible for the lack of availability of emotions (Klein, 1946) are not only essential to the comprehension of the material but indispensable.

III

I shall now discuss, briefly, some problems linked with 'anxiety' and the role of words and reconstructions in relation to the affects.

(a) 'Anxiety' in the psychoanalytic situation
Clinically, we recognize the existence of signal, primary, castration, separation, paranoid, depressive, neurotic and psychotic anxiety. Each type carries a specific meaning, function and origin. The list is a formidable one and not encouraging to our hope of finding a single basic theory of the affects. André Green (1973a, p. 104) has commented on the absence of such a theory in the writings of Melanie Klein, who has influenced many authors who have dealt with this subject. My understanding of this apparent omission is that the stress placed on the analysis of paranoid and depressive anxieties must be taken in conjunction with the concepts of primitive fantasies, early development and object relations. A theory of affects, as such, may be irrelevant to the Kleinian psychology, which could hardly be said to neglect them. However, some amongst our Kleinian colleagues create the impression that all one has to do in order to clarify the most obscure clinical situation is to locate the paranoid or depressive anxiety. It is

not always easy to relate this attitude to clinical experience. There are, for instance, individuals (of whom Mrs A is a clinical example) in whom anxiety dominates their lives to the point of freezing or pushing everything else out of the picture. When they come into analysis, we soon realize that we are not dealing with straightforward signal anxiety. It is more the case of anxiety being used as a screen to conceal other affects, rather than a particular idea or mental representation (see also Jones, 1929; Lewin, 1965). This is a massive effort on the part of the ego to block the affective path to the exploration and study of the thought processes which have gone into the formation of symptoms. To launch into an investigation of a precise genetic and developmental source of the anxiety could be misleading and confusing to the patient.

An interesting hypothesis recently advanced by Calef (1976; working in conjunction with Weinshel) if proved valid, might have interesting repercussions on our clinical work. From the starting point that some instinctual conflicts may terminate in unrepressed satisfactory resolutions (as part of character formation), this author argues that the signal affects determined by such conflicts would be conceived as reliable and trustworthy. In so far as neurotic conflict clouds perceptual consciousness and those functions which demand the development of affect signals, affective signals will be distorted. This in turn will lead to distortions of the more complex secondary affects. Should this hypothesis be correct, it follows that certain internal structures or functions, as they are functions of functions, may not be direct products of conflict and need not to be relegated to the Unconscious. According to Calef, we are dealing here with a form of internalization, not necessarily introjection. Some signal affects may therefore be considered as only indirect and not direct products of conflict.

(b) Words, affects and the psychoanalytic situation

> *. . . Words strain,*
> *Crack and sometimes break, under the burden,*
> *Under the tension, slip, slide, perish,*
> *Decay with imprecision, will not stay in place,*
> *Will not stay still.*

T. S. ELIOT, *Four Quartets*

Those who have experience in treating cases of sexual perversions and delinquency are quite familiar with the observation of the direct discharge of an impulse in a seemingly total absence of anxiety or guilt. Preverbal areas of disturbance, common in these conditions, are linked with feelings being resisted in an entirely autonomous way; the impulsive behaviour being designed to short-circuit affect development. Brierley (1951) has pointed out that affective language is older than words. She regards affects as part of a primitive system of the ego. Uncovering them, tracing their origin and interpreting their relation to the associated impulses and thoughts, permits the integration of the primitive ego into the principal ego. The difficulty here is that words will constantly fail us, particularly when they are most needed. The good analytic hour and the rapport with the psychotic or borderline patient will be disrupted by failure to find the correct words for describing a feeling state. Patient and analyst share the frustration. In general we tend to ascribe such difficulties to the material being derivative of some preverbal experience. Less attention has been paid to the possibility of the analyst having unconsciously recognized the patient's feeling in so far as it reminds him of a similar, personal and early preverbal experience. Help is impeded as even a long personal analysis may not succeed in supplying us with the exact and precise word which is needed at a given moment. In my supervisions I have noted that some very gifted but disturbed students have a capacity for dealing with such situations, perhaps because they have had very similar experiences in their own analysis. On the other hand, the less gifted but intellectually bound student may be inclined to use cliché or jargon expressions which may be quite difficult to eradicate. Bion (1976) has commented on our having to use words which are debased by common usage, and also on the fact that the analyst needs a discipline beyond that which can be provided by any training. He believes that forging words, which the analyst must keep in working order, will give him a language which he can use and value. It is perhaps in this use of technical language that the most serious collusion occurs between analyst and patient, as if each needed to create a barrier between feelings, impulses and thoughts.

Words are also at the centre of the controversy to which I have already made brief reference, concerning explosive affective situations, actual or threatened violence and a variety of acting in, which occur in the course of treating the more disturbed patients, especially those with borderline conditions. I believe that the absolutely correct interpretation which could quell the storm exists only in theory. In practice, a theoretically correct interpretation may be quite inadequate for the situation and should not be repeated in exactly the same form. Those who believe that a failure of an intervention to produce a change in a tense situation is always due to incorrect understanding, must either believe in magic or subscribe to a theoretical position which they dare not challenge. Because words are or are assumed to be ineffective, the analyst feels inclined to abandon the analytical stance and he may do so at the slightest sign of approaching trouble.

A parallel situation to that obtaining in psychoanalytic work occurs in the physical treatment of similar states. The neuroleptic drug fluoethixol decanoate, notable for its anti-psychotic action and anxiolytic effect in certain overactive and excitable patients, can have a biphasic effect on mood, low doses tending to be activating and high doses sedating. The following example shows the predicament we face when searching for the correct dosage in our interpretative work.

A girl in her early twenties, Miss B, had a history of sudden outbursts of violent behaviour requiring periods of isolation in her room or in hospital. She warned me about this in the first interview when she told me that her therapist had her ejected from his office by the police. She now wanted 'to get this man out of her system'. Within days she developed a state of mind towards the analyst which was a mixture of animosity and sexualization of the relationship. An interpretation of her increasing ambivalent dependence on the analyst-mother aimed at decreasing the erotization of the transference was followed by a session in which she screamed incessantly, keeping up a barrage of insult against him. Her behaviour was then linked with the interpretation given on the previous day, but I only succeeded in increasing what now seemed to be an expression of intolerable tension and narcissistic rage. Preparing for the next intervention, it occurred to me that people outside the room might be afraid. This led to my becoming aware that *I* was frightened, and I then began to consider the possibility of this feeling being due to projective identification. The situation became clear when she shouted that I had made her feel ugly and unattractive. I rejected the *idea* that this referred to physical ugliness and told her that my interpretation had aggravated her feelings of greed and dependence and as she anticipated frustration she felt angry and aggressive and in consequence ugly and unattractive inside herself. I felt considerable anxiety in making this type of intervention because I was not sure that the patient could tolerate my abrupt entry into her inner world, and I was also aware that I was dealing with a nearly, but not quite, conscious affect.

In dealing with Miss B and patients with such narcissistic problems, more than repression is involved in the analysis of their affects, which strike us forcibly as being related to tension phenomena. The most thorough exploration of the ambivalence, basic as it is, is not sufficient in relieving tension unless it is accompanied by the analysis of the inner world fantasies and of those 'primitive agonies (anxiety being not a strong enough word)' which Winnicott (1974) has described as lying behind 'the fear of a breakdown that has already been experienced'. In the case in point, a deeper interpretation had the required sedating effect, preferable to reassurance or calling the police. The patient left in a calm state with the feeling of having been understood. As the session was followed by sustained improvement, it is right to speculate on the possible change in the mental representation from that of a persecuting analyst-mother to one able to contain the aggression and greed.

A very different situation from the one just described arises when wordless communications, in the form of acting out and symptomatic actions, occur suddenly in an attempt by the patient to show that all is not lost in the course of analyses which appear satisfactory, both partners doing their duties. The only other clue that the affects are not brought into the analysis as a part of knowing and experiencing (Khan, 1969) is that the countertransference is seldom in question.

Space does not allow me to enter into a discussion of the connection between the lack of expression of the primary affects and psychosomatic states, and the clinically observed phenomenon of the closeness between explosive acting out and implosion leading to somatic manifestations, a Hobson's choice for so many unhappy individuals (see pp. 47–55 above; McDougall, 1974).

Some important questions remain. How do the words we use relate to an infant's or child's original experience? The language we use reflects the sophistication of the adult mind, and we know how we value the capacity in the analysand to abstract. What have we achieved when a patient responds to a correct interpretation of his repetitive compulsion, which is aimed at undoing an unpleasant weaning experience, saying, 'You are telling me that I am banging my head against a brick wall'? Is that what a baby feels at the time? Does it feel more than an adult? Are we not expecting an internal change to take place irrespective of verbal inadequacies? Are words the music of thoughts, as a woman said in acknowledgement of the analytic work done? On the other hand, are words, often such shallow and poor mediators of the affective states, all that important to the psychoanalytic process?

Years ago, I had a patient who seldom spoke during the second phase of a very long analysis. He broke his silence once, after some months, to say in answer to a further attempt at interpretation on my part, that I suffered from the delusion that words were necessary in psychoanalysis. We parted when he decided he was well enough to continue his analysis on his own. I never discovered whether he agreed or disagreed with my construction that in making me silent he was undoing the experience of having had a psychotic mother who had talked incessantly and irrelevantly all her life before being removed to a mental hospital. During the long silences I learnt to understand his tensions, moods, depressions and a host of non-verbal communications. I have never been able to pass on that emotional experience to my students or my colleagues.

(c) The role of affects in reconstruction
In a timely reappraisal of reconstruction in psychoanalysis, Greenacre (1975) clearly defines the obligatory contributions of the analysand and those of the analyst, which she finds more difficult to define. This is so because the analyst's thinking and cognitive processes are constantly under 'the ebb and flow of his personal and mental and emotional reactions. He may sometimes be clearly aware of this, at other times they are almost or completely subliminal. This part of the analytic work cannot be faked, computerized or even taped . . .' and, I would add, seldom, if ever, accurately reported. But more relevant to our topic is Greenacre's remark that it is 'the language of the specific reconstruction of actual emotional experiences that furnishes a reliving with a new perspective'. Having further noted that verbal communications must be the most important channel to be used towards the achievement of real knowing, she reminds us of the large number of non-verbal and preverbal communications available to the partners in the analytical relationship and asks 'not whether and how these physical eruptions may be analysed but rather how they operate in the basic transference relationship'. I have quoted extensively from this important paper because it touches on the core of the problem we face in the analysis of adults. Although it seems impossible to improve on Greenacre's final statement that the reconstruction brings the child and adult together, in the present writer's view this will not occur in every analysis. In a large number of cases it seems to happen more readily in the course of a second analysis, which almost invariably includes a reconstruction of the previous one. Many patients I have met had a past which they had never lived. A first analysis can restore the past to them, but the affects are swamped by an avalanche of recollections and intellectual constructions (often mainly contributed by the analyst) and reconstructions. The real working through of

old and discarded feeling states can in these patients take place only in the course of a second analysis.

Adherence to theoretical beliefs plays a part in the work of reconstruction of traumatic experiences, which have occurred in early life, in association with appropriate affective states. An example of this arose in the course of a discussion in the British Society, when it was agreed that fear of strangers was central to the understanding of the psychopathology of an adult patient. However, one speaker dated the traumatic experience to the eighth month of life whilst another felt that such fear *had* to be related to the paranoid position and therefore it would have to be put back a few months. It seems inevitable that this time difference in the theoretical arguments would itself reflect on the analytic situation and any feeling state which might then be recaptured. Five months are a large slice of an infant's life.

IV   AFTERTHOUGHTS

When we speak of the psychoanalytic situation, it is obvious that we are referring to the relationship of a special type which is born out of the specific, and in some way peculiar, nature of the encounter; the affects generated in it will, to some extent, reproduce those which occur or have occurred outside it. The mere fact that reciprocal actual sexual gratification is missing underlines the difference. The opportunity of thinking about the topic discussed in this paper has confirmed the view, which I have held throughout my psychoanalytic career, that any affect or feeling state exhibited by the analysand will have the analyst as the object, in fantasy or in person. It can therefore be best understood in terms of object relation theory. I am less convinced of the possibility of an affect being unrelated to an object, although in theory such an event could be observed outside the analytic relationship. I believe this could happen in the case of a *feeling dream* for example, in the absence of any particular imagery, but again it could well be that such a dream is derived from a pre-objectal state. With Brierley (1951) I would also say that it is the objects which are invested with affects rather than ideas being affectively charged.

Looking at the problem from the point of view of the therapist, it is my belief that although he will follow every lead offered by the patient, he will remain in control of the climate and temperature of the psychoanalytic situation. This requires the development of a special sensibility, a kind of internal pacemaker, which improves in its function with experience. This sensibility is of course part of the countertransference, but it has the special quality of operating mostly at a subliminal level and is therefore not in the immediate field of awareness of the therapist, as is the case with many other countertransference elements. A sudden and excessive demand, stimulated by the patient, will increase the affective load. The analyst's training will prevent immediate discharge and if all is well this internal information will maintain an appropriate level of fruitful emotional exchange. The average level of anxiety will be similarly regulated. Calef (1976) has gone even further in suggesting that a therapist uses 'the individual influencing machine' and 'that theoretical bias frequently functions more for the purpose of rationalizing the influencing machine than for the therapeutic work itself'. Although the term used by Calef is rather sinister, it deserves serious examination because of the indirect effect on the analysis of the affects generated at certain times in the psychoanalytic situation by the work of reconstruction. Although we are well aware that the affects are only one of many phenomena observed and developed in psychoanalysis, the different ways of handling them by those who practise contribute to the particular quality of the patient's total experience. A number of psychoanalysts (Ferenczi was the first amongst them) will provide a totally emotive analysis by utilizing all the available intellectual abilities in themselves and their patients. At the other end of the psychoanalytic spectrum are those who will rely on a clearly formulated theoretical and technical approach, reaching the basic emotions through the use of their brains. Both extreme groups have their detractors and poor imitators, whose psychoanalytic identity was perhaps never adequately established. Where a satisfactory identification is lacking, imitation may provide a substitute (Gaddini, 1969).

Psychoanalysis is an art but, unlike art itself, it cannot be isolated from meaning. Psychoanalysts, in common with artists, are dissatisfied with their capacity to interpret and externalize the total innermost experiences in themselves and their analysands. Unlike artists, however, they must constantly struggle with the imperative of distinguishing imagination from reality. It is almost a cliché to observe that even in the most talented, artistic expression confers no guarantee of freedom from emotional turbulence, neurosis or psychosis. Writers may long to give musical effect to the words they employ. Musicians, who claim the privilege of an ability to express feelings without being too troubled by precise meaning, will if pressed, confess to the superiority of language as the true mediator in object relations. Have not painters expressed their frustration by writing on their canvases? It is possible that in the case of an artist we are dealing with an exclusively albeit highly satisfactory process of reparation in relation to the internal object, leading to only affective tension being discharged. Psychoanalysis, contrary to commonly held fears, can be helpful to the artist in providing a further outlet in the psychoanalytic situation for the appropriate release of the affects. Greater integration derived from intellectual *and* emotional working through reduces acting out and symptomatic actions quite apart from mobilizing new areas in the personality. As many analysts know, this would enhance rather than impede artistic expression.

It cannot be of little value to remind ourselves that we are not alone in seeking appropriate affective discharges. As psychoanalysts, we are only too aware that our profession is not only impossible (Greenson, 1966a), but also extremely difficult.

9 THE SIGNIFICANCE OF TRANSSEXUALISM IN RELATION TO SOME BASIC PSYCHOANALYTIC CONCEPTS*

I INTRODUCTION

TRANSSEXUALISM HAS HITHERTO been largely ignored by psycho-analysts as being a defence against homosexuality or a bizarre and rare disorder of gender identity. In recent years a serious problem has arisen as a result of the publicity afforded to sex change operations and the unwelcome glamorization of such operations. The accumulation of clinical reports and information has not been accompanied by a substantial advancement in our theoretical understanding of the condition. When theory fails to develop at the same pace as clinical practice there will inevitably be adverse reper-cussions often leading to dangerous generalization and reflecting on the handling of, and approach to, each individual case.

The aim of this paper is to deal with those aspects of transsexualism which seem to challenge basic psychoanalytic concepts, and in particular castration anxiety, the oedipal complex and the role of conflict especially in relation to gender identity formation.

A further purpose is to stimulate amongst psychoanalysts the formation and expression of the psychoanalytic point of view. One recalls the time when prefrontal leucotomy was being hailed as a great advancement in the treatment of the mentally ill, neurotic and psychotic alike. This treatment is seldom used now and if lessons from the past are to be of value then a repetition of the indifference and *laissez-faire* attitude which was prevalent in the profession at that time should be avoided.

The idea of the mind being alien to the body is the essence of trans-

* This paper was first published in 1979 in the *International Review of Psycho-Analysis* 62: 379–99.

sexualism but opinions are well divided as to what actually constitutes it. This is not altogether surprising as we are dealing with a condition which in general lacks psychiatric phenomenology. Should psychiatric symptoms be present it may be difficult to ascertain whether they are the result rather than the cause of the disturbance. Once the desire for sex change has become the overwhelming preoccupation, prolonged observation is seldom possible through lack of co-operation.

The majority of workers in this field would regard as transsexual any child, adolescent or adult who expresses a claim to be trapped in the wrong biological body. However, it is wise to consider if there is evidence of an active, complete dislike or even lack of appreciation of primary and secondary characteristics of the appropriate sex. In the more extreme cases, there is a compelling and urgent desire for hormone treatment and plastic surgery with a total absence of castration anxiety and all the usual defences against it. For instance, fetishism seldom, if ever, occurs in a person who seeks sex change.

But transsexualism is not always so extreme. In its common and mildest form it occurs as a fantasy of belonging to the opposite sex and as such it is encountered in male and female individuals of all ages. It frequently happens that such fantasies are transient or at least that they occur with some periodicity but at times they are very persistent and associated with compulsive masturbation, when they are a symptom of a perversion or some other psychiatric condition. Those who are prone to such fantasies imagine themselves dressing, behaving and even engaging in sexual activities, in a manner appropriate to the other sex. There is no desire for surgical or hormone treatment; castration anxiety and a variety of defence mechanisms against it will be much in evidence.

It is relevant to note that the first description of what was a transsexual fantasy is to be found in the case of Schreber (Freud, 1911). Freud's lucid and forceful arguments in demonstrating the function of paranoia in warding off homosexual impulses may well have contributed to the delay in recognizing that in his delusional state, Schreber needed to reinforce his defences against homosexuality, by imagining that his body was changing into that of a woman. I would further suggest that the renewed investigations of the Schreber case by psychoanalysts have tended to support the view that transsexualism is nothing more than a defence against homosexual wishes which threaten the very sense of identity of the individual. It is not unreasonable for those who have not had first hand experience of the men and women who have given up their own gender identity, to assume that if a man believes himself to be a woman, he will be attracted to men and in consequence he should be regarded as homosexual. As cross-dressing is very common amongst transsexuals, it is understandable if one classified them as transvestites but the absence of sexual excitement will be an important clue in the differential diagnosis. Finally, we should recognize that some clinicians could well believe that only a psychotic will seek sex transformation.

The only real attempt to isolate this state of mind from such conditions as transvestism, latent homosexuality, psychosis, excessive femininity or masculinity, has come from Ralph Greenson (1968) and Robert Stoller. Stoller's findings and conclusions are set out in two volumes, *Sex and Gender* (1969) and *The Transsexual Experiment* (1975). This original presentation is outstanding for the richness of ideas and hypotheses backed by a great wealth of clinical evidence. The author's position is that 'if one takes care, one can find a rather precise clinical picture with underlying dynamics and aetiology' (Stoller, 1975, p. 2). He regards, perhaps somewhat surprisingly, the condition to be less complicated than other gender disorders and describes it as being intimately linked with a family constellation. It usually occurs in a beautiful boy, the son of a depressed mother who had felt unwanted in her early life. In infancy, the boy's experience with mother is blissful for both and they are symbiotic. Much imprinting and conditioning occurs at a very early age to a point where there is no vestige allowed for any masculinity at any time of the boy's development. The father is excluded from the relationship and this leads to a total lack of the oedipal relationship. The male transsexual's fate is sealed by the age of two or three, when extreme femininity will be present but in some cases this may be evident from the age of one. The infant is fated to serve as a treasured phallus for the mother who had suffered through the absence or rejection by her own father. On the other hand, this son is to be for her what her mother's breasts failed to be, a supplier of love (Stoller, 1975, p. 50). In the case of the girl, transsexualism does not make its appearance until later, as a rule around three or four years of age. The mother may have been uninterested in her daughter and father may have actively encouraged the development of masculine traits. The disorder looks more homosexual in its nature in the female than when seen in the male. This assertion is difficult to understand, as an essential element in this author's original contribution is his insistence that the presence of any heterosexual interest is a reason for exclusion from his categorization. His unchallengeable contention that we must look for different and separate psychopathology in the two sexes, leads him to state that in the case of the girl the disorder of gender identity is 'a defence against trauma – a depressed mother unable to care for her infant' (Stoller, 1975, p. 242) whilst there is a complete absence of trauma and conflict in the boy. It is difficult to regard as non-traumatic, the behaviour of a mother who actively distorts the process of separation and individuation.

This attempt to establish a dual psychopathology for both sexes is further reflected in the statement that there is a conflict that females are spared built into the sense of maleness. In my opinion, this view does not acknowledge the persistent, and in general successful attempts by girls to achieve separation from mother and their later struggles to avoid re-engulfment; struggles which at times are continued throughout life, whilst occasionally they may end in tragedy and/or transsexualism.

Stoller's diagnosis requirements reduce transsexualism to the state of a rare condition (if my understanding is correct, not even an illness) and I regard as highly controversial his final recommendation that as neither psychotherapy nor psychoanalysis has ever been reported as being of any value in treating transsexuals, those who fit into his description should be offered hormonal and surgical intervention, irrespective of age. There are some other major issues arising from this author's contention that the sense of belonging to one's sex is firmly set by powerful, silent, non-conflictual forces at work from birth. Although some may agree that 'there is no psychic structure adequate in the first months of life to carry the burden of such intricate fantasies as Kleinians require and that the infant is susceptible to the influences of imprinting and conditioning' (Stoller, 1975, p. 50), we must also speculate on the kind of psychological process capable of producing a scotomization of father (even a remote figure) and the type of identificatory mechanism resulting from a refusal by mother to let the son go.

There is also, in my view, a serious contradiction in the statement that castration anxiety is absent because there never was any masculinity and the admission that, although sex-transformed individuals improve socially and psychologically, their feeling of wellbeing is affected by the fact that surgery cannot extirpate either the memory of the male genitals or the sense of maleness. No explanation is offered for the fact that an existing sense of maleness fails to become the basis for castration anxiety, even if we accept Stoller's suggestion that the relationship with mother is completely desexualized.

I have reported in some detail, without necessarily doing full justice to it, what seems to me to be an authoritative statement from the only writer who has attempted fully to elucidate a complex disorder of gender identity.

Unfortunately his findings still await confirmation. For instance, in many cases the family constellation is conspicuously absent, as shown in a recent report on a series of fifty-six transsexuals who had surgery (Tsoi *et al.*, 1977), where no evidence was found of undue attachment to mother or lack of father figure or cross-gender assignment and rearing. None of the cases in the series had ever practised heterosexuality in their lives. Even if we accept Stoller's contention that it is preservation of one's sense of self, not one's anatomical appearance, which determines behaviour, much remains unexplained.

In my opinion it is counter-productive to restrict the diagnosis of transsexualism to a few cases as suggested by Stoller (1975) because this involves depriving us of the information to be gleaned from a study of all those who in increasing numbers seek sex change. Even when those cases of compulsive self-mutilation, excessive guilt and sexuality linked with religious fanaticism and delusional states have been excluded we are still left with a large number of individuals of both sexes who display a compelling desire for the obliteration of their primary and secondary sexual characteristics. Over the years therapists have come to recognize the ubiquitous nature of transsexual fantasies. In more recent times more and more people have been able to express an inherent dissatisfaction with their original gender identity in the knowledge that in doing so they no longer risk immediate admission to a psychiatric institution. In selecting clinical material for presentation I have tried to cover all aspects of what I regard as the transsexual syndrome.

II   CLINICAL MATERIAL

'Steve A' was an attractive, feminine, unmarried woman, twenty-four years of age when she was referred for psychoanalysis over twenty years ago, by a colleague who thought this to be the last resort in a case of hopeless neurotic conflict over homosexuality. She had been hospitalized for long periods since the age of seventeen and had become increasingly more depressed and anxious on account of her fascination for female breasts and recurrent thoughts that her sex was changing. Steve had made a poor start in life. At birth she was given an ordinary female Christian name, which was immediately abbreviated to a very masculine one, which had never left her. Her father, a regular Army officer, was seldom home and had little to do with her, although he was very close to her sister who was six years older. The mother, a woman who had been dominated by her own mother, tended to look at her younger daughter as her companion until late adolescence when Steve made her escape.

In the analysis the daily sessions were filled by repetitions such as 'Am I a man? Am I a woman? Please tell me.' She could not bear to be alone with girls, and every man, particularly the man she planned to marry, was suspected of being homosexual. Interpretations of her fear of homosexuality and her proneness to project her own impulses onto others were received either with abuse or by her storming out of the room. Having then little understanding of the important nature of the first communications on transsexualism (Ostow, 1953; Hamburger et al., 1953), I stubbornly persisted in my interpretations encouraged by the observation that as the patient was able to get in touch with her masculine feelings, her femininity was also beginning to blossom. When she finally did marry, in the third year of analysis, I believed that she was heading for disaster, especially because it was painfully clear to me that her husband was indeed not only obsessional but also very feminine. However, the analytical work slowly enabled Steve to acquire her own body as separate from her mother. Nevertheless she did not become fully convinced that she was a woman until she had her first child, a boy, who luckily turned out to be healthy. During the pregnancy, I had become aware of her seemingly ineradicable conception of her reproductive organs as being utterly useless or positively dangerous. Rather than the expected symbolic representation of the unborn baby as the longed for penis of her childhood, I was confronted by an alarming lack of internalization of anything of value. Yet, something was being salvaged by the analytical work, as she was able to control her disgust and allow her baby to be breast fed. Her disgust was, as it might be expected, a half-hearted attempt to protect her child from her poisonous milk. By the time a second child, a girl, was born she had lost her fear of being a lesbian and of changing sex. Sixteen years after the end of the analysis, which had lasted six years, 'Steve A' is well and her children are said to be normal. For a short period, some help was needed to enable her to make further adjustment to her husband's neurotic behaviour. Doubts remain with regard to the nature of this relationship, which I would suggest must have been based (and may still be so) on a successful exchange and reciprocal borrowing of masculine and feminine traits and desires. A similar observation was included in a study on sexual behaviour (Watson et al., 1977) where it is stated 'one male to female (transsexual) described a sexual relationship with a female to male patient, which would have looked to a third party as ordinary coitus, but which was satisfying to the participants because each could enjoy the fantasy of being the other, knowing the other's fantasy.' (See also the case of 'Miss N', in Appendix.) I cannot say whether Steve's husband enjoyed such fantasy but I know that my patient did. I have often speculated about this analysis since I have become familiar with the transsexual syndrome, and to re-examine it in this light appears to add a new dimension to it. My persistent interpretation of the patient's latent and conscious fears of homosexuality did not take into account that what she regarded as a catastrophe had not yet occurred. Had I been aware of what I now know, I should have also spent less time in considering the possibility that I was dealing with bisexuality. Finally, I would have had less difficulty in helping my patient to gain insight into the fact that her wish to change sex was not in order to be joined with her mother in sexual union but to prevent re-engulfment.

'Mr B', a professional man, married with children, suffered from an inability to ejaculate, except when masturbating, usually with the aid of transsexual fantasies. He cross-dressed very rarely and the amount of homosexual feelings discovered in the course of a long analysis was well within normal range. Castration fears were deep, well rooted and associated with counterphobic activities. Illness in early life, together with deficient maternal care and insensitive paternal influence, aggravated by unhappy experiences at public school at an early age had combined to keep him in a state of limbo between full genitality and impotence. An overstress or an insistence in interpreting the homosexual aspects both of his psychopathology and his florid transsexual fantasies would probably have led to a breakdown in the therapeutic relationship.

'Gerry C' was referred to the Portman Clinic, London, at the age of twenty-five, by a psychiatrist who thought his patient needed help on account of transsexualism and his repeated request for hormonal and surgical treatment. For as long as he could remember he had a desire to be treated as a girl. He started dressing in his younger sister's clothes in childhood, sometimes in the course of play with her but more often in secret. During the last two or three years the preoccupation with his transsexual wishes had become so intense that it interfered with his work at a teachers' training college. At the first interview, he looked white and frightened and spoke abruptly. His anxiety and display of aggressiveness increased when he was told that only psychotherapy would be offered to him. At the time I found it difficult to understand the source of his anxiety but he relaxed a little when I observed to him that he seemed to feel that I would actually harm him or hurt him in some way. He returned two weeks later apologizing for what he thought had been his appalling behaviour at the first interview but it was only several months later that the actual meaning of this incident could be understood. In due course I learnt that he had felt very close to mother whom he regarded as a very unhappy woman, who throughout life had suffered ill health. He also thought she had been extremely overprotective; on the other hand father had always shown little or no interest in him, leaving mother to deal with all family matters. His sister, eighteen months younger, was described as married with children, aggressive, domineering and a great deal more than a tomboy. His recollection also was that since the age of two-and-a-half he had been interested in everything that was feminine, a fact known to all members of his family. His secret cross-dressing had started around the age of five and by the time he had reached puberty he was convinced that he had been plagued by being a girl trapped in a male body. There was little sexual arousal at puberty and to date he had masturbated on less than a dozen occasions and 'always with an empty mind'. Late in adolescence, he had been able to acquire female clothes and he had worn them in the privacy of his room without ever experiencing any sexual excitement. From the start, the weekly sessions were dominated by his constant request for referral to a 'sex change clinic' and a rejection of my attempts to establish a working relationship. He finally failed to attend, but he approached me again a month later. Regular weekly sessions were resumed but this time I expressed an interest in meeting his family. He seemed delighted with the suggestion and an interview with mother was promptly arranged.

Mrs C was pleasant and helpful, showing considerable insight into her son's state of mind. She had indeed not been surprised to hear that Gerry wanted a sex change as she suspected he might be homosexual as there had been no girl in his life. With her husband she had recalled how at the age of eight he had appeared at a family party with his sister, dressed in each other's school uniform. She could not recall ever discovering him wearing his sister's clothes but she had been aware of her daughter's insistence on wearing her brother's. Gerry had been an attractive and beautiful child and she spontaneously admitted that she had been extremely close to him until she had given birth to her daughter, when he suddenly lost his speech, which until then had been very advanced. Later a long course of speech therapy extending over several years became necessary. Gerry had been very interested in everything his sister did and showed little overt signs of resenting her constant invasion of his territory; he had from the start been very protective of her. Mrs C's father had disappeared when she was just over two years old and her mother had quite a struggle in bringing up a large family. She had been very competitive with her two older brothers and recalled quite vividly how she had wished she had been born a boy. As she reached puberty she began to feel depressed but accepted her femininity readily. She married very young and was soon disappointed in her husband to a point when she had felt like leaving. Her migraine was very much part of her life.

Gerry's sister when interviewed turned out to be very feminine and deeply interested in her brother's predicament. She spontaneously said that she had advised him to go ahead and have the operation.

Although the weekly psychotherapy routine was well established, Gerry continued to exhibit frank anxiety, if not terror, at being in the room with me. He insisted he had nothing to say, adding he had no mind of his own. This statement, often repeated, was understood to be the direct expression and a residue of his original symbiotic relationship to mother, which had evolved into his profound identification with her. Slowly, he was able to express his doubt of the male role in relation to the female body, clearly revealing an utter lack of understanding of masculinity. In the context, he thought that to be masculine simply meant to impregnate a woman, but this held no particular interest or attraction for him and to say it was only repeating something that he had heard so often. One day he reported that he had been very surprised to hear a doctor on the radio stating that no physical harm could come to one from anal or vaginal penetration. This was followed by a declaration of his preference for female homosexuality, as something he might allow himself, if I relented and helped him to have the operation.

In his first dream, reported months after treatment had begun, *he was out on the road on his bicycle wearing female underwear, brassière, suspenders and panties. He is going backwards and forwards, wishing to avoid people knowing he is a man. Eventually, he meets two American Officers* (Gerry lives near an American camp) *and one of them asks him 'Is this something to do with the operation?' meaning a military operation in which they were involved, and then one tells him to take an alternative route. The scene then changes to someone (himself) losing his notes of a book he is writing; he starts to look for them but cannot find them anywhere, eventually discovering that he has left them at home.* In the second part of this dream there was an acknowledgement, that he is beginning to understand that the answer to his problem is to be found in what has happened in his home life, but there was also the encouraging sign that he was oscillating between wanting and not wanting the operation. A new phase in the treatment brought us near to some understanding of his difficult behaviour at its outset. As he put it, 'a very aggressive woman in him had quite simply come out', and it was imperative that he should find out whether I would be able to stand up to this woman. Although I suspected this meant that the woman he was identified with demanded that he should change his sex and that I should protect him, I did not interpret it. Further work showed that I was actually asked to take over the helpless male child part of Gerry. Yet another explanation was to be discovered in a later stage of the therapy, which presented me with considerable difficulty owing to sudden shifts in transference, made worse by the infrequency of the sessions.

Until now, there had been little evidence of oedipal anxieties. A sudden attraction for a girl at college brought a fresh outbreak of conscious fear of me which was quickly dispelled as soon as I was able to show him how he was seeing me as a father who did not allow him any sexual interest in women at college or at home. Shortly after this, a long forgotten episode in his early life was recalled. At the age of three-and-a-half he had been circumcised and had been in hospital for three days in great pain, his penis being very inflamed and hurting badly when he wanted to urinate. It was clear that the appearance of the hostile father in the transference had facilitated the recovery of this experience which must contain vestiges of the missing castration anxiety. I was then tempted to consider the possibility that I was dealing with a fairly straightforward case of latent homosexuality, but I reminded myself that Gerry's trauma had occurred long before the incident, which perhaps had finally destroyed any chance of spontaneous recovery. At any rate, concurrent with this episode, there was a recrudescence of compulsive transsexual fantasies and cross-dressing activities. Gerry had even reported having changed into female clothes in the Clinic's toilet while waiting for his session. On one occasion and with no warning apart from, 'I'll show you what I'm like', he quickly proceeded to take off his pullover and jeans revealing a sleeveless dress and black tights. From his briefcase came a wig and a pair of ladies' shoes, which he put on. He then resumed his seat, calm and composed, displaying no excitement whatever, looking at me inquiringly. I sat watching this strange transformation in a human being who apparently believed he could move freely from one identity to another, but I was also conscious of the hidden quality of a transitional phenomenon in what I was observing. In the circumstances I briefly commented on my role as an observing mirror of something that was going on now but that had probably originated in his mind when still an infant. He understandably showed little interest in this and soon after he took everything off again, got dressed in his usual unisex clothes and left. The following session was taken up by the incident and he told me that he wanted to show me how he could bring the feminine and the masculine parts of himself together and in harmony and that perhaps I would recommend him for surgery. But after further reflection, he commented that many people mistook him for his mother and wondered if I also thought he looked like her. Working through this material proved very fruitful in so far as we were able to discover that at the first interview he had quickly come to the conclusion that I wanted to separate these two parts of himself; in other words as a result of a sudden transference reaction he had experienced me as the father who wanted to separate him from his mother. What I had observed at that time was acute separation anxiety but here was also evidence that whatever happened to this young man in his early life did not succeed in obliterating all traces of the oedipal situation.

The most notable feature about this psychotherapy perhaps is that it was kept going over the years and that it was successful in removing the sense of compelling urgency for surgical intervention. It has also enabled the patient, through the analysis of his separation anxiety, to leave home and to pursue an occupation which fosters the expression of reparative drives hitherto absent.

It must be left to the reader to decide whether the total symptomatology as uncovered by analytical psychotherapy is compatible with a diagnosis of transsexualism. Leaving such detail aside the outstanding features of this case are: (1) The symbiotic relation or rather the fantasy of fusion between mother and son was brought to an end by the birth of a second child. (2) The son attempts to follow up the early fantasy with what appears as deep identification which was constantly threatened by mother's substantial withdrawal, although she continued to remain over-protective and controlling. (3) The failure to dis-identify with mother (Greenson, 1968) or in my view to cease imitating her cannot rest entirely on the latter. (4) The absence of castration anxiety is associated with a conception of the male genital as being potentially capable of causing injury. (5) The failure of heterosexual or homosexual impulses to appear is more difficult to understand, but is probably related to the primal scene experienced as violent and dangerous. It is certainly common in those cases where transsexual features are aimed at securing a permanent, though fictitious, union with the maternal image, a manoeuvre which appears to have been successful in this case, considering the lack of conscious separation anxiety.

'Jackie D' was nineteen years old when seen at his request with a view to sex reassignment. He was living with a criminal with whom he was having anal intercourse, which was satisfactory and disgusting at the same time, as he felt himself to be a woman and wanted ordinary sex with him. His account of his early history was confirmed by his mother, who said that she never thought it unnatural for her son to be interested in everything she did from the very beginning. He had made his first suicidal attempt at eleven, when told by a doctor he could not be a girl. He attempted suicide again two years later when informed he would have to wait until he was eighteen to be considered for an operation. Jackie refused to live as a woman but he uses heavy make-up and jewellery. His identification with mother is clearly shown by his ability at the age of twelve to look after father and an older brother, when mother deserted her family. After some sessions Jackie left in a rage declining the offer of regular therapy, which in any case had been undermined by the readiness of a psychiatric colleague to supply him with hormones and a promise of an operation at twenty-one. There was no evidence in this case of a symbiotic relationship with mother, who seemed quite capable of it. In fact, it was more probable that Jackie had been deprived of maternal and paternal love.

Whether he is a transsexual or an effeminate young man seems almost irrelevant when we consider that he is capable of accepting a passive homosexual relationship without any sense of loss of identity and at the same time he is quite fearless in seeking a new identity through the removal of his maleness, which he regards as altogether useless to him. Jackie's general behaviour and activities should be compared with the case described by Socarides (1970) who had actively engaged in homosexual practices from an early age, but found it unacceptable. Socarides writes 'the patient undergoes the dreaded castration, vicariously identifies with the powerful mother, neutralizes the fear of her and consciously enjoys the infantile wish for intercourse with father; escapes paranoid-like fear of aggression from hostile stranger men who could damage one in homosexual relations' (p. 347). Socarides goes on to state that transsexualism is evident in the homosexual who attempts to resolve his emotional conflicts through denial, a psychotic mechanism. This case report is notable as psychoanalysis was attempted but was prematurely ended by the patient.

'Miss E' had several years of psychoanalysis in the course of which she had secretly received hormonal treatment, before undergoing surgery which had been only partially successful. Miss E had been unable to continue with her professional work and lived with a woman as man and wife. The reason for the referral was a breakdown in this relationship owing to her partner's promiscuity and addiction to alcohol and drugs. Miss E rejected the idea that there had ever been a homosexual content in the relationship and resented the stress placed on it by the analyst. However, it is doubtful that this is sufficient to account for the failure of psychoanalysis in this case where transsexual features had been present since infancy, aggravated by her father's pleasure in her tomboyishness.

III DISCUSSION

A further selection of brief clinical descriptions of men and women who presented one or more features of the transsexual syndrome will be found in the Appendix but the difficulty remains of conveying to the reader the distress that goes with the belief of possessing a mind alien to one's body. It is also understandable that the differentiation of the condition from homosexuality or transvestism will not immediately be apparent. It is only in the course of the psychotherapeutic relationship or even extended assessment interviews that the observer will become aware of the absence of castration anxiety or of any sign of the sexual excitement which belongs to cross-dressing. There will also be no evidence of the hidden desire for revenge against women or the latent or the poorly concealed hostility against men that is present in the effeminate and passive male homosexual. This finding is valid in my experience even in those cases where the desire for gender reassignment makes its appearance in adolescence or later in life, when the precariousness of earlier adjustments and profound character defects are easily uncovered. Undoubtedly transsexualism and homosexuality have a great deal in common especially when the mother has become part of a narcissistic self-organization and the boy is seen to delegate the masculine part of himself to her, thus avoiding active participation in the destruction of father. Whereas envy and feelings of competition with mother will be prominent in the mental life of the homosexual they play little part in the male transsexual who will insist that as he is a woman he has no reason to envy women. A similar statement by a female transsexual carries less conviction in view of the shortcomings of plastic surgery in her case. It is perhaps the *apparent* strength and depth of identification with the parent of the opposite sex that has induced some observers to lay great stress on the role of envy and biological forces in the establishment of transsexualism. There seems to be little justification for this particularly as it is generally accepted that pathological masculine traits will appear later in the girl than will feminine tendencies in a boy. Whereas the pathological

identification with mother may seem almost inevitable when the relationship has been too close (at times approaching symbiosis) we have considerable difficulty in understanding why the girl who may have had a similar
experience will end up with a pathological identification with father and
therefore we must doubt the correctness of this assumption unless such
identification is clinically demonstrable.

The lack of a loving and loved father as a source of interference with the
opportunity for identification and identity formation was stressed by Greenson (1966b) in discussing the treatment of a transvestite boy. In my view the
role of father has particular relevance in the development of persistent
transsexual fantasies or serious disorders of gender identity, whether he is
remote and unavailable or excessively intrusive and masculine. In stating
this I have no intention of minimizing the importance of defective mother-
ing especially when it involves a tendency to encourage a pathological
gender role. In such instances, the relationship assumes a symbiotic quality
(fusion might be a better word) which finally evolves into an atmosphere of
ambivalence. If such a relationship still appears to the infant or child to be
or to have been blissful, it is through denial of the inherent sources of
frustration. Father's role is vital in controlling the intensity and persistence
of projections and identifications as they may arise in mother and baby. The
violence of such processes together with splitting and a profound disturbance of introjective mechanisms is made worse if the mother actively
prevents father from ever becoming a real person to the baby. There is in
fact little chance of internalizing a 'good breast' unless there is a father (or
something to represent him) so that the baby learns to feel 'it is not with me
it is also elsewhere.' It is therefore not a matter of regressing to the good
breast (Stoller, 1975, p. 289) but the lack of its introjection which is central
to the psychopathology of transsexualism. This disturbance will also inevitably lead to a faulty appraisal of the genital organs and genitality in both
sexes. Under the circumstances symbol formation will be affected in relation to several ego-functions. This was noted by Juliet Mitchell (1976) in a
thoughtful review of Stoller's *The Transsexual Experiment* where she points
out that it is not sufficient to say that the transsexual child is not psychotic
because he knows he has a penis, in so far as it is necessary to ascertain the
significance he attributes to the penis; in fact the transsexual appears to
have no symbolic idea of the penis. To underline the validity of this writer's
observations, I shall quote a relevant passage in Stoller's description from
the treatment of a little boy aged seven who clearly said he was *pretending*
(my italics) to be a girl and later he goes on to say that he does not know his

penis makes him a boy. 'You can never convince that stupid idiot, he will not listen, that's why he cannot get used to the idea of being a boy' (Stoller, 1975, p. 58). However it is not only a matter of a disturbed symbolization of the genital and its function. Should the fusion between mother and child continue well after the early weeks of the infant's life, the ego will become confused with the object. As Segal (1957) has pointed out: 'Symbol formation is an activity of the ego attempting to deal with the anxieties stirred by its relation to the object. That is primarily the fear of bad objects and the fear of the loss or inaccessibility of good objects. Disturbances in the ego's relation to objects are reflected in disturbances of symbol formation' (p. 392). Segal also stresses that a disturbed differentiation between the ego and the object leads 'to disturbances in differentiation between the symbol and the object symbolized and therefore to concrete thinking characteristic of psychoses', a point which she develops further in a later paper on symbolism (Segal, 1978); (see also Gallwey, 1979).

Although the personality and some basic ego functions of transsexuals are considerably disturbed, we could not regard them as psychotic but there is an unquestionable psychotic flavour and a suggestion of concrete thinking in their assertion that they actually think and feel as a member of the opposite sex. Paranoid and depressive anxieties are not far from the surface ('Steve A', 'Gerry C' and also clinical descriptions of 'Miss G', 'Miss H', 'Mr I', 'Mr L', 'Mr M' in Appendix) as is also separation anxiety, which in some cases appears to coalesce with a fear of annihilation or disintegration ('Gerry C', 'Miss H', 'Mr M' in Appendix). Many transsexuals in fact are locked in actual relationships which they find it unbearable to accommodate yet they are unable to end them ('Miss E', 'Miss H' and 'Mr L' in Appendix) (see also R. Green, 1974).

Neither cross-dressing nor homosexual relationships (although, as has already been pointed out, acknowledged as heterosexual) will bring relief to the pain and unhappiness of these people. Their state of mind should be compared with that of the transvestite who is attempting to give up his cross-dressing (Glasser, 1979a) or of the true homosexual (see pp. 108–115 above) who struggles hard to abandon the acting out of the deviation. In both instances, as the analysis progresses we become aware that beneath the castration anxiety lie the most profound disturbances in object relations and it is separation anxiety (often equalled to a fear of annihilation) which will finally mobilize all our attention. In my opinion it is this particular anxiety which is the basis for the appearance of the transsexual syndrome in males and females irrespective of age.

The boy whose mother has wittingly or unwittingly hampered the process of separation–individuation, after a phase of intense identification with her, needs to be *physically* the same as he is gradually more and more aware that he can only imitate her. To be given a new feminine body will reinforce the illusion of being forever fused with mother. Within the narcissistic organization (an important element in the personality and character structure of these individuals) the 'new body' will create a feeling of independence from the primary object. The plastic surgery is needed so that the grown man can say, 'I am not afraid of being separate; I have mother with me; I am *really* her.' If we compare this situation with that of the transvestite, who seeks to create that same illusion in order to escape from it (Glasser, 1979a) we shall understand why the demand for sex reassignment sometimes comes quite late after years of cross-dressing which has become less and less effective in relieving basic anxieties (see 'Mr L' in Appendix).

In the case of the girl we are probably dealing with even a more serious disturbance. This may be due to the profound despair that exists in some women never to be able to experience a body of their own. As the girl is physically the same as mother she needs to achieve full separation from her to be able to identify with the female and eventually maternal roles (P. King, personal communication). Her separation anxiety will keep her bound to mother and in desperation she will finally demand to be given a body which she can claim as her own. With the belief that she is a boy comes the resolution of the conflict over the desired and yet dreaded engulfment by mother. The girl can claim to have secured independence not only from mother but from father as well. In advancing this hypothesis, I am casting doubt on the validity of the assumption that the masculinity of the female transsexual is rooted in an identification with a father who prefers her to be a boy. This has not been very obvious in the women included in this clinical investigation. 'Steve A' for instance grew up in a wholly feminine environment whilst 'Miss G' and 'Miss N' complained of father's remoteness and ineffectualness. It is possible that in the case of 'Miss F' and 'Miss H' there was some direct encouragement by father to develop masculine interests. (In Radclyffe Hall's *The Well of Loneliness* (1926) the heroine is named Stephen at birth in deference to father's desire for a son. Perhaps this work ought to be regarded as an outstanding description of transsexualism rather than homosexuality.)

This brief outline of the psychodynamics of transsexualism, as I understand it, is not helpful in understanding the absence of castration anxiety and disregard for the consequences of the drastic plastic surgery (Feldman,

1977) to which an increasing number of men and women are willing to submit. In the case of the male transsexual, the explanation may lie in the severity of the projective and introjective identificatory processes which have caused so much confusion with the primary object in the early developmental stages. In the circumstances the subject will take over the object's cathexes and in consequence the boy will feel pride in all that is of interest to mother; the most direct result of this will be a lack of symbolization of the male genital. A similar situation will occur in the female, again as a result of violent projective identificatory mechanisms typical of those individuals who seek sex transformations. The capacity for taking over the quality and characteristics of the object continues unabated throughout adolescence and adult life. 'Gerry C' had no interest in men because he believed that his mother also lacked it and in turn acted as a girl because he thought this was what the mother wanted. 'Jackie D' instead was as promiscuous with men as his mother. 'Miss N' and 'Steve' made full use of massive projective identification in order to enjoy full heterosexual relations with partners who used similar identificatory mechanisms, being primarily homosexuals. It should be noted here that the reported observations of a mother treating the transsexual male child as her phallus is in keeping with the presence of marked projective identifications arising in the mother. Lastly, we should bear it in mind that the disturbance of symbol formation which has been discussed earlier in this paper, leading to concrete thinking will lend unbounded support to the bid for independence at all cost. The need for safety in separation and individuation may well go beyond the anxiety concerning the preservation of the body.

With regard to the Oedipus complex I could not fail to notice its presence in several cases I have observed in this series, notably those of 'Steve A', 'Gerry C', 'Miss H' in Appendix, but quite often I have noticed a studied avoidance of any discussion of the parent of the opposite sex ('Jackie D', 'Mr T', 'Mr L' and 'Miss X'). Lastly, I must admit that transsexualism only adds to the confusion in the debate concerning early ego development. As my view is that object relations are something with which the infant is inescapably involved from soon after he is born, it follows that it would be impossible to extricate the role of the environment from that of the psychic life of the individual who suffers from transsexualism.

IV   CONCLUDING REMARKS

In view of our limited knowledge of the transsexual syndrome, treatment can only be tentative. In the face of protestation that all problems would be solved by an operation the psychotherapist will be at a disadvantage as in the countertransference sympathy will overshadow empathy. Quite apart from this, our techniques must be kept under constant scrutiny. I have noted for instance that any premature attempt to take a history of the patient's early life and relationships is provocative and often leads to the premature and abrupt ending of the investigation. Others may be kept longer in treatment as they feel well protected by a profound amnesia for the first few years of life covering almost every conceivable activity or experience with the exception of: 'I always knew I was not a boy (or girl)'. Those who are not so protected will accept psychotherapy provided we do not show keenness in looking into the origins of the condition. My belief that this lack of curiosity is related to poorly repressed oedipal anxieties is based on clinical material which is far too limited and therefore awaits confirmation. A more serious threat to the therapeutic relationship comes from the unwillingness of the transsexual to engage in it. Negative transference reactions, a source of disappointment and pessimism for the therapist, can be sudden and unshakeable. In my view, as the transsexual is not psychotic, he is well aware of the bizarre quality of his current life relationships and will prefer not to have them subjected to analytical examination. He also fears that his pretences will be exposed, thus revealing little faith in the statement that the 'cure' lies in the acquisition of a new gender identity.

In summing up I wish to put forward the hypothesis that the transsexual syndrome is the precursor in some cases of transvestism and of homosexuality, these two conditions representing a spontaneous resolution of the more serious disturbance. The occurrence of transsexual fantasies in children should be taken seriously but not treated as if it were necessarily an expression of either transvestism or latent homosexuality. This would also apply to the handling of similar fantasies in adults.

Finally I must state that as I regard the transsexual syndrome as a personality and characterological disaster it cannot be corrected by mutilating operations which are often carried out in response to suicide threats amounting to blackmail. Unlike many other psychiatric conditions where the patient is clearly attempting to achieve a cure, here the patient requires the cure to be achieved by involving others, who are asked to play into the fantasy of adding to a pretension a distorted body, often a caricature of the real thing. When Winnicott (1952) wrote 'an environment developing falsely into a human being, hiding within itself a potential individual' (p. 100) he may well have written about transsexuals and the faulty environment in which they grow up. A new bodily appearance adds nothing to a false self. In my view as long as we know so little about this fascinating syndrome, we should refrain from adding our professional weight to solutions of questionable value but of an immeasurable nature. We should continue to observe facts, not forgetting the need to improve our psychotherapeutic techniques while clinical evidence is gathered.

APPENDIX

The following clinical descriptions are a selection drawn from cases referred to the Portman Clinic, London, as gender identity problems. Some were simply unhappy men and women but the majority were determined to pursue sex reassignment surgery. With few exceptions an offer of psychotherapy was made at the completion of the investigations.

'Miss F', aged thirty-three, had lived as a man and worked as a carpenter since age sixteen. She had lived with a woman as man and wife for five years. They had eloped to get married and the bride-to-be, aged nineteen, was not aware of 'Miss F's' real sexual identity. The presenting problem was mainly one of depression as they could not get married but there were social difficulties as well, as 'Miss F' was about to lose her job which she had held for years. Apart from her family, no one knew of their predicament. 'Miss F' had wanted to be a boy as far back as she could remember and had been very competitive and envious of two older brothers. No information could be obtained about her early relationship to mother but 'Miss F' spoke warmly of her father who had given her a motor cycle as a present. It had been a long wait until she was sixteen when she moved away from home to live the life of a man. When seen together with her partner, it was immediately apparent that 'Miss F's' strong masculine characteristics were highly complementary to her femininity. 'Miss F's' menstruation had never been noted by her partner, who was quite content with limited sexual activities. They were each frankly hostile to lesbians and male homosexuals respectively. Psychotherapy was of value in guiding them towards solving some social problems such as registration at a Labour Office and the legalization of the change of name. 'Miss F' was also satisfied to seek only a mastectomy and was reconciled to the idea of not pursuing further her request for full sex reassignment.

'Miss G', aged seventeen, had made several suicidal attempts, mostly aimed at protesting about her gender identity and role forced upon her by society. At the age of three, she had ceased to play with dolls and as she entered puberty she hated her developing breasts, resented menstruation and felt she should have a penis. For the past four years she had been incessantly preoccupied with her need to be given the body of a male. In a psychiatric assessment she was described as a manipulative, hysterical personality who was profoundly disturbed. Her problems were seen as possibly due to her emotional involvement with her aggressive, depressed and withdrawn mother. The offer of psychotherapy was met by one more suicidal attempt which resulted in her being taken to a special clinic. Her request for sex reassignment was accepted with the proviso that until the age of twenty-one she should manage with hormone therapy. This was on the basis of a further psychiatric assessment which diagnosed her to be free from psychiatric symptoms with the comment that her unhappiness was only due to having a male mind in a female body. The discrepancy of psychiatric opinions, with serious consequences, is a source of pain and distress which seems difficult to avoid in these cases (Feldman, 1977).

'Miss H', aged thirty-two had undergone hysterectomy, ovarectomy and mastectomy eleven years before her referral on account of deep depression, inability to work and a persistent hallucinatory state. 'Miss H's' appearance and demeanour were decisively and unmistakably male, enhanced by a profuse growth of beard. A highly intelligent individual with some artistic flair, she had worked as a child care officer until her change of identity, which she now bitterly regretted, although she would not consider the possibility of reverting to living the life of a woman. The expectation of further reconstructive surgery to the external genitalia had fallen through. Her reactive depression had suddenly developed into a fully-fledged schizophrenic illness five years earlier, with the delusion of being the Christ who had come to rescue all transsexuals, an idea which had gradually given way to the belief of being the devil. As a converted Roman Catholic 'Miss H' was tortured by the memory of a priest's recriminations after her confession that she had changed her sex. Her early life had been typical of a female transsexual. A poorly disguised deep attachment and closeness to mother was coupled with statements that father insisted she should stay with her and that she should be good and helpful. Her dislike for girls' toys and games was there from the start and by the age of five she was strong enough to spend a lot of time digging father's allotment. Young girls and women had been 'naturally attracted to her' from her adolescent years and in view of her intellectual abilities and charm it was not surprising that three professional women had been her common law wives since the gender identity change. The hopelessness of her mental state and the bankruptcy of her attempt to live up to what she now fully realized as having been a misfortune aggravated by an impossible pretence, prompted me to offer psychotherapy which I realized could not deal with the more severe aspects of her psychotic state. There had in fact been incidents which had brought her very near violent acting out in response to her paranoid state and hallucinatory experiences. Her attachment and dependence on the therapist was profound from the start showing the psychotic quality of her separation anxiety. For instance when an attempt at hospitalization was made it was necessary to promise formally that her weekly attendances would not be interrupted. All this seemed to belong to a delusional transference to the analyst-mother but a more serious complication arose when the 'voices' started to warn her about the danger of becoming too attached to the analyst-father. The background for this new transference development was that 'Miss H' had actually requested referral to me as from a public discussion she had been aware of my antagonism against sex change operations. This had meant to her that I preferred girls to remain so, unlike father who favoured her older brother to a point of sharing professional interests and a business with him. When an interpretation of my understanding of this aspect of the analytic relationship was offered to her, it was met by understandable rejection whereas she seemed more able to understand the nature of her profound anxiety provoked by her wish to be contained and cared for by the analyst-mother. It is clear that in this case surgery has brought no relief or anything approaching a solution to the patient's conflicts over fear of engulfment and separation from mother or her substitutes.

'Mr I', aged seventeen, looked feminine in his unisex clothes and appeared sufficiently secure in his attempt to conceal his masculine gender. He was depressed at having to live the life of a homosexual and would have liked to have surgical interventions if he had not been made apprehensive by the difficulties experienced by an operated male to female transsexual friend with whom he lived without any sexual contact. He insisted he had no information to give about his early life, which he could not remember in any case, except that his preference for girls' clothes and feminine things had been known to his parents 'all along'. An offer of psychotherapy was declined.

'Mr L', aged forty-one and twice married, with children, was referred for a second opinion with a strong recommendation for surgical and hormonal measures in view of frequent psychosomatic complaints traceable to unhappiness with his male status. He had been tormented by transsexual fantasies ever since his first wife had divorced him on account of his sexual incompetence. The fantasies had not been in any way reduced by an attempt to cross-dress which had taken him to transvestite clubs where he 'felt like a fish out of water'. He had also never experienced any sexual attraction for men but he had no particular abhorrence for it. 'Mr L', a gifted and creative individual, was clearly functioning below his potential and always struggling against a wish to do nothing. Although he was very co-operative in the treatment which was readily offered to him, there were extraordinary difficulties in view of his frequent threats of suicide and self-castration. At first his early history was an almost complete blank except that he seemed to have no positive or negative feelings of any kind for his parents and siblings. This was eventually replaced by a new account of his dealings with mother who was now emerging as an intruding dominating figure whilst father was uninterested in his son and unable to intervene. As the psychotherapeutic work progressed it became apparent that this man's poor work and social achievement and the premature ejaculation had the same common origin in an absence of a good introjected 'breast', bringing in its wake serious problems in the area of psychic reparation. Even more striking was the uncovering of an absence of any sense of value of the primary sexual characteristics, his one and only interest being in what a woman felt and her capacity to bear children. His lack of any cathexis towards his genitals was also shown by the absence of any excitement in cross-dressing with only few exceptions which were at puberty and even then only occasionally. At the time of writing a new feature has been uncovered in the periodicity of the occurrence of transsexual fantasies which seems to be linked with the onset of sadistic impulses towards his wife and women in general. 'Mr L's' psychotherapy has so far produced a change of attitude towards the desire for sex change, which has receded into the background. He is no longer depressed and at long last he is able to utilize his creativity and to make a good living as a potter. But transsexual fantasies are still at the centre of his psychic life.

'Mr M', aged twenty-two, was referred while hoping to have surgical interventions on account of court appearances on charges of deception. He looked very feminine in every way and he could well have passed as a woman. He had been living for four years as the common law wife of a man whose patience was constantly tried by 'Mr M's' compulsion to obtain money from men, pretending to be a female prostitute. He was the youngest of a large family and had been very close to mother in the early years of his life. This blissful union came to an end when at the age of five he was sent to school where he had great difficulties in settling down, suggestive of a school-phobia. Worse still, when he was seven mother left home to live with her lover. Father insisted that 'M' should stay with him but from that time he became a delinquent with innumerable court appearances. 'M's' aim in life was 'to become an exact replica of mother, who was beautiful and perfect'. He accepted psychotherapy because he realized that he needed help in various respects other than his gender identity problem. The outstanding feature of this case was the complete absence of castration anxiety together with the lack of any evidence of any masochistic or self-punishing tendencies. It is also worth noting that 'Mr M' felt that in all probability his partner was homosexual but he vehemently denied any possibility of himself being troubled by homosexuality. He reported the experience of wearing male clothes as that of being in 'drag'.

'Miss N' was a thirty-four-year-old musician, who had abandoned a successful career to embrace a new one which could allow her to dress and live as a male. She did not ask for a new gender identity as she had sufficient insight to realize that surgery could never be totally satisfactory for a woman but was only partially resigned to the fact that she had to accept herself as such, hence the depression for which she was seeking help. A good rapport was easily established and it soon transpired that she had been engaged in a symbiotic relationship with her mother who had also wished to have a musical career. She was totally devoted to her, escorting her everywhere whilst father stayed at home. A brief affair with a woman showed her that this was not what she wanted and since then she had a series of relationships with men who were allowed to have anal intercourse with her. A great deal of material about her early life emerged rather rapidly and with it a great deal of anger at being locked in a stifling relationship with mother but at the third interview she reported she needed no further help. Her current relationship with a middle-aged male homosexual, who did not regard her in any way as a woman, was more than enough to take care of her emotional and sexual needs.

10   ON SOME POSITIVE
ASPECTS OF THE
NEGATIVE THERAPEUTIC
REACTION*

Restoration of health is only the incubation of another malady.
T.S. ELIOT, *The Family Reunion*

IN THIS PAPER I wish to explore those aspects of the negative therapeutic reaction (NTR) which can be of value in revealing deep-seated fears about the meaning of health for certain patients. Quite apart from being indicative that something is seriously amiss in the analytic situation, the syndrome is complex clinically and conceptually. That it does occur is not open to doubt, although in recent years there has been a tendency to dismiss it as an irrelevant usage of a term to describe a course of psychoanalytic treatment which has failed. Analysts' opinions have been divided in attributing the failure to a special psychopathology in the patient or to faulty technique. Its confusion with various resistances is only too apparent in some case reports, just as it is clear that the term is applied even when therapy has not actually occurred. When the condition tends to be repetitive, it is possible to predict that a NTR will follow a piece of reconstruction or attempted integration, but in most cases it will occur when we least expect it, to coincide with the healing of a split or in the course of psychosynthesis. Freud (1919) insisted that synthesis is achieved in psychoanalytic treatment without any intervention, automatically and inevitably. He also suggested that 'Whenever we succeed in analysing a symptom into its elements, in freeing an instinctual impulse from one nexus, it does not remain in isolation, but immediately enters into a new one' (p. 161). As the psychosynthesis is not a wholly silent process it is understandable that there will bc somc acknowledgement of progress, or indeed of improvement, on

* This paper was first published in 1981 in the *International Journal of Psycho-Analysis* 62: 379–99.

the part of the patient or the analyst. The response will vary from patient to patient.

In common with most analysts I have formulated my own classification of NTRs out of the many I have encountered over the years. In general I am inclined to treat an immediate negative response to a piece of good analytic work, if it becomes apparent in the course of a session, as a resistance or a defensive manoeuvre. If more than a day has intervened before the 'reaction' is apparent, I alert myself to the need to look again at my understanding of the transference during the previous phase and to the possibility of some maladroitness in the handling of the countertransference. Special care needs to be taken in differentiating it from the frequent occurrence of relapses, the reappearance of aggressiveness, depression, or of a symptom which has been cleared up, in the course of termination. Should we be dealing with a NTR, it could well indicate that the core of the illness has not been reached. The worst reactions, of course, are known to occur in circumstances wholly unrelated to termination of the analysis, and frequently after a period of systematic, careful and intensive work associated with dynamic changes. As has so often been stated, the patient takes a step backward having taken two steps forward. Analysts agree in considering the condition as malignant, especially if it keeps recurring so as to lead to interminability of the analysis, but it will also be observed in deliberately long analyses. On the other hand, disagreements occur when we are trying to account for what is taking place, or when we attempt to conceptualize what lies behind our clinical observations. At this point our judgement is obfuscated by the countertransference, as unquestionably the essential element of a NTR is that the analytic work, which has lovingly and meticulously been carried out, is laid out in fragments before us. Some patients prefer this to a frank attack on the analyst and in so doing they magically protect him. The possibility of counter-attacking, thus aggravating the situation, is always there, often enough backed by a rigid theoretical belief as to what causes all this rush of destructiveness, or by fixed views of the patient's personality and character structure. The alternative is to become defensive which can be just as damaging to the analysis and the patient who becomes alarmed by his destructiveness.

Having arrived at the correct assessment of the situation, we have also reached a point of no return as the concept of NTR is a value system. Psychoanalysis is not reductive as a medical speciality and we must therefore ask ourselves whether we are too preoccupied with therapy at the expense of promoting the search for truth and the development of the personality. In any case we must take into account the fact that we do not hand over to the patient the responsibility for the analysis. We also tend to forget that whatever aggression is being displayed, it is not directed at the self, but is directed at the analyst, who in the eyes of the patient must still be felt to be capable of containing it, a point which I shall take up again later in the paper.

For several years, the only satisfactory explanation of this unfavourable outcome of our psychoanalytic work has been based on Freud's statements in *The Ego and the Id*, when he noted that an expression of hopefulness in the progress would make such patients worse. He added,

Something in these people sets itself against their recovery, and its approach is dreaded as though it were a danger . . . In the end we come to see we are dealing with what may be called a 'moral' factor, a sense of guilt, which is finding its satisfaction in the illness and refuses to give up the punishment of suffering . . . the patient does not feel guilty, he feels ill. (Freud, 1923, p. 49)

He further elaborated this point in the paper on 'The economic problem of masochism' (1924) in which he now refers to an *unconscious* sense of guilt, but at this stage he still considers 'the strength of such impulse as constituting one of the most serious resistances'. Here Freud appears to have altered his position as expounded in his paper on 'Remembering, repeating and working through' in which he had drawn attention to the problem of deterioration during treatment, postulating a possible reason in the return of the repressed and the patient's desire to prove to the analyst how dangerous the treatment is (Freud, 1914).

In the early 1930s analyses had become longer. Most analysts were now increasingly more interested in the earlier phases of development and, under the influence of Melanie Klein, deeper explorations of the personality and character were undertaken. The patients on the other hand, in many instances, continued to respond negatively in the face of progress and dynamic changes. It was left to Joan Rivière, a follower of Melanie Klein, to open up new fields of vision by putting forward the idea that problems of narcissism and self-esteem were involved in the NTR. She also suggested that such patients are driven by an excessive desire to make reparations to the internal objects, and in a sense they must take second place, thus rejecting any improvement (Rivière, 1936). My own understanding of this not unusual phenomenon is that the patients are desirous to make reparations but do so unwillingly, as this contains an implicit admission of guilt, and in the last resort they seem to expect that the analyst should do all the work of restoring and repairing the damaged internal objects. In this respect therefore I believe we are dealing here more with a resistance than a true NTR. A further attempt was made by Horney in 1936 by postulating the existence of a special masochistic type of personality who reacts in a variety of ways to good analytical work. In this outstanding contribution she introduced the idea of the patient being in rivalry and competition with the analyst, as well as the consideration that fear of success and failure could be related to expectation of provoking envy and rage in others.

In 'Analysis terminable and interminable', Freud placed a seal on the concept of the reaction which was to remain practically untouched for the next twenty years. The patient is no longer seen as regarding the therapy as a threat to his very being, as Freud now speaks of 'a force which is defending itself by every possible means against recovery and which is absolutely resolved to hold on to illness and suffering. One portion . . . has been recognized as the sense of guilt and need for punishment, and has been localized by us in the ego's relation to the superego. This is only a portion . . .' and considering

the phenomena of masochism immanent in so many people, the NTR and the sense of guilt found in so many neurotics, we shall no longer be able to adhere to the belief that mental events are exclusively governed by the desire for pleasure. These phenomena are unmistakable indications of the presence of a power in mental life which we call the instinct of aggression or of destruction according to its aims, and which we trace back to the original death instinct . . . (Freud, 1937, pp. 242–3)

Freud had often warned against excessive enthusiastic belief in the effectiveness of psychoanalysis as a specific therapy. However, I think we should note that at the beginning of the paper he refers extensively to the Wolf Man (Mack Brunswick's report on the second analysis had of course already appeared). Furthermore it is not often recalled that a preliminary statement on what was later to become the 'negative therapeutic reaction' had been included in 'The history of an infantile neurosis', when he wrote 'for he [The Wolf Man] showed a habit of producing transitory "negative reactions"; every time something had been conclusively cleared, he attempted to contradict the effect for a short while by an aggravation of the symptom which had been cleared up' (Freud, 1918, p. 69). Considering Freud's special interest in the Wolf Man, it could be argued that his disappointment in the poor therapeutic outcome was reflected in the countertransference, hence the rather gloomy and pessimistic view he expressed in his 1937 definitive assessment of the negative therapeutic reactions.

Analyses continued to be interminable, even if in many cases their interminability was now due to a different kind of patient seeking analysis which by necessity had to be longer. At the same time psychoanalysts became more and more aware of the need to understand the counter-transference which was sorely tried by the patient's unwillingness to give up his illness. It was left to Klein (1957) to reopen the issue in *Envy and Gratitude* with the following sentence: 'Envy, and the defences against it, play an important part in the negative therapeutic reaction, *in addition* to the factors discovered by Freud and further developed by Joan Rivière' (p. 185, my italics). She also underlines the fact that some 'patients, who in the transference situation, after having been decidedly helped by an inter-pretation, criticize it, until at last nothing good is left of it'. Klein lists a number of defences – such as idealization, the flight from the mother to other people, the devaluation of the object, the greedy internalization of the breast, stirring up envy in others, stifling of feelings of love and intensifying of hate – as part of the negative therapeutic reaction because they are powerful obstacles to the capacity to take in what the analyst has to give. This work is acknowledged as having thrown new light on the NTR, as a result of a new study of envy, but in an explanatory note we read that 'Melanie Klein considers that although envy can to some extent be analysed, it sets a limit to analytic success. This fact, therefore, places the final curb on the high optimism of her early papers of the twenties' (Klein, 1975, 3, p. 331). In spite of such sobering thoughts, most Kleinian analysts have tended to rely on the interpretation of the patient's envy as a mainstay in counteracting the patient's destructive attack on the analyst and his work, whilst the majority of analysts, particularly from North America, have tended to rely on Freud's concept of unconscious guilt and masochism as it is reflected in the writings of Brenner (1959) and Valenstein (1973). Olinick's paper (1964) is particularly notable for the review of literature and the assertion that the frankly hostile and negative attitude to the analyst (an excess of negativism) could well conceal latent or unconscious positive feelings. The paper is also interesting in that the author's recommended therapeutic management takes fully into account the countertransference as well as the effect of the patient's capacity to transmit his own fears of annihilation, which have been mobilized by the therapeutic interventions.

Asch's contribution (1976) is of considerable interest in so far as, although still focusing on the patient's masochistic ego, he stresses the link of unconscious guilt not only with oedipal wishes but also pre-oedipal crimes. He also sees the patient as being engaged in a battle with a depressed mother, defending himself against the regressive attraction of symbiotic fusion. Langs (1976) has also contributed a comprehensive review of the subject, particularly noting the shift of interest from the analysand's psychopathology to the bipersonal interaction between patient and analyst. Langs correctly distinguished true or classical NTRs relating to intra-psychic pathology within the patient, and to which the analyst does not significantly contribute. A second group he considers to be directly evoked and participated in by the analyst. I would comment here that, in my experience, in this second group we would perhaps find that the commonest and most prominent factor in the patient's pathology is his sado-masochism.

The increased investigation of borderline and narcissistic disorders has opened up new vistas on the NTR. The work of Rosenfeld (1975) deserves special mention for throwing fresh light on the significance of envy and narcissistic disturbances in causing the adverse reaction, finally tracing it back to attacks on the self derived from the narcissistic organization turning against the infantile dependent part of the self. This of course implies an identification with a mother who does not allow independence, clearly a source of possible countertransference responses or even iatrogenically induced negative reactions.

To sum up, in the early seventies the NTR had achieved the status of one of the 'Basic Psychoanalytic Concepts' (Sandler, Holder and Dare, 1970), but the literature of the period shows that the original formulation by Freud had undergone a number of amplifications which did not essentially dis-count the presence of unconscious guilt and a strong masochistic tendency. Such amplifications underscored (1) the fulfilment of unconscious wishes, mainly within the oedipal situation; (2) the prevalence of pre-oedipal and pregenital disturbance and of narcissistic disorders of personality; (3) that the latter would at times be associated with a surplus of envy, difficult to analyse; (4) the fact that all negative responses are anti-therapy and that great care needed to be exercised in differentiating the NTR from other forms of resistance; (5) that in the most severe cases the patients are confused between life and death and that they are more interested in surviving than in living, or even that some patients impress one as having an ego which is caught up in the death instinct; (6) the difficulty in making the patients recognize that we are dealing with a problem that is rooted in their early life with fantasies and fears of fusion with mother, and (7) that the examination of the countertransference was now considered as important as the investigation of transference.

The literature mentioned so far suggests a multiplicity of causes and no major agreement about the possibility of a common factor which could account for the sense of impending catastrophe and danger expressed by a patient in the wake of a good or even a reasonably satisfactory analytic experience, which manifests itself in an apparent urge to demolish all that has been accomplished, as well as a desire to cast doubts on the analyst's skill and integrity.

The topic was the subject of a thorough re-examination at the Third Conference of the European Psychoanalytical Federation held in London in 1979 when a number of excellent papers were presented under the unifying title of 'New Perspectives on the Negative Therapeutic Reaction'.

In his general introduction, Sandler (1979) suggested that this particular reaction to analytic work was identical with being 'wrecked by success in life' as shown by Freud in 1916, and he therefore concluded that 'improvement can be thought of as representing the gratification of an internally forbidden wish, and is consequently experienced as a threat' (see also Sandler, Dare and Holder, 1973). But he finally advised caution in dealing with the concept when exploring roots other than the sense of guilt as it had been contended by Freud as 'we may talk at cross purposes if we include all sorts of failures and all sorts of resistances' (p. 14).

In attempting to define the syndrome, Pontalis of France encouraged us to accept, as he put it, 'being starved and blind', thus acknowledging the legitimacy of the NTR, also implying that it is still of value, a point of view very close to my way of thinking. Although I could not agree with his contention that these patients are simply asking us to rid them of their mad sexuality, I would support his view that

In these cases, the transference . . . fully deserves its classification by Freud under the heading of *Agieren*. The transference relationship is stretched to its limit with sudden violent alteration in feeling: idealization and scorn, gratitude and rejection . . . There is no getting bored with these patients . . . But the analyst suffers. And the countertransference declares itself in the Agieren too. Only our body finds expression in diffuse tension, the immobilization of thoughts . . . (Pontalis, 1979, p. 25)

In another paper from France, Jean and Florence Bégoin (1979) spoke of 'the destructive rage of the baby within the patient, mad with pain and starvation . . . devitalized by greed and envy', thus again showing a tendency to ascribe the disturbance to excessive envy (p. 29). On the other hand their contribution was valuable in underlining the possibility of the existence of intense psychic suffering or latent anxiety, which the subject does not have the means to tackle. They also felt that the reaction can occur in the face of integration at any level, each time that psychic suffering outstrips the ego's capacity for defence and integration.

The next three contributions were notable for their assertion that there may be some value in the NTR which can be put to good use. A German contributor, following Margaret Mahler, took the view that the NTR represents 'the gesture of distancing, of the "no" which corresponds to the various phases of the process of separation as activated by the transference. It can either give expression to the wish for autonomy and separation or hide the wish for merging.' She concludes that the NTR should not be regarded as an obstacle but also as an opportunity to experience emotionally the faulty development of the detachment (from the dyad) in the transference and to come to terms with it by means of an elucidation with the accepting analyst (Grunert, 1979).

De Saussure (1979) took the view that patients 'who most easily feel narcissistically wounded by their insight are those who have been least successful in building images of themselves based on their own sensations and feelings . . . they look for signs which can give them, in fantasy rather than in experiences, images of themselves as triumphant and all powerful' (p. 43). This leads them to see themselves as becoming dangerous as a result of therapy. One of her patients had been helped by analysis but in another case, that of a man, 'there was no way of eliminating his symptom and reducing both the guilt and fear without causing him to feel deflated by the realization that he really was not menacing to the Gods.' Here we see also a useful contribution to the understanding of the puzzling clinging to conscious or unconscious feelings of guilt in spite of the great attention paid to it by most analysts.

Another speaker having taken a firm stance with regard to the causation of the syndrome, ascribing it to envy and narcissism, nevertheless concluded that 'even in severe forms, it can be very useful clinically, for it can lead both the analyst and the patients to become more accepting of attacks and more able to use them constructively. The negative reactions, in other words, need not be so negative' (Spillius, 1979, p. 37).

To sum up the work of this important conference, it could be said that the well known pessimism associated with this topic was somewhat dispelled. On the other hand, a striking feature was that it seemed easy to offer alternative explanations to account for the psychopathology of the many cases described at some length. This is a point which I wish to take up in the following clinical illustrations.

Mr A was sixty years old when, several years ago, he requested analysis on account of depression, insomnia and a variety of somatic symptoms. He had first gone into analysis at the age of twenty-eight and had terminated it after four years, having got 'as far as he could'. He had had four more periods of analytic therapy, ranging from a few weeks to three years. Whilst negotiating his analysis with me, he arranged for regular visits to psychiatrists to be treated with drugs and behaviour therapy. In spite of the grim prognostic outlook, I accepted him for analysis, although he stipulated, as a further show of his intense resistance, that there should be some fairly frequent interruptions to his five times a week attendance. There were some unusual circumstances in his history which stimulated my interest and curiosity. Mr A, a very successful business and family man with an enviable social life, had never been anything but miserable and unhappy: 'crippled by my inability to feel my emotions', as he said on our first encounter. At the end of the sixth month of his first analysis, his progress and response to the therapy had been such that his analyst commented that he was now about to enter a *second phase in his analysis*. He had left the session elated and as he walked away he felt he wanted to embrace every person in the street. At the next session, he felt overwhelmed by his positive feelings for his analyst but he felt rebuked and rejected by what he perceived as his 'stern comments'. This was quickly followed by the development of laryngeal spasms and sudden muscular contractions of the whole body creating enormous difficulty in speaking. Since then these symptoms had affected him only when in the presence of an analyst and he had come to regard them as the expression of the emotions which he could not otherwise feel. 'I am a wild animal roaring his dissatisfaction', he would say later in his analysis with me, when tempted to make one of his frequent attempts to undermine my belief in my technique or the acquisition of a new insight. My own observations suggest that although the 'spasms' were used at the service of a resistance against verbalizing his emotions, they were basically an expression of his wish to deride and anally attack any useful contribution originating from the analyst and in this context had become part of massive, endlessly repeated NTRs, brought forward by the first analyst's encouraging remark. The deeper analysis in due course of that event could be summed up as follows: 'To me it meant the end was coming. That man was everything to me. For the first time in my life I had found an anchor and it was slipping from my grasp.' Limitation of space does not allow me to outline the development of his analysis with me except for mentioning that once the major earlier resistances (psychiatric support, drug taking, interruptions, etc.) had been eliminated, I was subjected to the most violent destructive attempts to undermine everything I was doing. That he felt persecuted by me was obvious, but so was the fact that he had been persecuted by all the interpretations which he had received and which he was now dishing out or evacuating onto me. Here I was confronted with a major countertransference reaction in so far as I found myself attacking everything that he was saying, as he was repeating, in parrot-like fashion, all that he had been told over the years. In so doing, I suddenly realized that I was being used as a demolition worker, thus relieving him of the sense of guilt which had pursued him as a result of the destruction of so much analytic work in the past. An interpretation that he seemed intent upon collecting one more analytic scalp to add to his other trophies was followed by genuine surprise at first, so split off had his NTR been, but some weeks later, following one more destructive envious outburst, he brought a dream in which he had sacked all his executive staff. This had given him intense pleasure to the point of waking up with a full erection, the first in several months. The improvement in the sexual disturbance was followed by an abortive attempt to develop a very unpleasant psychosomatic symptom, reminiscent of the ulcerative colitis he had suffered in the past. However, with the slow progress came a realization that I still did not know which particular emotion Mr A claimed not to be able to be in touch with. The depression which hit him when confronted with an unavoidable break in the therapy suddenly became the key. The pain and the intense psychic suffering against which he had all along been defending himself, was that of being separate, which meant being abandoned and exposed to some unbearable catastrophic threat. When I first broached the subject he showed intense surprise and interest, adding that as far as he knew he had been aware for years of only a hankering for something from the past. He now remembered mentioning this towards the last stages of the first analysis and he recalled that the analyst ended the session with 'a snort of satisfaction in his voice saying we must know a lot more about this to understand more how that little boy was functioning'. He admitted that he took this as a warning to stay clear of the subject and from that day the thought of separation never entered his head. A pseudo-identification with the analyst had helped him to cope with breaking off analysis, always at a moment of danger of coming close to the real source of his psychic pain. His femininity, which had troubled him so much to the point of making him fear homosexuality, was again something which had protected him from the intolerable anxiety of having to give up the primary object. In infancy, this patient had never been actually separated from his mother. Weaning had been as traumatic as the birth of a sibling two years later.

I realize that the first analyst's comment 'you are entering a second phase in your analysis' did not only suggest progress but was also poor technique. However, it should be viewed in the light of technique over thirty years ago. In my opinion, the relevance of the comment is that it induced a recurrent, severe NTR, which remained hidden under a wealth of resistance for a great number of years.

In this patient the NTR could be interpreted according to any of the various propositions put forward by writers from Freud onwards. Mr A could certainly be considered as suffering from unconscious guilt and indeed could be regarded as having been wrecked by success. Yet he was no real wreck. He was certainly often operating within the range of sado-masochism and he displayed intense negativism. Some of the material not given here could show him as having no true image of himself, exactly as described by de Saussure (1979) as showing a preference for retaining an early narcissistic false image of himself, and indeed he did not lack envy or narcissistic disturbance. But in the last analysis, my conceptualization of his predicament was that the early separation from mother was a traumatic experience which had caused him intense unbearable pain from which he had been defending himself ever since.

My next clinical illustration comes from the long analysis of Mr B, a thirty-year-old man who had sought help on account of depression, inhibitions and difficulties in relating to men or women. The analysis had been marked by the most severe NTRs in response to any real progress, seldom remarked on by either of us. Over the years I had learnt the importance of taking care that integration or synthesis did not take place either too soon or too suddenly but above all I had learnt that such a patient psychically believed that *his* cure which had helped him to survive was preferable to anything I could offer. The material I am presenting was typical of this analysis, except that in recent times he had been able to enjoy his life, making use of his vast intellectual and physical resources which had been dormant for years. The core of the illness had been briefly touched on in the material but he still required further working through and understanding of it.

Mr B had returned from a brief but very happy and successful holiday in a better frame of mind. He was unusually silent during the Monday and Tuesday sessions when he had mentioned being happy to see his regular girlfriend but also having been glad to have spent an evening with his previous girlfriend whom he still longed for and of whom he felt I disapproved. He did not know why he was so quiet, and noted the absence of dreams. On Wednesday I ventured to say that he was marking time, as he had often done in the past, particularly because things had gone better for him lately. [I immediately regretted saying this because Mr B feared wasting every second of his analysis, but I felt it was necessary to open things up in this way as I suspected that he was almost due to take a step or two back and I hoped to forestall it.] Mr B found my comment about marking time highly provocative, but he produced a rush of associations including a detailed account of seeing a film remarkable for its extraordinary violence. In response I took up the point well known to both of us that he was borrowing from the film to tell me about his anxiety in relation to his aggressiveness and violence. On Thursday a great deal of material was uncovered with regard to the violent feelings and intense excitement aroused by the mere presence of his ex-girlfriend. For the very first time I believed we had got very closely in touch with his violence, not simply aggression or hostility which had been subjected to very careful analysis over the years. He appeared greatly relieved by the analytical work done and as he was leaving the room he turned around saying quite distinctly 'Thank you'. On Friday morning he was again in a deeply disgruntled, sulky and grumbling mood. He felt a whole week had been wasted and I could not deny that, as I had said he had been marking time. My immediate response was one of intense anger, so intense that I could not fail to notice it. This was helpful as I could then use it in formulating my next intervention, but I noted a slight increased hardness in the tone of my voice. I pointed out that since my earlier remark about marking time we had done quite a bit of work and that we had learnt a great deal about the true reason for his continuing to hanker after a girl who could provoke him into rages, a girl who could if necessary look after herself, giving as much as she took, in the way of verbal violence or of torturing him with her depression. [This was an indirect reference to his masochism in repeating here the experience of having grown up with a depressed mother.] I added that in the course of a day all that work had ceased to have a meaning for him and all he seemed to want to do now was to destroy the analytic work we had done and in consequence he seemed to want to destroy me and my beliefs. The session ended in a mood of depression and despondency expressed by the patient, and in anxiety for me in view of vague suicidal threats.

There was little change over the next few days, until Mr B was once more able to reopen the issue of his struggle to control his violent feelings, but we both knew that somehow we could now go a little further than we had been able to go in the past. In a later session Mr B blurted it out that in commenting on his violence I sounded like Satan telling Jesus: 'If you are the Son of God, jump off the Temple Mount and see what happens.' He went on to say that some earlier remarks about his hesitation in beating his opponents in a recent tournament were just as bad. At this point I could still understand that this fresh outbreak of NTR once more seemed to be related to the equation of cure with total release of all his feelings and aggressiveness, and I was wondering where I had been wrong. Rather defensively I reminded him that it had seemed odd that he could lose every game considering that he had been invited to play the top players of his club. I reminded him of his fear of provoking envy by winning all the time. He cut me off, saying he was not interested in that; he was much more interested in the good thing I had said about his wanting to destroy me and the analysis. He said: 'If I accept what you say I'll accept everything; I'll become just a little boy again; I'll be so dependent that I could never stand up again and that I don't want.'

Now the material was lending itself to a new conceptualization and this could have been along the lines of Rosenfeld's (1975) formulations, i.e. that envy and narcissism were dominating the picture and that the narcissistic organization was now attacking the dependent child in the patient. As already mentioned, Mr B had often displayed envy and was certainly to be regarded as being quite narcissistic, and he did appear to attack the dependent child in himself. But in the light of my overall knowledge of him, I felt he had to reject the positive help which I was offering as this was the road to independence which he still felt had been his undoing. Every step towards insight was equal to being allowed to grow up and this he could not accept. In his early life he had been highly precocious and every move towards independence was accepted immediately, and probably prematurely. My impression at the time was that he was speaking on behalf of a harsh superego that was instructing him to make a show of independence whilst all the time he still felt a strong pull towards an illusory merging and fusion with the analyst as the idealized primary object. Mr B on this occasion could well understand how his hostile sudden reaction, which was meant to proclaim his bid for independence, was a sure way of going backwards rather than forward. His place on my couch was safe for a little while yet. Strangely this was also a magical way of protecting his analyst and himself. My countertransference reaction, of course, was also provided with the foundation for my interpretation as I was obviously as angry as *he was* for having to comply with the demands of his superego that he should give up his dependence. This kind of reverse process in the transference (cf. King, 1978) is of the utmost importance as it may lead the analyst to be less than aware of the struggle for dependency-independence that is going on in the patient and could well be responsible for those cases of iatrogenically induced interminable analyses.

The analysis of Mr B's NTR was once more, as it had been in the past, of great value for bringing us in due course closer to the core of his psychopathology: the re-experiencing of the intense pain of separation from the primary object. In this case I have no doubts that the original experience has been protracted and highly traumatic, and, as a result of reconstruction in the analysis, I have reason to believe that it was associated by great closeness to mother with intense excitation and gratification but with sudden and abrupt moments of rejection and finally total separation. His mother's illness no doubt played a part in creating a situation of trauma and pain of an unbearable degree. I believe this patient had no memory of his traumatic experience except for the pain which he had to avoid re-living in the transference. Whatever pain he caused himself through his isolation and inability to feel when relating to people was nothing in comparison to the earlier psychic suffering.

DISCUSSION

In selecting these two clinical illustrations, I hoped to show how our observations can be conceptualized in various ways but I also propose to use them as a basis for the exploration of whatever common factor may exist in the NTR. Most analysts would consider it likely that patients who respond badly to good progress are suffering from severe character disorder and that in general narcissistic disturbances are widespread and profound. Is the reaction simply revealing that a stressful situation is at hand, or is it that it bears the hallmark of a person's character? After all, in the face of stress we do reveal ourselves, but what is there in these patients that can make us at times overlook that they are under stress? Is it correct to say, as I have heard it stated, that any patient who behaves in this manner is perverse? Does not such a view and some other attempts at conceptualization ignore the patient's obvious sense of danger resulting from the analytic work? Why do we so readily disagree with those who write about this exasperating development, which is such a threat to the analytic situation? Is it because we all have different views about life, early life in fact, and what constitutes mental health, and because we think differently about what analysis can do or cannot do for our patients? It is doubtful whether there is only one answer to each question.

In my opinion the NTR is a resistance in so far as it interrupts the analysis, but it is a very special kind of resistance which can prove helpful in several ways. For instance, it could be useful in isolating those interminable cases where an unanalysable core is present, making us question the advisability of analysis. It is of unquestionable value in alerting us to the need to keep a keen eye on the state of the transference (especially in long analyses). It is a reminder that catastrophic reactions sometimes are due to not realizing that a fantasy of fusion has been dominating the transference and the patient has suddenly felt separate from us. It forces us, for instance, to examine more carefully what kind of object we are to the patient, who may even treat us as a concrete internal object, so much part of themselves. The hardest task, of course, will often be to show the patient what kind of narcissistic object we are and then to show them that we are not that object. This will at times be indicative that something has been neglected in the spectrum of narcissistic envy, but here I would differ from Kleinian writers as I regard it necessary to consider in some cases the alternative possibility that the envy which is emerging so forcefully could be occurring within the range of a reversal of transference roles. Mr B is a good example of such an eventuality as he seemed determined that I should feel the impact of his internalized envious superego. There was strong evidence in his history as constructed in the analysis, suggesting that his depressed mother could well have been envious of the attention he was receiving as a baby. I am aware that so far I have stressed the value to the analyst of this condition in monitoring his countertransference.

To focus once more on the patient's pathology, it is clear that some patients react particularly badly to the fact that once a piece of work has been carried out, which might include bringing something into consciousness or the mending of a split and so on, the analyst leaves it to the patient to choose what he does with it. When the defences have been stretched to intolerable limits, some analysands respond by giving us fair warning that something has not been understood in all its implications; or that it has not proved *digestible*; or that it has not been sufficiently worked through; or that it is so painful as to force them to make everything null and void; or that even death may be preferable, as more often than not analysis is for them a life-line.

Simply to state that the patient cannot accept growing, living or achieving success and that the trouble is mainly due to the unconscious guilt, linked with the fulfilment of oedipal wishes, is understating the case or distorting it even more than it is psychotically distorted by the patients. To me it is obvious that the patient does not know how to convey to us the strength of his stress and emotions, and he puts us to a most severe test by challenging our tolerance and know-how. Under the circumstances, I fully support Pontalis's suggestion briefly outlined earlier in this paper, that we are dealing with a form of acting out in the transference. Do not our patients display evidence of being dominated by their unconscious wishes and fantasies, refusing to acknowledge their origins? Are they not behaving under the impact of the repetition compulsion? And is it not true that we have great difficulty in getting the patient to understand that the transference is of the utmost importance as a precipitating factor for his aggressive and destructive behaviour? The fact that the patient is using words rather than simply acting is not against such a possibility. We still need to unravel the hidden communication in what he says and does within the transference context. In common with other patients who use acting out as a special way of communicating with us when they feel that no other way is open to them, patients in the grip of a NTR also tend to somatize their conflicts and feelings as an alternative to the actuality of acting out (cf. pp. 35– 49 above).

In introducing the concept of acting out as a basis for understating our patient's anxiety in response to some favourable development in the therapy we have a first common factor, underlying such a variety of behaviour and possible psychopathology to account for it. A second factor is to be found, in my view, in the overwhelming evidence that the patient is defending himself against a danger or threat and he is attacking us and the analysis, as attack will always be regarded as the best line of defence.

At one time I favoured the view that the threat was coming from a faulty synthesis or the not understood significance of integrating previously split off parts of oneself. Whilst not underestimating the challenge to a patient of learning to live with something unacceptable or even unlikeable, as it is in the case of integration; or that he may be over-anxious about literally creating something new for himself, as a result of psychosynthesis, I think that in all such instances, the NTR is amenable to the ordinary care and attention of a well conducted analysis. In all other cases when the reaction is repetitive to the point of leading to interminable therapy, I believe we are dealing with a defence associated with the threat of unendurable pain and psychic suffering. There may have been some trauma or some experience which rightly or wrongly has come to be regarded as traumatic. The pain involved is excruciating and is remembered sufficiently clearly to be avoided at all costs, but the memory of the event to which it relates is often neither accessible nor available (as in most cases of early separation from mother, disturbed weaning, etc.). This is, I think, in keeping with the view held by the majority of analysts that we are dealing with a malignancy which clearly antedates the oedipal situation. This will also account for the difficulty in helping the patient to recognize that what he or she may be experiencing is related to early life.

My dissatisfaction with the use of the concept of integrative failure in accounting for the more intractable NTR has been somewhat dispelled and clarified by a recent paper by Gaddini, in which he takes Winnicott's work on the maturation process as the basis for his arguments. It will be recalled that Winnicott (1974) stressed the difference between non-integration and disintegration, the latter presupposing some degree of integration. Gaddini underlines the importance of distinguishing between splits which follow integration and those cases of splitting when no integration has actually taken place, which are more amenable to therapeutic intervention. He particularly notes how 'the pathological anxiety of the loss of the self is also fed by the tendency towards integration, which implies a fearful recognition of separation for ever. Integration in pathological conditions then appears as a fatal step beyond return, which is the passage from survival, even if precarious, to the final catastrophe.' This author further suggests that

it may be useful to distinguish between two contrasting and concomitant aspects of pathological anxiety of loss of the self, namely, anxiety of non-integration and anxiety of integration. Obviously, it is the latter which represents the true pathological aspect: it is stronger than the anxiety of non-integration, and prevents the natural developmental process, and contributes in an essential way to the maintaining of the non-integration state as an extreme defence. (Gaddini, 1981)

It will immediately be apparent that Gaddini's remarks will explain not only some mishaps in dealing with severe cases of NTRs but will also throw some light on all those intractable anxieties which are so resistant to treatment. We are still in the dark, however, as to why so much hostility is released by patients who are clearly distressed, anxious and overwhelmed by pain and psychic suffering. It is possible that the hostility is an expression of inner tension and danger, meant to mobilize the analyst's attention, at the same time challenging his capacity to contain the patient's worst fears. This is an opportunity for turning what is unquestionably negative into something positive.

Looking back into the 1930s, we are impressed by the progress which has occurred since those early observations into pronounced negativisms and the rejection of therapeutic gains and insights by some patients. Today, we are a great deal more aware of the psychoanalyst's affective responses to the patient's need to continue to be ill but to some extent we rely on assumptions to account for it fully. Perhaps in clinging to illness some patients succeed in magically staving off death, and this may even be true when all the evidence suggests that they are flirting or drawn towards death. For these patients, to live means that now or sometime in the future they will die, and in consequence they opt for survival in preference to a full and contented life. However, in the majority of cases, where the NTR makes its appearance again and again, it would seem that removing the obstacles to health is not quite enough to make people healthy. Our ability to help them is still limited, in spite of our extensive knowledge of the meaning of illness, which has been prominent in the work of the pioneers of psychoanalysis and their followers in the last decades. It is just possible that in the future we shall pay greater attention to the meaning of health, even if we were unlikely to agree on a definition of health which would appeal to all of us.

11 FROM DENIAL TO SELF-AWARENESS
A 20 Years' Study of Childhood Delinquency Evolving into Adult Neurosis*

T WENTY YEARS AGO two children, a girl aged ten-and-a-half and her brother a year older, were referred for psychotherapy to the Portman Clinic, London, with a long history of behaviour disorder, delinquency and severely disturbed family background. In the case of the boy, analytical psychotherapy was terminated after two years with good results, whilst the girl's treatment, having been brought to an end after three years, was resumed shortly afterwards and continued at intervals until 1979. Although it is possible that this report may stimulate a discussion on the value and limitation of psychotherapy in the management of delinquent children, my main concern is in showing the evolution of the delinquency into a neurosis, a development which could only be dealt with by prolonged psychotherapy.

To make the presentation easier, I have adopted the artificial method of dividing it into three phases, though in reality the development was gradual and contact was almost uninterrupted throughout the period.

THE FIRST PHASE

Jenny was nearly fourteen years of age when I took over her psychotherapy, as her previous analyst was no longer available. I had known her family since September 1960, when the children were referred for psychiatric assessment. The family lived in a large terraced house in a London suburb. The father, an intelligent man in his early fifties had been unemployed for years on the grounds of ill-health. He was regarded by his general prac-

* This paper was first published in 1981 in the *British Journal of Medical Psychology* 54: 175–86.

titioner as a bad influence on his children and also as a malingerer, in spite of numerous ailments such as 'shell-shock', duodenal ulcer, chronic bronchitis, etc. The mother, a little younger and less intelligent than her husband, had been sterilized after a too rapid series of pregnancies, which had left her in indifferent health. The family income was minimal but money was regarded as of little importance; for instance, father had neglected to collect a small inheritance from a relative.

There were six children. The eldest, aged eighteen who had suffered from meningitis as a child, was working as a storekeeper. He had been taken to court from time to time for a variety of reasons, including sexual assaults on his sister, aged seventeen, clearly a mental defective with hardly any schooling. She stayed at home, doing all the housework which was neglected by the mother. Next came the two children, whose delinquent behaviour had caused the referral to the clinic. James, aged eleven and a half, a frail little boy whose IQ was 145, had suffered from poliomyelitis in childhood and was still showing some degree of paralysis in one leg. Jenny, aged ten and a half, a pretty child with an IQ of 140, had otitis media and earlier on had suffered from rheumatic fever and nephritis. Next came a girl, aged six, apparently in good health, and a boy, aged five, expected to become a permanent invalid on account of Pink's Disease.

James and Jenny were responsible for mobilizing an army of social workers and probation officers as a result of their delinquent activities. The immediate reason for their appearance in a children's court was the stealing of a large quantity of ropes, as well as of a bunch of keys which they had used to break into the local offices of the Electricity Board. When in these premises, they left some of the stolen ropes behind, which enabled the police to trace the origin of both burglaries. During the investigations the two children had taken the police to a local park, where the stolen keys were found buried under a tree. It then emerged that the brother and sister had been in the habit of roaming around the streets after school for some years. They had also shop-lifted, quite regularly, often bringing home things to the parents, who would return them to the shops. Although the parents seemed to have no control over them they often lectured them on the basis of their strong religious beliefs; but the two children had invented a religion of their own which exonerated them from any sense of guilt in relation to their stealing activities. The probation officer who was ultimately responsible for the case soon noticed the extreme secretiveness of his two clients and felt unable to deal with them. They went to the same school. James was uniformly praised for his behaviour and good steady work. All the teachers loved him, but also admitted not being able to get through to him and in general regarded him as being lonely. Jenny, on the other hand, was unanimously disliked and was said to be a liar and spiteful; no notice was taken of her state of utter boredom. During the assessment interviews, it was soon clear that both children were well ahead of the teaching which was being provided for them. An important decision had to be taken, which finally led to James being moved to a grammar school, as he was regarded as 'university material', whilst Jenny was kept where she was, as she was not expected to get anywhere. The court issued a supervision order for two years with a strong recommendation for treatment. Twice a week analytic psychotherapy was immediately undertaken by two experienced child psychotherapists. At this point, the clinic social workers took over the task of keeping in regular touch with the family. I had at the time some overall responsibility for the whole case, but without any contact with the children. The home visits by the social workers often unearthed worrying evidence of the parents' disturbed states of mind. Mother was now quite ill with alleged thyroid deficiency which kept her in bed all the time. Father, off work, restless and prone to shouting at and beating all the children at the slightest provocation, also seemed to have a special dislike of Jenny.

James's psychotherapy was uneventful and continued for two years. He attended regularly, bringing books to read and at first talking to the therapist very little. He responded well to a non-intrusive approach, making excellent use of the last six months of treatment. In the case of his sister, however, the psychotherapy soon took a dramatic turn; everyone in the clinic knew of her sessions, as she would often rush out of the consulting room shouting insults and obscenities, proclaiming her hatred and dislike of Miss X, her psychotherapist. Years later, Jenny told me how she could not bear all the talk about 'mummies and daddies, breasts and envy and so on'. Although there may have been some justification in her feelings of being infantilized by being asked 'to draw whatever she wished', it was obvious to all at the time that she reacted to the anxiety mobilized in the sessions with states of manic excitement. Quite often, on her return home after the sessions, she would speak contemptuously of her therapist to her parents, imitating her and threatening never to go again. This produced hostility in the parents who would complain to the social worker that the treatment was making the child worse. The parents also insisted that it was their duty to tell their daughter about sexual matters, yet they were fearful of her developing sexuality, being intimidated by her flippant talk about sex. The child's confusion was being transmitted to the parents but all attempts by the social worker to help were resented and rejected out of hand.

By the time Jenny was thirteen, the supervision order had expired and her first bout of psychotherapy, which had lasted three years, was brought to an end. I was once more faced with the problem of deciding whether the two children should stay at home or be sent to a special school. The decision was all the more difficult as they had, as far as we could tell, stopped offending, and to prove that the home was altogether uncongenial could have involved us in litigation, which might have been harmful to the children. In the last resort, we decided to rely on our ability to keep in touch with the family without intruding too much.

Sporadic contacts over almost two years suggested that our two delinquents were holding their own, in spite of unchanged family and home surroundings. Then, quite suddenly, they were both referred for reassessment. James had got on extremely well at his new school and was now getting ready for his final examinations. There had been some recurrence of behaviour disorders, mainly bad tempers and an inability to get on with people, but James was adamant in rejecting any further offer of help.

In the case of Jenny, the reasons for the new referral were more urgent as she had been ill again with nephritis and when in hospital had made quite a nuisance of herself. Her talk of sex and intimacies between boys and girls was regarded as precocious and scandalous by the ward Sister. Mother had also confided to the nurses that she was not to be trusted, explaining that she had been out late at night with boys and possibly men and in consequence neither parent could tolerate her presence at home any longer.

At nearly fifteen Jenny was a beautiful and attractive young woman, charming and seductive. Our first interview late in 1964 left me rather perplexed as there was no attempt to conceal her need for help. Although the level of the exchanges appeared to be superficial, she told me a great deal about the home situation, mainly concerning her father's paying too much attention to her. She now revealed that since she was twelve years old her father's behaviour had worried her and that she herself had to make sure he would leave her alone. Since that time her relationship with her mother had deteriorated, whilst father had once more become hostile towards her. At this interview, I also learnt that she continued to shop-lift regularly until she went into hospital, when the help she had received had induced her to modify her anti-social outlook on life. The second interview, a week later, convinced me of the need to offer Jenny a second course of psychotherapy, as she had bruises around her eyes, sustained in the course of a wild fight with father. Although she presented herself as a victim, she did not conceal the fact that her behaviour had probably been extremely provocative. The treatment which then began was to last some three years.

THE SECOND PHASE

Some general comments on the individual psychotherapy of pre-adolescents and adolescents is called for here. It is well known that such an approach is beset by all kinds of complications, especially when the family as a whole is capable of accepting only a minimal degree of intervention by social and psychiatric agencies. On the other hand, individual treatment, even when clearly indicated, will not always be successful, particularly when it is linked with a supervision order, as the patient will see it as a judicial measure. Even when this does not apply, young persons may be altogether overwhelmed by the procedures, which involve a degree of intimacy to which they are not accustomed, or, on the other hand, such intimacy may prove at the same time too exciting and frustrating. Young persons are also very secretive and all child psychotherapists are aware that in the last resort success or failure depends on whether the patient is ready for treatment. When we offered analytic psychotherapy to these children in the first instance, we had taken into account, as I noted at the time, 'that they had been fighting for their lives against being swallowed up by their sordid surroundings'. Their particularly high intelligence and intellectual ability was another important factor, which I expect would not be disregarded even now that the principle *family therapy or nothing* appears to become more and more prevalent.

When I came to reassess Jenny's position, everything could be taken as a warning as to the futility of attempting further psychotherapy in preference to removal from home. Her persistent stealing was ominous to say the least and there was little evidence that the first bout of treatment had made much impact on her. Yet, there was enough to suggest that hope was still motivating this girl, for better and for worse. Her stealing and the offensive and brash behaviour while in hospital had to be understood in terms of hope that something other than punishment might be forthcoming. Her voluntary return to the clinic was in itself encouraging and hopeful, suggesting that her previous therapy had not been entirely wasted. I further concluded that, in accepting the resumption of psychotherapy, Jenny must have felt ready for it.

The early sessions of this new phase were occupied by what had taken place with Miss X. This was part of a conscious and brazen attempt to seduce the analyst-father into a collusive alliance to make fun of and exclude Miss X, standing for the hostile mother. Unconsciously, we later discovered, this was an attempt to pre-empt the possibility that I, too, might offer interpretations at a primitive oral level, in view of her ever-present feelings of deprivation and undeniable greed. Furthermore, the retrospective analysis of the ambivalence which at one time had created so much anxiety and confusion proved helpful, in spite of the fact that it led to the first appearance of negative feelings towards me, as I came to replace Miss X as the symbol of everything she feared and hated in her mother. This is of course not uncommon in a second treatment when integration of insights which have been stored up in a split-off or dissociated state becomes possible.

As the therapy progressed, I learnt that my patient was very active sexually but only in fantasy, as she was to remain a virgin for the next three years. She was ashamed to admit it but she was also resentful that anyone should have suspected otherwise. Problems related to her envy of boys and her dissatisfaction with herself as a female were emerging, mostly in relation to her despair about engaging in appropriate reparative acts (her poor school record was part of this failure). This was clearly shown in a dream in which mother was in the sea and was about to drown; Jenny jumps in but mother swims back, needing no help. Prominent in the material at the time was also her greed and resentment at not receiving as much attention as she wished. Its appearance in the transference was quickly followed by acting out at school, when she drew pictures on a girl's blouse. She did not think the girl would mind, as her mother would wash it for her.

To defend herself against dealing with her ambivalence towards her mother, Jenny turned all her attention to her father and the therapist. She finally tried to compensate for her frustrations by developing a number of friendships with boys, provoking father to act again in a jealous way towards her. Jenny was more than pleased with the result of this massive projective identification of her own jealousy and, in defending her position, explained that after all boys helped her to grow up normally. The importance of this communication, which concealed my patient's anxiety about homosexuality, escaped me at the time and it was some years before it could be fully examined. Even more serious was my failure in understanding that Jenny was *using* boys, rather than relating to them, as this was part of a character defect which was to prove a stumbling block to her capacity to make adult relationships and to her development of genital sexuality.

After the initial shock of having to adjust to the new analytic relationship, Jenny soon developed new ways of dealing with it. Rather than producing the frenzied manic behaviour which had characterized her response to Miss X's interpretations, she now switched off or would say politely, 'I'll think about it.' My notes during the summer of 1965 show that she was silent throughout the whole session, but a week later reported that before that session she had a dream about the analyst, the type of dream most patients have sooner or later. Its analysis brought on a state of depression which was dealt with by a further attempt at erotization of the relationship to me. My response was to show her how she was defending herself against dependency feelings towards the analyst-mother and, as could be expected, this was met with sarcasm and recollections of Miss X's interpretations, but eventually she took flight into memories of her close relationship with her brother and how as a little girl she fantasized about setting up house with James and adopting a baby. With the admission that as a child she craved for love as she did now, she told me how she stole compulsively with her brother; how they often set dustbins on fire at the back of houses; how once they tried to hang a cat. But as soon as she was beginning to lift the veil covering up the childhood activities, she would become distant and withdrawn. Mood swings had been unmistakably apparent for some time but as we entered the second year of psychotherapy Jenny was quite depressed. She was also unable to remember her dreams but, with her usual resourcefulness, she stole dreams from a close friend and brought them to me. We both knew that she was under pressure, nevertheless it was disturbing to learn that she had been caught travelling on the underground trains without paying the appropriate fare. Jenny had found a way of going anywhere for the price of a penny, and, not suprisingly, she did not wish me to know that she had appeared in court again. The parents, instead, duly reported it to the social worker, somewhat triumphantly, so much so that my case notes reflect the countertransference anxiety that we might be forced to remove the patient from home and that treatment would be discontinued.

At that time the home situation was fairly critical. Jenny's relationship with father was continuing to deteriorate and was made worse by the loss of support from James who was now spending less time at home. She was also becoming aware of feelings of shame and embarrassment at her rivalry and envy of her brother as a male, but she also felt some guilt because he seemed to have little interest in girls. Although mother was less frankly hostile she was still no help to my patient.

Mother had been confined to her room for two years, staying in bed all the time, surrounded by a large number of radio sets which she purchased compulsively in spite of the family's shortage of money. The mother's bizarre behaviour, which had been confirmed by our social worker, to some extent amused her daughter, who could now say that mother was a kindly sort of person and very maternal. In the course of the next few years I found myself agreeing with this assessment but I also concluded that this odd woman, who was good with babies, could also withdraw abruptly from them as they grew older.

Jenny stopped coming regularly at seventeen after leaving school with excellent results and in order to go to training college. During the next two years she kept in touch by writing, always letting me know where she was. It was only then that I realized that there had been a serious omission in the psychotherapy, as it was obvious that neither of us had taken steps to terminate it. A feeling of depression and uncertainty about the future was the reason for a request for an appointment early in 1969, and in the course of a few sessions we dealt with a recrudescence of dependency which she had tried to get rid of in a manic way by frequent visits to Italian restaurants. As usual, the patient's capacity for quick understanding was mistaken by myself (and Jenny) as *insight* and that caused me to accede to her request that she should manage on her own, in spite of my uneasy feeling about difficulties which had arisen in a relationship with a young man. Some months passed without any communication, but later that year Jenny came to see me with the news that she was three months pregnant and that she was going to have an abortion. The transference implication of this important event in my patient's life was of little interest to her as she embarked on a major piece of acting out in forcing others to prove that she was not fit to be a mother. My immediate offer of further psychotherapy was not taken up until two months later.

Neither of us could fail to notice that a pattern had developed, based on her need to seek help and yet reject it at the same time. Her greed made her fear rejection by me, as much as she feared becoming too involved in a relationship with me as the analyst-mother, which seemed threatening to her sense of being: there was no danger of her identity being threatened as this was still somewhat nebulous, with little, if any, integration of her femininity and masculinity. Jenny's capacity for massive denial and the magical and omnipotent way of dealing with her anxiety and conflicts was only partly responsible for my failure to deal with some of the patient's central predicaments. It is true though that the limitation imposed by the patient on the frequency of our meetings was beginning to take its toll, as it put pressure on me to do too much in a short period of time, and often too little, as I could not see what I should have seen. For instance, I am sure that when I was told of the pending abortion, I missed the point that perhaps Jenny would have preferred me to suggest a solution which would have enabled her to keep the baby, instead of my passive acceptance of the inevitable. However, when she subsequently claimed that the abortion had left her wholly untouched, we both knew she was lying, but it was too late.

Insight was still not part of a true experience for my patient. Although we were both aware of what was happening, the sporadic attendance pattern continued, except that now her work commitments were given as the reason for her departure. She was making excellent progress in her career and claimed to have a full social life. She had, of course, become a responsible citizen but not a wholly happy person. She was competitive and full of rivalry with men at the intellectual level but she also resented them wanting her body and, in some cases, her mind as well. Although she reported as having a good sexual life which was never casual or promiscuous, my impression was that she did not truly enjoy it.

As the years passed, Jenny often mentioned not wanting to have children because she could not cope with them (she had never looked after her younger siblings) and was scathing of marriage, which meant loss of her independence. On the whole, her identity was still in the balance as, although she had found a suitable outlet for her femininity in her work, she was still unable to use her masculinity, which in any case was not a strong feature of her personality. A clue to her dissatisfaction with this part of herself came from the casual reporting that she had a lesbian affair with a girl of the same age and that it had made no real impression on her. She had been the pursuer and had taken the male role, and unquestionably her disappointment was due to having to recognize that her wishes and fantasies had little to do with reality. The only explanation of her partial satisfaction when having sexual relations with men was that she projected and identified herself with the man, so that she lost contact with her feminine self. Or, as Khan (1974a) has suggested, a patient with Jenny's character problems may be fully capable of experiencing sexual orgasm, but not ego orgasm.

Giving up denial and the reliance on omnipotence for the solution to her conflicts was a very gradual process, which was leaving behind a trail of depression and a deep sense of despair. Towards the end of 1975, I suggested to Jenny that she was now ready for psychoanalysis as I could see that no further progress could be expected from once-a-week psychotherapy on an irregular basis. She took the suggestion calmly but her curt reply that she would think about it did not promise well.

After a silence lasting several months, a letter came from a distant country where my patient had emigrated. She sounded enthusiastic about her work and new life, but there were vague hints of difficulties in her personal relationships. In my reply, I offered to refer her to a colleague locally but she did not follow it up.

THE THIRD PHASE

Early in 1978 Jenny wrote from a London address, wondering whether she could have some sessions during her sabbatical leave. An interview was arranged and I was left in no doubt as to her conscious apprehension at the thought of psychoanalysis. However, she accepted gladly my stipulation that it was either a question of several months' psychotherapy or nothing. This new attempt was to last just over a year, extending up to my retirement from the clinic in the autumn of 1979, and it gave us the opportunity of tackling the problem of termination. Two factors contributed to a more favourable outcome of our efforts. Jenny had returned to England on account of increasing awareness of feelings of alienation within herself and in relation to the world around her. From my point of view, I felt more comfortable, not having to yield to the pressure of the limitation of time.

Jenny's well-groomed appearance and her fast sportscar were part of a need to project an image of self-assurance and self-reliance, in order to conceal deep unhappiness and the conviction that she lacked something in herself. She was well *aware* of her problems, showing her usual good *insight* into them. But, as Khan (1969) has pointed out, *self-awareness* by itself is an insufficient source of experience. The absence of true experiencing was painfully obvious in the careful report of a protracted love affair with a man whose wife had been her friend, whilst living with a young scientist who had followed her to London, hoping to marry her. This she could not do as she loved the other man, but again in her tangled relationships she was showing her unwillingness to permanently commit herself. All this of course was highly suggestive that oedipal conflicts reactivated in the transference were acted out as a result of incomplete and unsatisfactory working through. Jenny did not reject this interpretation, but the discovery that she had left London shortly after her brother James had got married seemed to open up new avenues for investigation. We soon started looking again at the delinquent activities which had created a special bond with James. As we know, being so bored at school, they looked around for something to amuse themselves. They soon discovered that it was easy to steal the lunch boxes of labourers on building sites. They would then retire to a local park and eat the stolen food, hiding in the bushes. They also entered the cloakrooms of several factories, stealing whatever money they could find. By the time James was nine and Jenny eight years old, they planned their crimes with care. When they stole £35 they did not know what to do with it. They bought a bag, made it look old, put the money in it and took it to a local police station, where a kindly policeman, having praised them, told them to come back in a month's time, in case no one claimed it. They set fire to dustbins at the back of shops and houses, having agreed to give the same description of an imaginary man in case they were caught and questioned separately by the police. They planned their crimes at night, talking to each other through a thin dividing wall, but before falling asleep Jenny would tell James long stories, mostly about her adventures with boys. With the recovery of these memories, she was now rediscovering her adoration of her brother, which had clearly acted as a firm barrier against oedipal feelings. The whole experience with James had stayed dissociated and had been further buried under the many events, ever since their respective therapies had broken into the relationship. She could now cry with feeling, recalling the heartbreak and disappointment when she discovered her brother's interest in girls. She still claimed that, even after his marriage, when they got together there was something between them which escaped other people's notice. At a deeper level there was a great deal more to this brother-and-sister love story, as James had become an indistinguishable part of herself, onto whom she projected her masculinity and with whom she could identify. His availability at all times supported and allowed her to deny her dislike of herself as a female. Not surprisingly, interpretations alerting her to her penis envy fell on sterile ground. It was clear and painful to her to know why she had felt herself to be lacking something during the last few years. Unfortunately I had overlooked some clues about all this in the previous phase, as one of the stolen dreams she had brought me came from a friend who had a twin brother, a fact that had caused intense envy in her. Jenny still thought, without much conviction, that perhaps all her troubles were due to her homosexuality, but this was an attempt to avoid facing up to the hopelessness of her way of relating to men, aggravated by an almost paranoid attitude to the idea of total commitment.

A considerable increase in self-awareness and reflectiveness was giving a new meaning to what now seemed to be her previous spurious insight. This was also reflected in her behaviour during the sessions, when she would be silent for long periods without making me feel that she was either withdrawn or remote. Nevertheless this caused me anxiety, as I did not feel I could always be in touch with her depression. This anxiety was more than justified when, having left a session in a preoccupied and pensive state of mind, Jenny drove her car into the path of another vehicle at a crossroads half a mile from the clinic. Both cars were completely wrecked but all those involved miraculously escaped. Although suicidal thoughts and feelings had been frequently discussed, my patient insisted that the accident had nothing to do with that, it was only that she was 'thinking the whole thing out'. I believe what was preoccupying her at the time was the prospect of ending her treatment, of which she had been given fair warning but which she had difficulty in accepting.

Late in August 1979, Jenny mentioned she was planning to go abroad again, which meant resuming the old relationship with the married man. I reminded her that we had little time left to straighten her problems as I would be retiring in October. Her reply was 'So soon?', adding that she did not wish to think about it, as it was so unfair. In response to a lot of abuse and accusations, I said that apparently she would have accepted my disappearance if it had been due to illness or death, but not otherwise. She thought this was so obvious that it was hardly worth mentioning: had I died she could shout, scream and rave for a while; as it was, she was helpless. I then began to link her present experience with the helplessness of weaning, but before I could complete my interpretation, she shouted, 'There we go again, just like the other witch.' In a more petulant mood, she continued to pour out accusations of unfairness and injustice, insisting that it had nothing to do with her poor mother, when it was all the therapist's fault. It then occurred to me to say that her anger was not so much in losing me but that someone else could have access to me whilst it was denied to her. She looked thoughtful as she quietly left the room after this interpretation which was based on my conviction that Jenny's depression was rooted in early oedipal conflicts.

My patient created a muddle around her next appointment which put her in a position of either being rejected or being treated as a special patient. In my interpretation of her behaviour I added that she was looking for excuses to be angry and that she wished to make me feel guilty. She responded, 'Why should I never take notice when you tell me I am greedy; my mother said it often enough but she was far too giving; a bit like you, I suppose.'

At long last, I realized that the open-ended arrangement in Jenny's therapy had not been entirely such a good idea after all, and I put it to her that it probably made her feel very special and guilty. She did not argue against this but told me something quite new. As a child, she was not quite sure at what age as it went on for years, at around seven o'clock in the evening she would lie down on the floor, daydreaming of being really special, with people milling around her, making a lot of fuss of her. People would bring her things and do things for her. She had never told anyone, not even James who could never understand what she was up to lying down like that. Her behaviour was probably prompted by having spent some time in hospital in her childhood, but I also asked myself how often she had dreamt that daydream again when lying on the couch at seven o'clock in the evening, her favourite appointment time.

The end was approaching, and Jenny felt very pessimistic about her future, particularly because she saw little chance of accepting the loss of her independence. My own pessimism instead was related to a suspicion that there had not been a sufficient working through of her anxieties about femininity. In the course of the last three sessions she admitted that she had been reflecting a great deal on what we had discussed lately and felt easier and perhaps readier to accept loss, but she now wondered if that had been the reason for never wanting a baby, because she could not keep it attached to herself for ever. She also recognized that being able to return to me whenever she wished had come very close to the fulfilment of the desire never to give me up whilst retaining her independence. However, as we parted, I still felt that my patient's unfulfilled wish for merging with a loved person, her mother, her psychotherapists, anyone who offered her love and protection, was unbounded and still awaiting resolution.

DISCUSSION

The complexity of this case is such that only some salient points can be taken up in a discussion. Its management should, of course, be looked at in terms of trends in child psychiatry twenty years ago. Undoubtedly in 1980 the approach might be different, not only because of the absolutism of some family therapists but also because of pressure on psychotherapy time and increased demands for it. (The *Concise Oxford Dictionary*'s definition of absolutism is that God acts absolutely in the affairs of salvation.)

By all standards, it can be said that the family which is only tangentially part of this report had reasonable support throughout their children's early psychotherapies.

Casting aside these and other sociological aspects, we must address ourselves to the origin and nature of their delinquency as it presented to us in 1960 and as it subsequently emerged in Jenny's psychotherapy. The delinquency was serious, protracted, and for some years it went unnoticed in the adult world, suggesting a wish not to be caught; there was in fact deception, planning and secrecy. Both children had suffered deprivation through being members of a large family in poor circumstances, and trauma as a result of the parents' psychological disturbance. On the other hand they had a fair start in life, as repeatedly acknowledged by my patient. This lends support to Winnicott's view on the origin of the anti-social tendency, when he writes:

At the basis of the anti-social tendency is a good early experience that has been lost. Surely, it is an essential feature that the infant has reacted to a capacity to perceive that the cause of the disaster lies in the environmental failure. Correct knowledge that the cause of depression or disintegration is an external one, and not an internal one, is responsible for the personality distortion and for the urge to seek a cure by new environmental provisions. The state of ego maturity enabling perception of this kind determines the development of an anti-social tendency instead of a psychotic illness. (Winnicott, 1956, p. 313)

This statement, which in my opinion is applicable only to some cases of delinquency, seems to fit rather well with my observations of Jenny.

On the basis of reports from a variety of sources, it is possible to conclude that my patient reacted to depression in infancy with particular liveliness, restlessness and tension, which were to become marked personality traits. Mother's last two pregnancies aggravated the depression, also causing intense envy and jealousy which finally drove Jenny to seek escape into delinquency, with her brother as a willing partner. The omnipotent denial which fuelled the manic behaviour over several years was not noted until Jenny entered regular psychotherapy. We know how this girl throughout the years was able to exercise her omnipotent control over the environment by provoking all sorts of reactions in those who came in contact with her. It was the denial, however, that was the fulcrum of her self-cure attempt, by nullifying conscious anxieties and by eliminating any sense of guilt in psychic and real terms, considering the intensity of the criminal activities. On the other hand, the price Jenny paid for this effective method of defence was a lack of awareness and of true experiencing of herself, an unbearable disability which was to grow worse as she grew older.

But we still have to account for the conscious and unconscious meaning of the two children's delinquent acts, which to some extent strike the observer as being, if not substitutes, at least derivatives of phallic masturbation. There are even many elements suggesting that, under Jenny's leadership, they came to share some acting out of primal scene fantasies (the secret eating of stolen food; the placing of money in a bag to be retrieved later). In essence, however, our little patients were engaged in dangerous, compulsive, exciting games. When the subject was first broached with me, Jenny volunteered the information that there was nothing sexual to what they were doing. As I had appeared to query this, she promptly had it confirmed by James who spontaneously said they were only seeking excitement. We are of course familiar with the fact that in young persons the confluence of physiological and mental happenings often lead to states of excitement and tension which are discharged through sexual or delinquent acts (Limentani, 1984). Further enlightenment about the nature of these children's *games* can again be found in Winnicott's paper on 'The capacity to be alone' where he writes, 'It is a pity to omit reference to the vast difference that exists between the happy playing of children and the play of children who get compulsively excited and who can be seen near to an instinctual experience . . .' He goes on to say, 'By contrast, a deprived child with anti-social tendency . . . is unable to enjoy play because the body becomes physically involved. A physical climax is needed and every parent knows when nothing brings an excited game to an end except a smack – which provides a false climax but a very useful one' (Winnicott, 1958, p. 419). James and Jenny were exposed to father's proneness to administer physical punishment to them but, as it did not immediately coincide with the delinquent acts, the compulsion to offend was endless and irresistible.

We should now examine the different reactions that followed the court appearance and referrals to the clinic. James reacted with some degree of compliance, almost as if the long-delayed latency was setting in, so that eventually his entry into puberty was quite orderly, as far as we could judge. For Jenny, instead, her immediate reaction was one of rebellion and an intensification of the behaviour disorder, which was further aggravated by the onset of puberty and which was to last for several years. The fact that father, as the daughter was growing up, was paying too much attention to her at first, and that later he became openly hostile and violent towards her, did not help matters. Jenny also alleged that her father had sexually interfered with her when she was not quite five years old. Although this statement must be treated with some scepticism, his behaviour in later years suggests that the daughter may have told us the truth. I certainly felt that one of the curative aspects of my relationship with Jenny was that she felt secure in it and in her feelings for me as a father substitute figure. But in the last resort, it was the disturbed relationship with mother that had to be worked through in the therapeutic process as it seemed to reverberate on every aspect of her emotional development. Quite apart from interfering with the idea of being a woman, and possibly a mother, it seemed to affect her capacity to give herself to a man. A passage from Anna Freud's (1952) paper on 'A connection between the states of negativism and of emotional surrender' is very relevant. She writes:

> The passive surrender to the love object may signify a return from the love object proper to its forerunner in the emotional development of the infant, i.e. the primary identification with the love object. This is a regressive step which implies threats to the intactness of the ego, i.e. a loss of personal characteristics which are merged with the characteristics of the love object. The individual defends himself against it by rejection of all objects. (p. 265)

It was this particular aspect of Jenny's emotional development which became entangled in the analytic relationship and profoundly affected the transference and countertransference.

During the psychotherapy, whilst she was still a child, she displayed anger and distress and frequently used the manic defence as almost the one and only protection against involvement with the therapist. In later phases, she defended herself with silence or by sitting up in preference to lying on the couch. At a conscious level, my affective response to my patient's attempts to protect something very private in herself was to provide her with an opportunity of using me as she wished, i.e. as often and when necessary, which I expected would allow her to understand her greed, guilt and wish for denial without feeling too persecuted. Over the years I have acknowledged the possibility that unconsciously I was resisting Jenny's constant impulse to reject me and her attempts to omnipotently force me into rejecting her. I believe my patient was helped by this collusion, as the primary object-analyst neither rejected her nor engulfed her.

CONCLUSIONS AND A POSTSCRIPT

Delinquency is rooted in denial and a belief in the magical and omnipotent solutions of anxiety, conflicts and particularly of the problems related to helplessness. For the subject of this report, the struggle to acquire a sufficient degree of self-awareness to enable her to see herself as she really was, with all her anxiety, depression and guilt, was especially difficult and hard. To give up her previous modes of self-cure meant being plunged into neurotic conflicts of such magnitude as to make them appear insoluble to her. Suicidal thoughts, a source of anxiety to both of us during the termination phase, could be brought into the sessions and it was encouraging that she could understand them in terms of deflected aggression or as an attempt to force me to change my mind, i.e. to cancel my retirement from the clinic. As her insight increased, I was left in no doubt that she was truly experiencing herself as a whole person, but there was still something missing. As Khan so well describes in his paper on 'Vicissitudes of being, knowing and experiencing in the therapeutic situation', 'Knowing is more than the mental reportage of self-awareness or verbalization of memories of life experience . . . there is a quality of ego cathexis plus imagination added to the remembered facts or the mental representations of past experiences for the experience of knowing to crystallize' (Khan, 1969, p. 209). This was still missing in my patient when the treatment was ended, and for this reason this narrative takes us only as far as Jenny's acquisition of the experience of self-awareness.

POSTSCRIPT (1988)

As a postscript I shall briefly describe the events that have followed since therapeutic contact stopped in October 1979. A week or two later my patient sent me a card which pictured some elephants. Inside there was a brief note which said:

> It is hard as always to find words to say thank you – for always being there as long as you were able (a mere fifteen years). I know that giving you up is not losing you – unless I lose a part of myself. I will write, not as often as I would like and will think of you more than I should. Please take care and be happy.

At Christmas came another brief note with wishes and the news that she would not be going abroad after all. She was in fact planning to make a new life in England. I suppose the elephants on the card were there to say that she hoped her good memory of the treatment would outlast the pain of termination. In a case such as Jenny's if there is hope, there is life. This forecast proved correct, as five years later Jenny was happily married and the mother of a baby daughter.

12 TO THE LIMITS OF MALE HETEROSEXUALITY
The Vagina-Man*

THE MEN I DESCRIBE in this paper may go through life without acknowledging any difficulty with their heterosexuality. They are intelligent,
gifted and usually untroubled by the variations of their sexual drives, or the
occasional fleeting interest in people of their own sex. Their femininity,
only faintly noticeable to others, is as a rule well integrated and often put to
good use in their professional lives. On the debit side, although they are
capable of fairly lasting and deeply satisfying relationships with women, we
find a high divorce rate and frequent changes of partners. Some of them can
be exceptionally promiscuous, exploiting their capacity to attract women in
a wholly effortless manner. Their promiscuity has a striking oral quality, in
so far as they give the impression of being sexually insatiable, thus confirm-
ing the psychoanalytic observation of the equation penis=mouth. Many of
them are little affected by an orgasmic incompetence which is hidden by a
reasonable sexual performance. All these men are incapable of a full
homosexual contact, though some have experimented with boys in childhood or early adolescence, but never intensely.

Brief reference should be made to their partners, who are mostly said to
be strikingly beautiful, rather masculine, and intellectually powerful
women. Whilst this description fits into the popular or psychoanalytic
definition of the phallic woman, no notable features are reported about the
partners of the promiscuous males, except for their willingness to engage in
frequent, casual sexual intercourse.

Life stresses, physical illness and especially a breakdown in the relation-

* This paper was first published in 1984 in the *Journal of Analytic Psychotherapy and Psychopathology* 2: 115–29.

ship with a partner, make these people aware of the areas of darkness in their heterosexuality. Should they seek help, the added stress of the therapeutic situation highlights anxieties about their femininity and threatened homosexuality. Their early life invariably shows the presence of some traumatic experiences, but the picture of early object relations that emerges within the transference is in no way suggestive of true homosexuality (see pp. 114–32 above). There is, for instance, no evidence that the latent homosexuality, if present, is being used as a defence against paranoid anxieties; there is no suggestion of seductive behaviour on the part of mother; there are no allegations of a very weak, or alternatively terrifying, father figure. On the other hand, and this may seem a contradiction, there is a great deal of evidence that mother was somewhat masculine, if not a phallic type of woman, who also treated her child as her phallus. My observations also suggest that these mothers are possessive but capable of temperamental withdrawals and sudden rejections.

In the course of psychoanalytic treatment, the extent of the disturbance is brought to light, notably on account of a secret wish to be a woman, associated with profound envy of everything female. In some instances the desire to be a woman is accompanied by an even more jealously guarded secret of possessing a fantasy vagina, when not only the anus and the mouth, but also the eye, the ear and the urethral orifice are endowed with receptive qualities similar to those of the vagina. It should be noted that in the majority of cases this fantasy has been subjected to repression. In some cases this part-object identification is implicit but well concealed by the whole object identification.

If my notion of a vagina-man, the counterpart of the phallic woman, proves acceptable, we shall have to consider the reasons for the fact that the fantasy of having a vagina has not received the attention which it deserves. I can only offer some tentative explanations. In the first instance it is possible that the overwhelming orality displayed by these men in their analyses, coupled with our enslavement to conventional and generally accepted beliefs, has contributed to the neglect. On the other hand, the refinement of psychoanalytic techniques with a better understanding of the implications of projective and introjective identification has contributed to the clarification of the symptomatology described in this paper.

Furthermore, the greater freedom enjoyed by men and women in expressing their desire to cross the boundaries of sexual genders, has encouraged the bringing into consciousness of fantasies which were until now subjected to denial, suppression and repression. The lesson to be learnt from the studies of transsexualism has not yet been absorbed by psychoanalysts. Is it not to be expected that many men could prefer to indulge in perverse fantasies of belonging to the other sex, avoiding the fear of castration, and worst of all, the mutilation of their bodies?

CLINICAL ILLUSTRATIONS

(1)   Alan was thirty years old when he began a psychoanalysis on account of difficulty in sustaining relationships with women and work inhibitions. His heterosexuality was not questioned until the third year of analysis, when it became apparent that his sexual experiences, though they could not be criticized in any way, were not accompanied by much satisfaction. It turned out that during intercourse his almost exclusive interest was focused on what the partner felt. The fact that he had no male friends and that in the transference he experienced ill-concealed anxiety towards the analyst as a man, naturally led to a careful investigation of latent homosexuality. This lack of male friends seemed to make little or no difference to his capacity to be in male company. Alan was in every way a male in physical appearance and deportment; yet he felt that his femininity was immediately noticeable to anyone who met him. That his girl friends did not share his view was of no reassurance to him. There had been, in fact, a succession of affairs, lasting for long spells, with allegedly very beautiful women who without exception were remarkably intelligent, masculine and career-orientated. None of them had any interest in having children, which suited him well.

Alan's passivity and pervasive orality had been carefully and relentlessly analysed. Again there had been little change but, in view of many other improvements, as we reached the ninth year of the analysis, we decided to give ourselves one year's notice of termination. Alan was now under severe pressure and not only because he feared he might be incapable of mourning me, just as at one time he had not been able to cope with his mother's death. He was worried because, having lived with a girl for three years, he had to decide whether he should marry her. He had no wish to interfere with her career, but he thought they should have a family. He feared ending up staying at home looking after the baby and hated the prospect of giving up his work. There were also other problems, as his professional success had brought him more responsibility, which he felt he should accept as a real man, but he still felt unequal to the task. His rapidly increasing passivity was reflected in the analysis, when he would lie motionless on the couch with his legs wide apart, demanding to be given interpretations whilst attempting to get inside my mind by urging me to express opinions on all sorts of problems. Alan bitterly complained that as a result of the analysis he was in the unpleasant position of having to give all the time, when all he wanted to do was to be at the receiving end. This material was at first understood in the light of the impending separation, still a long way off, but the situation remained unchanged. On the other hand, the emphasis began to shift towards a renewed intensity of his anxieties about his femininity. I made some very incomplete notes at the time, concentrating on what was relevant for me to some work I was doing with transsexuals.

Alan announced at the start of a session that he had some big things to talk about but promptly took up other matters in an attempt to divert attention from himself. I allowed him to get back on course, on his own, as in the countertransference I was getting a feeling that I was being forced into a role of a powerful, controlling female, the dominating figure in his infancy and love life. He then said he had seen Shaw's 'Man and Superman' and had been deeply impressed because the woman in the play knew how to choose her man, someone who was charming, talked easily and freely to people. True, the man was feminine, but he handled his femininity very well. He wished he could be like that. I commented that as usual he was trying to deal with his problem by referring to someone else, as if we had not become sufficiently familiar with his anxiety. I ended up with a clumsy remark that for him to be feminine meant to be homosexual and that was the issue he wanted to avoid with me. As usual Alan readily agreed, but this time he did not proceed to attack and destroy what I had given him, as he was clearly preoccupied with other thoughts. As he got immersed into explaining his views on feminine women, it occurred to me that he was equating femininity with passivity, a common enough notion, and not with homosexuality. Alan received this modest enlightenment with a furious outburst, complaining that I had never given him such an important explanation before. At the time it did not occur to either of us that none of his past women friends had been in the least passive, either in their personal lives or sexually. His current partner, however, had caused him considerable alarm because she was forcing him into a more active position by never taking the initiative about sexual matters.

This session seemed to give Alan a sense of freedom about talking of his desire to be a woman and some time later he said: 'I feel I have been a vacuum cleaner . . . that is my idea of having a huge, bottomless vagina. But I want to know, where is everything I have taken in. When I watch my girl friend and you [the analyst], it looks as if you have everything in your minds . . . it grows and grows . . .' Alan was at long last getting affectively in touch with his envy of the genital woman, mother who had the paternal phallus and all the babies.

There is nothing particularly unusual about this material, which is meant to show how ten years had gone by before the patient felt he could talk about his fantasy of having a vagina. It was not clear to me how long the fantasy had been conscious and I have no recollection of it having appeared in any dream, although the patient dreamt profusely. I should point out that the fantasy occupied a great deal of space in the analysis but for not more than a few sessions. After that it seemed as if it was of no particular importance, and for that reason I failed to make any further notes. Several months later, however, I made a note, commenting on how 'There are times when I lose contact with Alan, usually after a *good* interpretation. He seems to become absorbed by his own thoughts, due to his desire to discover how I have reached a certain conclusion. It strikes me as if he is reliving his relationship with women.' It was indeed through the comprehension and the accurate analysis of the projective and introjective identifications, in the transference, that the true nature of the patient's relationships with women was revealed and understood. From the beginning of the analysis Alan wished to impress me with his associations, dreams, and his behaviour in the session, and in due course with his capacity to give himself some interpretations. He often readily admitted that he wished to be as exciting as possible 'for the good of the work we are doing', he would say. On such occasions a good response from me was felt by him to be similar to a woman's orgasm. This kind of experience would make him feel well satisfied with his session. In the countertransference I often felt the patient wished to force me into a feminine and passive position, making me hope I would receive something from him that would get us out of a stagnating situation. Whilst he was able to get rid of some of his passivity in the manner I have just described, he was less successful about his femininity. Apart from all this, the patient at times impressed me as behaving as something like an analytic phallus, thus reliving his very special relationship with his mother.

Alan and his mother had, in fact, been very attached to one another, in the first two years of his life, but he had felt rejected when she had a second child. Through the transference, it had been possible to reconstruct that his mother had treated him as her phallus.

This patient falls within my notion of the vagina-man, the male who relies on his heterosexual inclinations, supported by an identification with the woman (the primal object) in order to escape from threats of homosexuality. Alan was a charming man who, according to his own admission when he was a little more honest and spontaneous, could be very popular with both men and women, yet I doubt he would ever succeed in being really friendly with a man. His need to equate femininity with passivity was absolutely essential as part of a defensive manoeuvre against homosexuality. This defence was also very effective in containing his castration anxiety, which was little in evidence in his analysis. I believe this was the reason for the conscious appearance of the fantasy of his identification with the partial object (the maternal vagina), at a time when he felt very exposed within the transference and his life situations. I have already alluded to, and have tried to show in this brief account of the analysis of this patient, how an excessive preoccupation with homosexuality and the pressure to interpret it within the transference, can lead us astray. In the case of my patient, I was quite certain that his psychopathology was not typical of a homosexual. I shall add that there was nothing whatever that had occurred to him during the first years of his life, to make me even remotely consider the possibility that I was dealing with a person who was close to the pathology of trans-sexualism.

(2) John was a highly intelligent young man, an intellectual with a remarkable capacity for absorbing knowledge. He was curious and inquisitive about things and people and was most sensitive to changes and sounds. In his childhood he had undergone abdominal surgery and it seemed fair to assume that this had mobilized severe castration fears. Yet his sexual development had, in general, been normal and since adolescence he had enjoyed a very active sexual life. His home background was regarded as having been good, but from the beginning of the analysis it was clear that he had been the object of much ambivalent attention on the part of his mother.

Questioning thoughts about his heterosexuality had appeared early in the analysis. The following sessions are meant to show how the patient had been fighting a defensive battle against castration fears and threats from a powerful mother, from whom he had difficulty in separating. The unknown quantity of a gentle but firm father added to his problems.

Session 1: The patient dreams of being with a woman who has the face of a girl (sic) with lots of freckles. She was delightful and acted very sexually, rubbing her body against his. He could feel her wetness. He associated the woman in the dream with a girl with whom he had had a similar experience. Recalling that the only flaw in his sexual development was a complete absence of nocturnal pollutions, I began an interpretation on these lines, but the patient interrupted me, saying: 'You are curious about that, aren't you? All that is in your mind, not mine.' I said he was quite satisfied that it should be the woman who was wet and not himself, and it seemed as if he wished me to go on being as confused as he was about it.

Session 2: Next day John expressed disappointment that I had failed to show my appreciation for his self-control, to the point of stopping himself from having an orgasm. He claimed he could do the same with all his partners, waiting for a signal from them.

Session 3: A few days later, after being silent for a while, John said: 'I had a dream once, when I was in therapy. I had a vagina and I was giving birth to a baby. The baby spoke with a very cultured accent and started telling me some riddles that I could not solve.' In his associations, the patient remembered that he had the dream at a time when he was very involved with a male friend at university. They probably were very much in love with each other and he could not understand why they had not had an affair. As he hesitated, I took the opportunity of drawing his attention to the fact that at the time he seemed to have a fantasy of being a woman and having a baby. Perhaps he could not easily think of having sex with a man. John responded: 'Funny you should say that, as I remember standing in front of a mirror at the time, thinking, "Look at that body, I could make love to it."' He suddenly felt embarrassed and fell silent. I interpreted that it was not clear to me whether the image in the dream wished to make love to him, or the other way around, not that it mattered much but I also thought he felt there was something of that nature developing between us.

I should note here that the incident reported in this session is the only occasion when the patient had felt close to becoming involved in a homosexual act.

Session 4: Next day the patient started by praising the analysis because he felt free to be what he wanted on the couch. 'If I want to be a woman, so be it, it does not matter', he said. A dream of the previous night came to his mind. He was in a garden. In a corner there was a birds' bath with lots of penises in it. He tells himself he does not want them.

Session 5: The session began with the report of a dream which the patient had shortly after hearing a radio broadcast about a British ship being turned away from a port because it was carrying nuclear weapons. 'I was on a beach,' he said, 'and there was a pretty pussy cat, jumping about. It was loaded with nuclear bombs or a microchip. It could have gone off any moment. There was a most beautiful, small object that could be made to fly; it was made of silver. Later, it was put inside a phantom jet.' He associated the silver object with a nickname his mother had for him. 'Pretty phallic, don't you think?' he asked. He now reminded me that in the past we had discovered how a cat stood for his femininity which got out of control now and again. He then started laughing, saying: 'I had not thought of it until now, but can't you see that the phantom jet is my phantom vagina, with that small, beautiful silver thing shooting out of it . . .'

The sessions reported were important for several reasons. They provided some direct evidence that the patient's mother had treated him as her phallus in his early life (see the association to the small object in session 5). In the countertransference I had often felt that some of his heterosexual exploits were intended to fill me with admiration and vicarious satisfaction. The father was constantly being kept out of the picture, but he seemed to return now and again under the guise of the phallus hidden in mother's body. The threat from the paternal phallus and all the anxieties related to it are met with a revival of an identification with the whole or the part object (the vagina).

The patient's attitude was summed up some months later when, quite spontaneously, he said that the only way he found really safe and satisfactory to deal with powerful masculine women, was to 'feel like a woman, or better still, to become like a woman'. Nothing else would do with them, or indeed with the analyst, who would admirably fit into the image of a combined male and female figure. Hence his need to impress me with his pleasure in being a woman on the couch, if he so wished (see end of session 4).

Several months later, I had the opportunity of showing to the patient that he wished me to know that he was still seeking phallic women as a good match for his fantasy vagina. The patient replied, pointing out that he could not follow what I was saying. Had I confused him with someone else, he asked. After a silence, he began vaguely to remember mentioning such a fantasy *ages ago*, but he still could not remember what made me say that so firmly. I then found it necessary to remind him of his dream about the phantom jet, etc., and this was followed by immediate recognition, making it unnecessary for me to give further details.

It would seem, therefore, that the fantasy I am describing in this paper is liable to be suppressed or disavowed, or even re-repressed, but that it can reappear into consciousness equally suddenly.

(3)   Francis was a middle-aged man who had spent the last twenty years of his life chasing a great many women, very successfully. On entering analysis

his problem was one of vacillation, in so far as he never had less than a masculine and feminine woman to choose a partner from. This had enabled him to remain a bachelor, indulging his sado-masochistic tendencies at the same time. In the analysis he was soon to discover that his psychic femininity was not only his secret, but also a stumbling block to his capacity to relate to men and women. His unhappy home life as a child was still haunting him. His father, who had publicly admitted to having been a homosexual until his marriage, treated his mother abominably. Francis was convinced that his father expected him, and indeed wanted him, to be a homosexual, but he hated the idea. Throughout his adolescence he was troubled by his attraction for boys of his own age and still experienced embarrassing feelings with some men. It was not long before a strong resistance developed in the analysis, easily traced to a florid homosexual transference. Nevertheless, this was helpful in recapturing some early screen memories. For instance, as a child of three, the patient often played a game which consisted of putting father's penis to his ear, pretending it was a telephone. He also remembered how rubbing his back against that of his mother would be 'extraordinarily soothing', especially if he had been frightened (no detail of the source of the fear was given). This is the history that is often given by practising homosexuals, but Francis was able to avoid this outcome by allowing free rein to his fantasy of being a woman, besides acting it out in his relationships with his partners, through projective and introjective identification. In the transference the soothing interpretations were highly sexualized experiences when the analyst's voice would reach him through his ear (which he often *equated* with the female genital), whereas the more unpleasant interpretations were experienced as unwelcome anal attacks.

(4) This clinical illustration will demonstrate how the vagina-man can at times reach the very extreme limit of heterosexuality, bringing him dangerously close to homosexuality. In these instances, the desire to be a woman is not associated with a fantasy of having a vagina, but is more directly experienced as a conscious, passive desire for penetration by another man. It is perhaps the threat of castration anxiety coming from members of both sexes that leads them away from fulfilling the desire.

Oscar had become impotent with his wife and other women, following a surgical operation on the genital-urinary system. This had occurred during a long analysis which had been stagnating for some time, owing to the patient's sexualization of the relationship with the analyst, which was experienced as reciprocal sodomization. He frequently achieved orgasm without an erection, simply by stimulating his anus. He would succeeed in having an erection if his wife inserted a finger in his anus, but still could not achieve penetration. He regarded his wife, a career-orientated woman, as being 'absolutely phallic', not at all interested in having children, which did not displease him. Oscar was a charming, middle-aged man. He was brilliant, sensitive, and professionally successful, but plagued by guilt which prevented him from enjoying his achievements. He read voraciously and absorbed all in his environment with his mind and eyes that missed little. He had managed to keep his masculine aggressiveness under control by exploiting his femininity to the point of making himself utterly passive and dominated by large numbers of people. His early object relations were disastrous. The father was an effeminate, ineffectual man, intellectually brilliant and highly respected within his own professional circle. He represented the maternal side of the parental couple, whilst mother was the decision-maker and the active partner. Oscar was deeply confused, as he always had been from the age of five when an older boy had handled his penis, to show him what sex was like. In late adolescence he got involved in some work with a homosexual and he recalls how fascinated he was by the stories this man recounted of his sexual encounters with large numbers of men. The operation had left him a feeling of having had a bad pregnancy, and as he said this, he would feel his abdomen. The insertion of a catheter was just what he had imagined it would be like to be penetrated anally.

I have described in some detail this man's desires and fears about homosexuality, as it seemed in direct contrast with his earlier life which had been one of remarkably active heterosexual pursuits. As he was only seen in consultation, it was not possible to have a clear picture of his early sexual development, although he insisted that in spite of his sexual confusion, he had never experienced any particular difficulties, certainly nothing like what had happened to him since the operation had deeply affected him.

DISCUSSION

The men described in the clinical illustrations share a sufficient number of qualities and characteristics to allow me to put forward the hypothesis of a vagina-man who is, to some extent, to be considered the counterpart of the classical concept of the phallic woman. It is well known that the latter is mainly a pre-oedipal fantasy, that the woman (mother) is endowed with a phallus (external or internal). In later life, it is met in men who feel masochistic and submissive towards women. There is, however, also the woman who considers herself, or is considered by others, to be endowed with phallic attributes, consciously or unconsciously. In my view an analogous situation occurs in those men who consider themselves to be endowed with very strong feminine attributes, a belief which can at times be shared by others. But that is where the analogy with the phallic woman ends, in so far as in this latter case we are dealing with a much more primitive kind of fantasy.

The vagina-man is basically narcissistic, intelligent, charming and friendly. He is easily affected by contacts with people, when he becomes engulfing or engulfed. Some of his character traits could be regarded as oral: he reads voraciously; he looks at things with unfailing avidity; he insatiably seeks the company of others, especially that of women, in or outside a sexual context. He is feminine, but his femininity is almost entirely psychic; yet he is vulnerable in so far as he fears it is noticeable to others. Only occasionally do women remark on his femininity. The vagina-man is attentive to women and as a result of it, his sexual performance is in general better than average, but his own pleasure is somewhat diminished by the envy of what the partner is experiencing, coupled with a desire to know exactly what that experience is.

His partner is usually a masculine woman, who has a distinct preference for the more feminine male. It is interesting that both John and Francis had championed the cause of feminism to the delight of their lady friends.

An outstanding feature of the personality of the vagina-man is his passivity. This is in no way a problem in relation to the more phallic type of woman because of the opportunity to be feminine without having to compete whilst offering himself as the presumably desired phallus. On the other hand, the passivity is an unwelcome character trait when relating to men, especially those in authority. The anxiety is mainly one of being controlled rather than of homosexual submission. At one time Alan was less afraid of ending up as a homosexual than of being controlled by men in his professional life; on the whole, he would always feel reassured by his heterosexuality.

As I have already indicated throughout this paper, I believe that projective and introjective identifications play a dominant role in negotiating all that is needed in establishing and maintaining the counterphobic measures so necessary to the vagina-man's survival. In some instances it will be the control or anxiety which is defended against as it implies a disintegration and loss of identity. On the other hand many other cases will show the main source of anxiety to be the inability to give up the primal object. I should stress that the analysis of men with this symptomatology, without exception, reveals the presence of at times severe narcissistic disturbance. They cannot, however, be regarded as suffering from nacissistic personality disorders, at least as I understand Kohut's definition of this nosological category. Neither do they come close to Joyce McDougall's description of 'some narcissistic perturbation, which results from perpetual oscillation between the two poles of libidinal investment, the constant swing from narcissistic libido to object libido'. The patients described by this writer have a 'sexuality which is secretive and obscure, or marked by indifference . . .' (McDougall, 1982, p. 381).

The reader could well be wondering whether the individuals I have described should be regarded as bisexual. The fact that all human beings have a number of psychic characteristics belonging to both sexes continues to receive attention from psychoanalysts and the general public. More often than not this generalization leads to preconceived ideas about the social roles of males and females, thus tending to confuse the issue. Any behaviour which is passive, intuitive, submissive or masochistic is feminine, whilst active, sadistic, intellectual and penetrative behaviour is typical of masculine attributes. These attributes, however, also vary from one society to another. In any case, the concept of bisexuality is something that Freud may well have come to regret after he introduced it at the instigation of his friend Fliess, as he never seems to be quite at home with it. This could have been due to the incomplete state of knowledge of embryology, biology and physiology at the time he was writing the *Three Essays*. In a footnote to the differentiation between men and women, he states ' . . . in human beings pure masculinity or femininity is not to be found either in a psychological or a biological sense' (Freud, 1905a, p. 220). But in 1930 he writes:

> The theory of bisexuality is still surrounded by many obscurities and we cannot but feel it as a serious impediment in psychoanalysis that it has not yet found any link with the theory of the instinct. However this may be, if we assume it as a fact that each individual seeks to satisfy both male and female wishes in his sexual life, we are prepared for the possibility that those [two sets of] demands are not fulfilled by the same object . . .
> (Freud, 1930, p. 106)

The notion of the vagina-man shows that some individuals are capable of satisfying their needs in one object, and in some ways it lends support to the somewhat unsatisfactory concept of bisexuality which, given its prevalence in psychoanalytic thinking, would seem to be almost indispensable.

In my view, our understanding of bisexuality can be improved by the adoption of a concept which covers a constellation of symptoms, behaviour patterns and personality traits to be found in men who manage to exist at the limits of heterosexuality. My conclusions are based on observations of a very large number of individuals I have met in psychoanalysis and psychotherapy during the past thirty years that could not be included as clinical illustrations. The fantasy of having a vagina is not wholly necessary to the hypothesis and in any case, even if it is part of their psychic life, it may never come into consciousness. I am in no way advocating the neglect of analysing latent homosexuality or homosexual impulses as they may appear in the transference relationship. I nevertheless hope that the acceptance of this concept could lead us to review some of our stereotyped ideas about homosexuality, or of many cases of promiscuity. Its acceptance also means that we do not need to take a romantic view of Don Juan as someone who was hoping to find the ideal woman (the primal object), to the last; neither do we need to accuse him of being a latent homosexual. Perhaps Don Juan is nothing more than a man who has found a way of avoiding the outbreak of some primitive anxiety which threatens to destroy him, by turning to the pursuit of a chimera.

13 ON SOME ASPECTS OF HUMAN VIOLENCE*

A S VIOLENCE APPEARS to have a particular attraction for human beings, not all its manifestations should be regarded as abnormal. Let us consider, for instance, acts committed in the course of wars, revolutions, and even terrorism, when a different view will be taken according to the side taken by the observer.

My interest in this theme is derived from a sense of unease caused by serious contradictions about what experts have to say on this topic. Some will argue that any attempt to understand human violence is a waste of time, whilst others insist that we should take into account the rights of individuals against those who wish to protect the interests of the community, and so on.

I do not wish to appear an alarmist, even if I refer to the unchecked increase in violence in all kinds of societies right across the globe. On the other hand, I feel that we should not ignore the fact that many of us no longer feel safe in the environment in which we live. The prevalence of violent material offered by the media to the public, whether it is based on fact or fiction, needs to be justified and explained. It is possible that these so-called artistic expressions, or the desire to disseminate the truth, are not harmful; indeed, it will be contended that they provide a useful outlet to the aggressivity of the majority. Others will observe this phenomenon with apprehension and fear. Ernest Jones tried to assume an unbiased position, in 1915, when he posed many questions in his essay on 'War and sublimation': 'In war, things are done by a large number of men on both sides, of a kind that is totally foreign to their accustomed standard of ethical conduct

* This paper was read at the Department of Psychotherapy, University of Naples, in May 1984.

—204—

during peace, and the question arises, what is the source of the impulses thus vented and the relationship to the controlling forces of civilized life?' Jones goes on to note that

similar impulses are to be readily detected in the conduct and mental attitude of most children in the first few years of life, although their significance here had, for certain reasons, been greatly underestimated. It should be evident that if an adult were to display the same disregard for the rights and feelings of others, the same indecency and cruelty, and egotism as that characteristic of the infant, he would very definitely rank as an asocial animal. (pp. 77–8)

Jones continues: 'There can be no doubt that the asocial impulses we are discussing are part of inherited characteristics of mankind, and it is throughout intelligible that both the infant and the savage stand in this respect nearer to the animals from which we descend.' (pp. 77–8)

More recently, psychiatry has taken refuge in ethology in an attempt to throw some light on the behaviour of human beings, hoping that animal observation would show us that a world without violence is inconceivable. It will certainly be easy to show that animals can be cruel to members of their own and other species. I believe, though, that to have it confirmed that mammals are violent and that they are capable of killing their offspring, will not help us to understand the horrifying brutality of some men and women towards their children.

There will always be instances of individual behaviour which are utterly similar to that of domestic or wild animals. To illustrate this point, I shall use an imaginary situation of a couple who are peacefully walking in a crowded city street in a poor area. The man, obviously strong and well dressed, has his arm around the woman. Quite suddenly a tremendous blow from behind throws him to the ground, forcing him to drag the woman with him. On turning around suprised and shocked, he is confronted by a small coloured man, armed with a broken bottle, hurling insults at him. The victim of the assault does not react except for asking a question such as 'Why did you do that?' I would argue that in this imaginary example this calm behaviour would cause the attacker to fall silent and to walk away. On the other hand this act of unprovoked aggression could have led to an arrest and in this case it is to be hoped that the physical and mental examination would have thrown some light on this episode of impulsive violence. In the absence of any information we shall ask ourselves if the man was drunk, psychotic, drugged, and so on. In any case, our speculations could also lead us to think that it was only a matter of a masochist in search of adventures. However, this kind of incident could be used as an example of all coloured people being violent, as if white members of the human race are never so. Of course, it could be argued that the aggressor was poor and that the victim appeared wealthy in comparison, as if rich people are incapable of being violent. I shall return to this example because there may be other ways of interpreting it.

No sooner had I made a note of this incident than a newspaper article attracted my attention. It stated that 'the pestilential followers of Chelsea Football Club continue to live up to their fame. Yesterday they threw themselves into an orgy of destruction . . . four policemen ended up in hospital. Some members of the crowd shouted "Animals"' (*Sunday Express*, 4 September 1983). Reflecting on this report, I reminded myself that over a great many years when I worked at a clinic for social deviants, only one of those so-called animals had been referred to me. In general, I had been told that such bloody battles, prevalent in stadiums right across Europe, were better left to sociologists and the magistrates. But is it really possible to believe that group pride and its identification with a football team, whether on the winning or the losing side, is a satisfactory explanation for the filling up of hospitals and police stations at the weekends?

In my view it is altogether impossible to generalize on instances of collective brutality or group sadism. This will prove all the more difficult when the violence is expressed against a sexual background, or when it is triggered off by political, racial, economic tensions, or even partisan attitudes arising from sport encounters. The only notable common denominator will be based on the fact that a group which embraces violence in order to express emotions, allows its components to avoid a sense of personal guilt and responsibility. I should add that in such instances it would appear that personal guilt goes into a state of temporary suspension. There are some exceptions. Within institutions, such as prisons, remand homes, psychiatric hospitals, etc., it is at times easy to trace the factor, or shall we say the fuse, that causes the explosion. There will also be no difficulty in distinguishing violence from the function of normal aggression in adolescence; neither shall we ignore the disastrous effects of humiliations, restrictions and chronic resentments often leading to revenge actions. All these factors, though, will be acknowledged as only mitigating circumstances, both by psychiatrists and by the administrators of justice whose responsibility it is to ascertain the gravity of a crime.

In recent times, sociologists have come closer to psychologists and psychoanalysts, in underlining the problematic nature of defining an act of violence. Professor Percy Cohen, an eminent sociologist of the London School of Economics, notes how an act is not violent unless it is clearly apparent that the perpetrator of the act intended to inflict physical damage on a person. This definition ignores unconscious motivation, but he notes that the difference between conscious and unconscious acts is always poorly delineated within certain cultures, when some violent acts are coloured by ambiguity (Cohen, 1983). This writer quotes the ethnographer, Chagnon, as saying that 'Among the Yanomanö husbands beat their wives, burn them and, sometimes, kill them. Yet, we are told, women measure their husbands' concern in terms of minor beatings they sustain; and we are also told that Chagnon overheard one woman commenting to another that her husband must really care for her since he has beaten her on the head so frequently' (p. 6). But Cohen is critical of the above observations which do not contain sufficient explanation of the behaviour of the Yanomanö husbands in relation to others in general. He further suggests that there could be another explanation, such as that Yanomanö women, fearing extreme forms of violence, are grateful for small mercies when submitting to some lesser form of it and express gratitude by treating head-beating as a sign of affection (p. 6).

I have quoted from this author at length because he has some interesting things to say about the reliability of comparative statements. He writes:

> It seems to give great satisfaction to us to know that other cultures are more violent than our own; it is one of the ways of denying the violent actions which we, or those close to us, do commit, or which we fear that we might commit. How comforting for the British to know, or to think that they know, that America is more violent than Britain; for European mainlanders to know that they are less violent than the islanders of Sicily, Corsica and Sardinia; for whites to know that they are less violent than coloured people, and so on. (p. 12)

Contemporary sociologists do reject comparative statements, mainly because they do not believe in the reliability of statistics, any more than the average citizen in any country. Statistics do lead us to formulate theories based on *cultural* elements. These theories, on the other hand, do not take into account that culture is internalized and is eventually transformed and associated with specific personal characteristics, as it occurs amongst Corsicans or Sicilians, who are well known for their impulsive and aggressive nature. In practice we often come across such contradictions which often originate from authoritative sources. In 1984 the London *Times* published an article in which it was stated that 'the desolation and the violence of Belfast and other cities in Northern Ireland is reflected in the children's games . . .' Some psychologists have perhaps been far too optimistic if they believed that young people would adapt and grow normally in an atmosphere of constant violence. A psychologist, Margaret Marrow, warns that 'we must teach the children how to play. It is very common to see children use construction bricks, in play, as bombs.' A twelve-year-old girl returning to the city from the country said, 'As soon as I returned home I saw a man who had been shot in the knees. It was much more exciting here.' (We note the thirst for excitement, which is ever so important in puberty and adolescence.) *The Times* continues, recalling how 'fourteen-year-olds in the North of England are no more or no less anxious than those in Ireland . . . where they are accustomed to violence' (*The Times*, 5 January 1984). Whom shall we believe, or shall we simply ask ourselves, how do we measure anxiety in the young?

All that has preceded does not contradict the assertion that if the individual grows up accepting violence as a way of resolving conflicts of all kinds, it will always be more probable that the violence will become a way of living like any other. Hopper (1981) has drawn attention to some factors which lead to such an outcome, including (1) feelings of relative deprivation with respect to economic and status goals; (2) feelings of discontent which are socially specific and which are sometimes known as feelings of alienation, that is to say personal powerlessness, social powerlessness, isolation, self-estrangement, etc. Few would question the validity of these factors, always to be found in the eruption of violence in individuals and groups. In the last resort these tendencies will be directly linked with the capacity of the authorities to impose principles of order, legality and justice.

If sociology has little to contribute to the understanding of this worrying aspect of human behaviour, what have the other sciences to offer? In recent years neurophysiology has supplied us with reports and information of great significance and importance. I shall make only passing reference to the obvious and well known associations between some organic diseases, and some forms of violence linked to genetic factors. I shall note, instead, the importance of those researches which have shown how the explosive behaviour in non-psychotic individuals may be associated with cerebral dysfunction, without any evidence of clinical manifestations.

Turning to criminology, I cannot avoid expressing my profound disappointment in the persisting disagreement between psychoanalysts and psychiatrists regarding the definition of madness, or the disorders of personality. In 1983, a man was tried in London for the murder of seventeen people who, having nowhere to live, had accepted hospitality in his private home. All the victims were homosexuals, but it is not clear whether he had sexual relations with his victims. He would kill them at night, hiding the body which he would in due course cut up and boil, burning or throwing away the remainders in the lavatory, or even depositing parcels in the neighbouring streets. During the day this man behaved normally, going to work with the utmost regularity. It was this apparent element of normal behaviour which led some eminent psychiatrists to state that this man was not psychotic and therefore not a proper person to be detained in an institution for the criminally insane. It was clear from the published court reports that the evidence given by a psychoanalyst experienced in forensic psychiatry, that the crimes had been committed in a state of splitting, and a desire to obliterate some unwanted parts of the aggressor's self, quite compatible with normal behaviour at other times, was incomprehensible to judge, jury and criminologists.

Nevertheless, it is my impression that modern criminologists in the USA and Britain have shifted their position in separating off the most violent crimes from individual pathologies, and that greater importance is attributed to subcultural factors associated with economic and social forces. I would not deny their importance but it has been my experience in times of low unemployment to observe character disturbances as being responsible for an incapacity to accept discipline at work, but this finding is of little interest to a criminologist. Furthermore, is it not true that only *certain* individuals react violently to being insulted, and all the more so when their self-esteem is under threat? It is well known, too, that threats to the individual's integrity and self-esteem can provoke reactions even more violent and unexpected than physical dangers. I believe it is necessary to take due note of the above observations, as to ignore personal factors attributable to personality and character could lead us into assuming that many conditions are untreatable when they could well be so.

But what had Freud to say about all this? It will not be surprising that he had expressed his opinion very clearly in reply to an invitation from Einstein to exchange views on the question: 'Is there any way of delivering mankind from the menace of war?' (Letter from Einstein, in Freud, 1932, p. 199). 'It is a general principle', Freud wrote, 'that conflicts of interest between men are settled by the use of violence. This is true of the whole animal kingdom, from which men have no business to exclude themselves . . .' (1932, p. 204). Having examined the advantage of eliminating the opposition by brute violence, or violence supported by intellect, Freud continues:

> There was a path from violence to right, or law . . . It is my belief that there was only the path which led by way of the fact that the superior strength of a single individual could be rivalled by the union of several weak ones . . . Thus we see that right is the might of the community. It is still violence, ready to be directed against the individual who resists it . . . The only real difference is the fact that what prevails is the violence of the community . . . Thus on the way to right and legality, right is the right of the community. (Freud, 1932, p. 205)

Freud refers to Einstein's astonishment, expressed in his letter, that 'it is so easy to make men enthusiastic about a war and that there could be . . . an instinct for hatred and destruction' (p. 201). Answering, Freud wrote: 'I can only express my agreement. We believe in the existence of an instinct of that kind and have in fact been occupied during the last few years in studying its manifestations . . . Human instincts are only of two kinds; those which seek to preserve and unite (erotic or sexual) and those which we group together as aggressive or destructive' (p. 209). Clearly a pessimistic position; nevertheless Freud did acknowledge the fact that the self-preservation instincts can make use of aggressivity to reach their aims; the love instinct will be reinforced by the instinct of dominance to reach the object.

Freud's ideas did not change to the end of his life and it was left to his followers to unravel the problems left by the leader. Amongst them there is the problem concerning the issue of aggression being a primary force, perhaps inborn, or a reaction to frustration. There are some further questions. For instance, how can we distinguish aggressivity from hate, hostility and sadism? What has been resolved by the statement that sadism results from a fusion of libido with aggression? We shall have to admit that sadism is not always easy to comprehend because we do not precisely know how inflicting pain causes pleasure. This pleasure is at times obviously due to the effect which it has on another person, thus indicating how the aggressor is identified with the victim. But in another case, the pleasure appears to be derived from the sense of power over the victim. However, what is always present is the total absence of guilt, which had not escaped Freud in the course of introducing the concept of the superego, so clearly distinguishable from the conscience which belongs to ethical principles and the confessional. The superego, besides containing unconscious elements, retains all the injunctions and inhibitions derived from the individual's past. It will never accurately reproduce, though, those elements which originate from the infantile introjections of parental figures or their substitutes, because it will also contain elements which reflect the infant's aggressivity.

In describing the internal world in 'An outline of psychoanalysis', Freud pointed out how

> a portion of the external world has, at least partially, been abandoned as an object and has instead, by identification, been taken into the ego and thus becomes an integral part of the internal world. This new psychical agency continues to carry the functions which have hitherto been performed by the people (the abandoned objects) in the external world: it observes the ego, gives it orders, judges it and threatens it with punishments, exactly like the parents whose place it has taken. We call this agency the *superego* and are aware of it in its judicial functions as our *conscience*. (Freud, 1940, p. 205)

I need not expand on the well known observation that when the superego takes the ego as the object for its aggression, an unbearable sense of guilt will ensue, which in its extreme form will lead to suicide. On the other hand, the externalization of aggression can find a suitable target in those persons who symbolize the superego, such as the school authorities, political parties, the police, prison officers, nurses in psychiatric hospital, social workers, and so on. Those who are prone to violence will not stop at distinguishing those who are critical from those who frustrated them, whether they are friends or foes, parents or lovers. A poor development of the superego will also create specific problems, perhaps with less severe consequences.

Modern psychoanalysis has gone much further, postulating the precursors of the superego active in the earlier phases of development (the pregenital or pre-oedipal). The prototype of object relations, given to us by Freud in his description of the ego and superego interrelationship, is finally developed by Melanie Klein in the theory of the Object. According to Laplanche and Pontalis (1973), the fact that object relations have dominated psychoanalytic thinking in recent years, is due to a greater awareness of the interaction between the individual and the environment. Michael Balint (1935) had indeed outlined the significance and the importance of these interactions which are subject to constant internalization. With the deepening of observations, we have become increasingly more aware of the shaping of the objects within ourselves and how these objects contribute to what we are. For instance, a boy will grow up taking as a model a brutal father, or an indifferent mother; or a girl will assume all the feminine characteristics of her mother, or the masculine elements of her father, etc. Whilst Melanie Klein will promote the study of object relations, it will be Fairbairn who will show how it is not a mother, father, the maternal breast or the paternal phallus which is internalized. What is internalized is the *relationship* which the individual has had, or has, with them as partial or total objects. In more recent times, Winnicott and Bion have contributed to the enrichment of the theory of the object. I shall use this brief incursion into the study of mental processes from a dynamic point of view to illustrate how some episodes of violence which defy comprehension can be profitably unravelled.

The case I described above of a coloured man who displayed considerable violence towards a stranger lends itself to some speculation. We shall assume that in the course of a depth interview it will become apparent how this individual had been profoundly jealous and envious of the relationship between his parents and that he had internalized both them and their relationship with strong feelings of aggression and exclusion. Any stress condition caused by drugs, alcohol, economic factors, etc., could induce this young man to feel provoked at the sight of two young persons walking in the streets with their arms around each other.

Let us also briefly consider how those eruptions of violence affect groups of young people who appear to act without any real reason or provocation, when our understanding of the psychodynamics of adolescence will come to our rescue. Here is a typical example.

Not many years ago a group of young people left their village in southern Russia to visit a discothèque only a few kilometres away. Upon reaching their destination, they attacked the local youths without the slightest provocation. They finally set fire to the place, leaving behind a number of dead and wounded. The culprits were duly apprehended and taken to prison where they were interviewed by psychologists. All of them gave the same explanation for their strange behaviour. Boredom, they all said without ever contradicting themselves, as if they had their excuse ready well in advance. If we accept their explanation we can put it to good use in promoting appropriate preventive measures to avoid a repetition of similar incidents. We shall probably hold the view that it is necessary to keep young people occupied and that we should do our utmost to keep them amused.

On the other hand, if we bear in mind the fact that boredom is only a symptom endemic amongst young people, we take a different view. Boredom is, after all, the first line of defence against states of excitement in adolescence when it may have no precise objective. The inability to find an adequate outlet for those states of excitation is most likely to induce states of depression which can be mistaken for boredom, both by the subjects and onlookers.

Elsewhere I have expressed my views on the limitations of psychoanalysis, but here I do not wish to create the impression that psychotherapy is utilizable or applicable to all instances of violent behaviour and crimes. But I do share the interest of a very experienced colleague, Mervin Glasser (personal communication), in making the public aware that violent people have a mind. In keeping with this aim, I shall once more express my conviction that a knowledge of elementary psychodynamic principles will be of considerable help to those who have to deal with anti-social behaviour, even when it is the result of genetic, physical, psychotic, social or personal factors. A degree of familiarity with modern psychodynamics will be essential to those who advise the administrators of justice in assessing the possibility of recidivism. Far too often we hear of dangerous persons being released from custody on the strength of a period of hospital treatment associated with some drug therapy. This is a field where the co-operation between psychiatrists and psychoanalysts could turn out to be invaluable. It is not unknown for a lack of communication between social agencies, doctors and psychiatrists to lie behind the occurrence of foreseeable tragedies. In my view, lack of co-ordination between those organizations and individuals who are involved in the prevention and treatment of crime is to be deprecated.

The need to co-operate in this field will be all the more apparent if we consider that there is a true lack of information about the causes of violence in countries where it would be possible to gather some reliable information. Very often the true causes are subjected to distortions or are made to disappear to protect groups or individuals, or even for political or ideological reasons.

In concluding I shall add some brief comments on the emotional reactions of those who have a duty and responsibility to control other people's violence. These reactions, not always conscious, can become a source of untold and unmeasurable difficulties. (In the case of psychiatrists, psychologists and psychoanalysts, these spontaneous and inevitable reactions assume respectability and are contained in the term 'countertransference'.) To ignore, or deny, such reactions is not only dangerous but could cause even worse episodes of violence. I was not in the least surprised to be told by a high-ranking police officer that he was very scared when confronting a hostile crowd. I admired him all the more when he repeated this statement in public. Fear, when we are not aware of it, induces violence, just like boredom, poverty, frustrations, jealousy, envy and many other human sentiments. The presence of these spontaneous and natural reactions, or their denial, will be reflected in what we do, or in our way of conceptualizing these problems, creating some insurmountable voids. I cannot expect that this brief and incomplete exploration of a disagreeable and tough territory, will be followed by a wholehearted acceptance of the psychodynamic principles which I have supported. Nevertheless, it may have served a purpose if it leads to further arguments and discussions.

14 ON THE PSYCHODYNAMICS OF DRUG DEPENDENCE*

A S THE CAUSES OF DRUG dependence are multiform and exceedingly complex, I shall refer to them only briefly in this essay. Many readers, perhaps, have some idea as to what causes drug addiction, and concurrently will hold definite views on how to prevent or treat it.

It is hard to maintain an unbiased and balanced attitude to the problem, which inevitably attracts the attention of the press because of its tragic consequences. The ordinary person will rightly become emotional if he or she is at the receiving end of thefts perpetrated to obtain drugs. The euphoria resulting from drug-taking stimulates vandalism and attacks on persons, often causing understandable public outcry.

In general, the epidemic which has hit the world during this second half of the century has caused a great deal of thinking which has not yet come to fruition. In the past, it was generally accepted that the compulsion to take drugs was linked with psychopathic characteristics. Nowadays only the more severe cases are thought to have a pathological nucleus with a clearly defined mental disturbance. Even then we must distinguish them from those cases where there is physical or mental stress, and we shall often be confronted by a temporary disability. The anxious person will take any drug; the psychopath will turn to whatever drug accelerates the mental processes; whilst the persistent use of morphine is suggestive of a psychotic disturbance on a depressive background.

The greatest source of social anxiety, of course, is the realization that one in three schoolchildren will try some drug or other (Greaves, 1985). The fact that thousands of young persons seem to slip into the habit of taking

* This paper was first published in 1986 in *Free Associations* 5: 48–65.

drugs has been accounted for by some as attributable to experimentation or juvenile exuberance, but I think we ought to cast some doubt on such a simplistic explanation. On the other hand, the coincidence of drug abuse and adolescent depression is so common as to be very impressive. In many instances the dependence seems to be associated with a well-defined adolescent crisis. In this case we should note the concomitant occurrence of lack of energy, apathy and introversion. Childhood has been left behind, but adult life is not to be seen so clearly ahead. Adults are not always at the disposal of the young to help, and are far too often identified with authority. This state of affairs engenders a state of isolation, and few adolescents will readily admit that it can be aggravated by taking drugs.

Studies of drug dependence are often perplexing in so far as they may selectively stress cultural, environmental and constitutional elements, ignoring the fact that they interact within the inner and external world of each individual, creating the most adept terrain for the condition. We should also bear in mind that it is not necessary to be a deprived child to fall prey to dependence. Treatment centres nowadays are accustomed to admitting the children of the aristocracy, the rich and the poor. Patients will come from broken or united families.

Simple statistics can often confirm empirical observations. A 1972 study at a special London clinic on sixty consecutive patients showed that they had commenced their drug use before the age of twenty-one. Forty-one per cent of the subjects had been separated from a parent for at least one year before the age of sixteen, while fifty-eight per cent had offended before becoming addicted and had experienced parental loss. Paternal loss exceeded maternal loss. The survey also showed occurrence of violence in forty per cent of the cases, and a high incidence of court appearances (ninety-two per cent). All patients were multiple drug users – referred from a wide area in and beyond London – emerging from a background of disturbance, parental loss, truancy, unapprehended theft and sibling criminality (Boyd, 1972).

Modern conditions in which people live – overcrowding, the monotony of certain forms of work, or its absence – contribute to worsen a situation which (on the other hand) began to deteriorate from the sixties, when we thought world affairs and standards of living were about to take a turn for the better. But already in the early seventies we were beginning to notice more and more the effects of competition, emotional and nervous tensions, as well as the notable reactions to the new permissiveness in the sexual sphere.

The imperceptible, subtle alteration of our attitudes to sex and violence, and to personal relationships within the family and society, have found the majority of adolescents in a state of unpreparedness which has added to the usual turmoil of their inner worlds. It is interesting that, although young people have been given greater freedom and increased opportunities to follow their instinctual drives, this has not been followed by more tolerance of dependence on parents, which is there until adulthood is reached.

Inevitably we hear a great deal about the abuse of drugs as a form of rebellion, with all the usual references to external enemies, fighting the police, etc. On the other hand, we also note the increasing lack of parental guidance and the scarcity of acceptable authority figures. At the same time, we cannot fail to notice how some young persons become the tools for parental rebellion. As I have already pointed out, no social class is excluded. Indeed, we could venture to say that the very marked occurrence of drug dependence amongst the higher strata of society is beginning to look like a tendency to reject the hypocrisy of that social environment and of a protected existence. The current awareness that this condition knows no barriers in terms of social and cultural background, and that age, colour or creed are of little or no importance, has thrown a new light onto our understanding of the problem.

Sociologists will correctly draw attention to the occurrence of mounting individual and group tensions, with manifest aggressiveness and even the outbreak of group violence in connection with widespread drug abuse. It is interesting, though, that aggressiveness is at first kept at bay by the use of chemical substances, but in due course it worsens in response to the ghetto conditions which are the ever-common milieu for the addicts. The early reduction of violence has now been replaced by its increase. The flower people of the sixties have become the muggers of the eighties.

The younger section of the world population appears to be justifiably concerned with the constantly increasing amount of violence in contemporary society – irrespective of its occurrence in the form of wars, racial strife or repression by law-enforcement agencies – yet they seem to be ready to use violence to demonstrate against violence itself. The operative factor here must be the well-worn defensive mechanism of identification with the aggressor. But the ordinary citizen is even inclined to feel attacked and to regard as aggressive the displays of passivity, non-committal and opting-out attitudes adopted by youthful members of the community who tend to identify themselves with drug movements. Such contradictory behaviour possibly indicates a persistence of similar internal conflicts about aggressiveness, which are part and parcel of human development. Drug abuse, as I shall attempt to show, is very much concerned with ways of dealing with this aggressiveness.

As readers are no doubt aware, everything I have said so far is open to doubts and counterarguments. In fact, personal reactions and dogmatic statements are not unknown when drug dependence is under discussion. For this reason, I thought it might be more profitable to concentrate on what is ascertainable from the evidence gathered from detailed observation of addicts who have been subjected to psychotherapy or psychoanalysis. The subject is of particular interest because, as it happens, it is directly related to the development of psychoanalytic thinking.

In the *Confessions of an English Opium Eater*, Thomas De Quincey (1822) writes: 'I hanker too much after a state of happiness for both myself and others; I cannot face misery, whether my own or not, with an eye of sufficient firmness; and am little capable of surmounting present pain for the sake of any recessionary benefit.'

Concealed in this statement, proffered by the most famous addict the world has ever known, are the most basic ingredients of the psychopathology of drug dependence: the relentless search for an ideal existence not unlike a nirvana state; the denial of anything that might interfere with the belief that such a state exists; and an intrinsic ego-weakness. Few would question the view that magical thinking is involved in believing that a chemical substance would make everything right and that it would solve the most complex personal problems, including the matter of existing. In reality, the addict is severely split within himself as he succeeds in believing that he is calm and unaffected by what goes on around him; demonstrating at the same time that the only way he can go through with life is by being either asleep or not fully conscious.

This kind of contradiction runs through the psychopathology of the addict. His claims that his difficulties arise outside himself and his attempts to localize them in the external world are often successful in mobilizing the sympathy, and even the help, of relatives, friends and social agencies. But this is belied by his wish to alter the internal state through intoxicating means, and further evidence will be offered to show that a great deal more is involved in drug-taking than the creation of euphoria and oblivion.

As the condition progresses, the attempts to externalize or project a desperate internal state are intensified. The addict then withdraws from contact with society into the subcultural drug group which has its own *mores*, language and anti-social trends, totally acceptable to its members. In advanced and often terminal conditions the squalid surroundings, the filth and misery in which the addict is found are a fairly accurate reproduction of the inner world in which he is a prisoner.

In a discussion of psychodynamics, the specific action of the intoxicant must not be underestimated. Freud (1930) summed up the situation very clearly in *Civilization and its Discontents*:

> . . . in the last analysis, all suffering is nothing else than sensation . . . the crudest but also the most effective amongst these methods of influence is the chemical one – intoxication. I do not think that anyone completely understands its mechanism; but it is a fact that there are foreign substances which when present in blood or tissues, directly cause us pleasurable sensation; and they also alter the conditions governing our sensibility, that we become incapable of receiving unpleasurable impulses. (p. 78)

Freud goes on to say that the service rendered by the intoxicating media in the struggle for happiness and keeping misery at a distance is so highly prized as a benefit that individuals and peoples alike have given them an established place in the economics of their libido.

It is acknowledged that it was Freud who was responsible for discovering the most important link in the chain of events underlying drug dependence. In *Three Essays on the Theory of Sexuality*, he had linked oral eroticism in men with their desire for smoking and drinking (Freud, 1905a). This discovery was to become the nucleus for many subsequent psychoanalytical investigations, which clearly demonstrated how severe drug abuse is associated not only with oral fixation, but also with disturbance in the other developmental stages and a variety of conditions, notably homosexuality and manic-depressive psychosis (Abraham, 1926; Glover, 1932; Benedek, 1936).

Rado's contribution (1926) was outstanding in that it clarified the mechanism by which oral eroticism is still present and gratified, even when the intoxicant is introduced into the organism by means other than oral ones. This is achieved by promoting a feeling of well-being similar to that produced by drinking and eating to satisfaction. This author also noted the connection with sexual excitement, and even more relevantly commented: 'Once the intoxicant has become a sexual aim, the subject has fallen victim to the craving.' Rado underlines this observation with the remark that the elimination of genital interests undermines genital potency and finally leads to a turning away from real love-objects which are no longer of any interest.

Fenichel (1945a), agreeing with Rado, notes how with the breaking up of the genital organization 'an extraordinary regression begins'. The various points of fixation determine which fields of infantile sexuality (i.e. Oedipus complex, masturbation conflicts and, especially, oral or anal impulses) come to the fore and in the end 'the libido remains in the form of an amorphous erotic tension energy.' Fenichel believes that the effect of the drug rests on the fact that it is felt as food and warmth and that eventually all of reality may come to reside in the hypodermic needle. It follows that what he has described is rooted in oral dependence and constitutes the essence of drug addiction, whilst all other features are incidental.

Whilst not challenging the views which have been put forward so far, contemporary psychoanalysts would regard them as incomplete, as they do not take sufficiently into account the very complex psychodynamic mechanisms as frequently encountered in the course of psychoanalytical therapy, and particularly the ambivalent attitude to the drug itself displayed by those who misuse it. This comes across very clearly in subcultural language when the pedlar, or 'pusher', is often known as 'mother', but what he sells is referred to as 'shit', 'crap', 'junk', 'weed', 'grass', 'mud', 'dope', etc. If challenged, few abusers would regard the object of their craving as food and would accept the term 'poison' for it.

A novel approach, though, had already come from Glover (1932), who had shown how the addict's own hate impulses do not prevent him from becoming identified with the object (mother or the breast), towards whom he feels so ambivalent – which constitutes a dangerous psychic state. Glover was also the first to point out the different ways in which a toxic substance can be used. He realized that apart from the immediate physiologically induced sense of relief that comes from a pill, an injection or sniffing an inebriating substance, the drug symbolizes an ideal, magical, omnipotent object. At an unconscious level, its incorporation is used to control and assuage the severely disturbed internal relationships. In this respect, the intoxicant has a well-defined function aimed at the control of aggressive and sadistic charges. But this is not all, as at an even deeper level the substance which stupefies and dulls the senses is in reality expected to cure by destruction.

To recapitulate: Glover's discovery not only confirmed the presence of libidinal components in drug symbolism, but also showed that the attributes of intoxicants invariably contain a combination of libidinal and aggressive (sadistic) components, hitherto unsuspected. He actually based his argument on the principle that the most non-noxious food can become injurious and destructive if misused, and he gives an example of the patient who refuses to follow a diet. This suggests that in the choice of a noxious habit, the element of sadism is decisive; the drug becomes a substance (unconsciously a part-object equated with the maternal breast) with sadistic properties, which can exist both in the outer world and within the body, but which exercises its sadistic powers only when inside. The addiction then, according to this author, represents a peculiar mixture of psychic danger and reassurance.

This important study has also contributed to the elucidation of the occurrence of drug abuse in association with homosexuality (Hartmann, 1925). Early psychoanalytic work had uncovered the psychodynamic factor of homosexuality as a defence against hate and aggression. It also has a similar function even when a homosexual fantasy system remains at a wholly unconscious level. The regular use of drugs, however, appears to join forces with such fantasies in fighting off aggressiveness, hate and unusual amounts of sadism. In the course of the psychotherapy of addicts, we often notice how the eruption into consciousness of the homosexual fantasies is linked with an increase of the compulsion.

The pervasive presence of sadistic charges – as it has been outlined – cannot be allowed to overshadow the masochistic elements in the makeup of the addict, which now become clear as he is not unaware of the danger to which he is exposing himself. They are also inherent in the practice of alternating abuse with withdrawal and abstinence. We must note here that a characteristic of the addict's personality is his masochistic way of relating to his external world. Drug-dependent individuals are prone to tolerate ill-treatment from those who supply them with the drugs, and show little or no reaction to the squalid surroundings in which they often live. Some of the therapeutic interventions that are offered to them at times exploit such masochistic tendencies.

Psychoanalysts who belong to the Kleinian school have attempted to clarify this situation by placing great stress on the manic mechanisms used by the addict to control paranoid anxieties such as idealization, identification with an ideal object and the omnipotent control of objects.

Rosenfeld (1960) has pointed out that under the influence of manic mechanisms all frustration and anxieties, particularly persecutory anxiety, are denied, and the bad aggressive part of the self is split off. The pharmacotoxic effect of the drug is used to reinforce the omnipotence and the mechanisms of denial and splitting. Rosenfeld believes that the addict regresses to a phase of infancy when the infant uses hallucinatory wish-fulfilment fantasy in dealing with anxiety – not to a state of satisfaction of the infant at the breast, as suggested by previous investigators. The substance is used as an artificial aid in the production of hallucination, just as the baby uses the thumb to hallucinate an ideal breast.

But there is another important aspect of drug-taking which is related to paranoid anxieties and sadistic impulses, when it is then felt to be a bad, destructive substance. In such cases the pharmacotoxic effect is used to increase the omnipotent powers of the destructive drive. In their psychoanalyses, these patients reveal a totally bad and disrupted inner world, under the dominance of destructive forces. The external poison is needed to fight the poison inside; a feeling of helplessness is created which is readily communicated to the therapist. With regard to the relation of addiction to depression, Rosenfeld believes that a central factor is an identification with an ill or dead object. The drug is said to stand for such an object, which is then incorporated. In the present writer's experience, this is a generalization of a phenomenon which can be observed only in a small number of cases, considering the prevalence of depression and depressive moods in drug-dependent individuals.

Mention must be made here of one more psychodynamic factor: the extreme tendency towards the splitting of the ego, due to its inherent weakness. The most disturbing and direct consequences of this tendency is the impulse to project both good and bad parts of the self onto people and the environment in general, leading to much acting out and disastrous external relationships. The implications and the effects of these manoeuvres in relation to the individual's position within society have been noted at the beginning of this essay.

To recapitulate our findings so far: psychoanalytic exploration of the deepest layers of the addict's mental life will unfailingly reveal a complex situation dominated by a sadistic relationship between the patient and his internalized objects (equals a representation of an object or image which has acquired the meaning of an external object), a source of acute persecutory anxiety. In other words, the addict is struggling with persistent, unresolved problems which characterize his relationship as an infant to his mother. This scenario is evolved in a background of primitive fantasies associated with very intense ambivalence towards the object (mother). This is reflected in the individual's behaviour, where sado-masochistic tendencies are clearly observable by an outsider, who is alarmed by the addict's capacity to harm himself and others. To all intents and purposes the compulsive use of an intoxicant is comparable to the relationship of an infant to the mother, which may have a blissful appearance on the surface but in some instances conceals a cauldron of hidden and explosive dangers.

What has been described so far are the psychodynamic factors which we are likely to encounter in the more severe cases of drug dependence. In the majority of cases we are dealing with essentially borderline conditions; in the last resort they can also be regarded as a defence against fully fledged psychotic reactions. Be that as it may, we would, of course, be unlikely to find a similar cluster of psychopathological phenomena in a mild case of habituation where a person needs a narcotic at bedtime, or in the experimenter and weekend user who might abuse intoxicants for only a short period of life. On the other hand, certain basic anxieties – conflicts over aggressive drives, confusion about sexual aims, etc. – are to be found in all cases and it will then be a matter of degree and quality, or even chance, whether specific psychological disturbances will appear.

The type of noxious substance involved plays an important role, and in practice even the most experienced psychiatrist is placed in a difficult position, as it is almost impossible to distinguish between the underlying psychopathology and symptoms arising from pharmacotoxic effects. A case in point is met in connection with misuse of LSD by a person who is in an unsettled state of mind, characterized by vague anxiety, unspecified fears and inhibitions. The euphoria which accompanies the experience of taking LSD can be interpreted as the manic defence against the release of persecutory anxieties – at times quite terrifying – brought out by the hallucinogen. Turning to another chemical substance in order to find relief from a chemically induced psychological disturbance is an easy way out. The choice in this event will probably be cannabis or a tranquillizer, alternating with the amphetamines. A vicious circle is established in an attempt to ward off the threatened mental breakdown (or disintegration) and this soon becomes the central psychodynamic element in the total picture of dependence, not always clearly visible to the observer. I am referring here to the problem of escalation, which we need to take into account when we are considering the possible legalization of certain drugs.

In the case of young persons the position is quite mystifying, as the conscious and unconscious psychological changes attributable to adolescence may be in the process of evolution, or may still be present in the form of troublesome residues and are not made clearer by exposure to pharmacotoxic influences. Adolescence is also a time of life when curiosity about the functions of the body and mind is accompanied by fears and anxieties of a profound, and at times overwhelming, quality. Unbounded energy becomes confused with aggression and, rather than attempting to deal with it, the solution of damping it down with a sedative will appear infinitely more attractive and safe. Should the initial attempts to get rid of sexual feelings through casual contacts prove unsatisfactory, the result is a flooding of despair, emptiness and desolation, which can be temporarily – but instantaneously – relieved by the concrete ingestion of a pill, or the injection of a drug which will bring blissful sleep.

But this is not all. The revival of bisexual conflicts is met either with promiscuity or an almost complete withdrawal, which is sustained by a loss of feeling and inability to communicate. This is likely to promote a desire to seek out other persons who are in a similar predicament, in the hope of alleviating the experience through sharing it. Not infrequently, drug-taking becomes the only bond of significance, and therefore the only experience to be shared.

Communication between members of the group remains unimproved but breaking the law – through smoking cannabis; or doing something daring by mobilizing the forces of the unconscious with a dose of LSD; or defying one's conscience with the aid of amphetamine – becomes the cementing force within the group, giving illusory courage and fresh hope. In spite of its artificiality, the group tends to act as a shield and protecting force, particularly because it is capable of absorbing a great deal that is unacceptable to each individual member. Mechanisms of projective identification are very common under these conditions, as they allow each person in the group to project himself or his problems into someone else, which accounts for the unusual combination of selling and misusing drugs at the same time. The position of the 'pusher' becomes more understandable, in so far as he literally pushes the urgent longing for the drug into others. Perhaps this widespread occurrence of projective identification is the real reason why true communication does not take place but, on the other hand, the mechanism produces some immediate relief from internal pressures.

Having taken all these elements into account, it is necessary to stress that drug dependence in early or late adolescence has its roots in the depression which is so overwhelmingly common during this developmental phase. Once more we become aware that the demarcation between normal and abnormal is very undefined. In those instances where adolescent depression is based on a symbiotic tie with the omnipotent, need-satisfying mother (the pre-oedipal mother of Freudian psychology), we also find shame, inadequacies and a weak, helpless ego with narcissistic object-relationships and a marked element of oral dependence, which contributes to the serious-ness of the psychopathology (Anthony, 1970). This syndrome is frequently met in that small group of drug-dependent adolescents who are exposed to the dangers of escalation, once they start 'experimenting' with noxious substances (Limentani, 1973).

Closer to normal development is the adolescent depression which is linked with a revival of the oedipal guilt. Other accompanying features will be a wish to destroy the idealized image of parents; defiance of authority; aggression against the self in which both the self and incorporated objects are annihilated. The very nature of the disturbance is such that communi-cation with the adult world is lost. Behaviour disorders, minor or major acts of delinquency, and some degree of sexual promiscuity have always been characteristic of this age group – more so in recent times – but unhappily, in the last few years, drug abuse has become one of its major features. Adults in our contemporary world seem altogether unable to provide help, but we should note that young people are not turning to them for it. Perhaps we have reached a point where adolescents are stating in no uncertain terms that they have no faith or belief in the capacity of the adult world to give them the help and support they need. The widespread abuse of drugs is their answer; the despair, hopelessness and sense of urgency of the message should not be missed.

The responsibility resting on those who are in contact with young people – therapeutic community workers, psychiatrists, psychotherapists, and so on – has increased to a spectacular degree during the last few years. The pervasive pessimism that affects everyone who has to deal with a severe case of addiction was understandable in the early stages of the current epidemic, being based on earlier, more limited, experience. This pessimism was much in evidence in the early sixties, and it certainly influenced the authorities in an approach dominated by *laissez-faire* and despairing attitudes.

Nevertheless, with the spreading of the phenomenon we had to recognize that – even amongst the most serious cases of drug dependence – there were many who could interrupt it and finally cast it aside. What was also surpris-ing to some of us was that some young persons actually came to us request-ing therapy, usually when they had become aware of not being able to go it alone, so to speak. The problem will always be how and whether to inter-vene, taking into consideration our scanty resources – especially in the field of psychotherapy.

To counteract some of the prejudice and scepticism which surrounds the treatment of drug dependence by psychological means, I shall now present a brief résumé of the psychoanalysis of a young man whose various addictions appeared to be a serious threat, not only to the outcome of the therapy, but also to his own personal life and career.

Ian was twenty years old when he was referred to me with anxiety and depressive symptoms. His failure to pursue his studies at a major university, the main reason for coming to this country from overseas, caused me to wonder whether he had severe character and personality defects. He had told me of his interest in 'experimenting' with drugs such as cannabis and LSD, but only as the five-times-a-week analysis progressed did I become aware of his habituation to a large variety of drugs, including intravenous methedrine and heroin. His experiences under LSD had proved extremely frightening to this patient, as in them he found evidence of the insanity which had been one of his outstanding fears. As the working alliance developed, the detailed analysis of many 'trip' experiences and of his very heavy use of cannabis was made possible. In due course it became clear that the latter habit had become incapacitating. Treatment was concluded after three years. His own follow-up and spontaneous summary of the analysis, shortly after termination, is of some interest. This is what he wrote:

> After the last session I remembered the first time I met you. I wore a suit and dark glasses. I expected a lecture. Was I going to lie on the couch, just like I'd seen in the movies. Was this going to be a verbal, academic experience. I would be talking about how at three I fell off the stairs, and so on. For the next two months I was wondering if I felt any different. Now I AM IN ANALYSIS, big capital A. Can people tell, I asked myself, as I walked. I know I walked like someone who had swallowed a magical pill. In those days I was lonely, and scared of meeting people. So I got a TV set and read lots of books. I ate in restaurants at first. Then I bought a small stove. Having bought the thing I couldn't cook, not in those days. I was lonely and gradually I learnt analysis was difficult. Because I was having it I was THE SMARTEST man in the world. I knew things others didn't know. I had theories about life. One at a time I told you about these theories. I would tell myself: I shall impress my ANALYST. I tried, but they didn't impress you. I must admit the first two to three months I thought you were stupid. You said the most obvious things and showed the mentality of a child. It didn't even make sense. I turned around once and you had your eyes closed. I kept turning around till I accused you of being asleep. You said nothing, but a couple of minutes later you alluded to it. Eventually I felt better and so I got myself a girl

friend and it was satisfactory. I then thought a man is not a man unless he is copulating. Having a beard helped in making me feel more like a man. You remember I also decided to take my examinations as I was feeling so confident.

Life was difficult for Ian, who did not relate very easily either to men or women. Eventually he met some friends who were regular drug users. After recalling how he missed sessions, waking up one minute after the session was due to end, he recalls:

Another friend came and I took an acid trip with him and, again, I told myself: Ah, now I really see what is happening. In fact, I saw nothing. I stared at a red object; that was a child staring at mother. I came back and told you I felt very guilty. That is when it all started again . . . I was getting to be known, as I was acting very stoned when I was stoned. I went to live with a friend and his girl friend. That's when it started to deteriorate. I'd sleep on the floor. They offered me to sleep in their bed. I wanted to make love to M. I was sexually very hung up. I nearly took her away. We had plenty of shit [marijuana], X, my friend, went away, came back with acid. Then another day he came back with the works; ampoules of methedrine. He was fixing all the time and I'd drink all the time. I didn't want to fix. Finally I said OK but I won't do it myself. So he fixed me with two ampoules. I still didn't want to do it as I figured I would get hurt. About that time we were fixing with meth. We would go to London and come back with 60 ampoules. Then he got some H [heroin]. I never took more than a pill at a time. I was so proud now I had really made it and I had started regular habits, carrying the works and all that. I was very clean and I used a very special needle. This went on and on and I came to you only once or twice. I was wearing a scarf, to use it as a tourniquet.

Things were going from bad to worse for Ian and, 'Finally, I'd taken so much methedrine I completely freaked out. Such a confusion. I could take more and it would make little difference. I was obsessed with the works, the syringe and spikes. I'd seen you once or twice and I saw my father once or twice, etc. He nearly died of shock.'

Ian had indeed missed a lot of sessions, but I persisted and told him I would be there all the same. After that, there was some improvement. Ian managed to cut himself off from the others. He was now on tranquillizers to help his weaning. He writes:

> I was poisoning myself with them some more. I was trembling like a leaf. I was scared to walk out. I was wearing a tie to look like other people. I started thinking all hippies were queer and I was out of it. I can't remember what I talked about in the analysis. I gave you little scraps of information. I know we figured something out about pills and it helped. I still didn't want to say it was wrong to take methedrine. I went back home for a vacation and I was taking sedatives. I did things but didn't see anybody I knew. In October I had a relapse. I met a hippy who had a fix of amphetamine powder which he had watered down. That was very bad. Perhaps I got jaundice then. One big thing was sex. All men were trying to rape me.

In his letter he recalls how he demanded to be made potent by me, just before meeting a girl, and he recaptures some of his aggressive feelings. Later he met the girl he was to marry and began to settle down in the analysis again. In the closing lines he writes:

> Then from one day to the next I started doing things and it has steadily progressed. I thought at first I would have to be rigid with myself, like a Puritan priest or a Calvinist, but it turned out to be totally different. It's a moral code which gets absorbed. You can still be flexible with yourself. Finally I decided to stop the analysis. I couldn't quite see what else I could say. There was a point where I had to break off. It's all very well clinging to a 'breast'. I also thought it would quicken my convalescence. As a matter of fact, I felt the time had come to take a real course of psychology with you. I wanted to have it all to take it away with me. During the last week or so it lessened a lot; I wasn't trying to pull things out of you any more.

Some years went by before I heard again from this patient. He then informed me that he had continued to make good progress and that he was leading a useful existence, making good use of the university experience he had gained in England. He had also married and had a family.

Why a patient should write his own account of the course of his analysis is open to speculation. Knowing what had been at the centre of the treatment at the time of our parting allows me to venture some explanation. Ian

—228—

wanted me to know that he had been able to preserve the good analysis inside himself, side by side with the memories of bad times. This is, in fact, my reason for presenting it here. I thought Ian's very long letter – which I have not reproduced in full – did give some idea of the internal struggle to fight off the treatment which was going on side by side with the fight against the drug dependence. It is obvious that the therapist must not accept the destructive rejection on the part of the patient, just as he must be prepared to let the patient go when the time has come. The aim of the therapy is, in the last resort, basically that of showing how ambivalence and destructiveness, which form the core of drug dependence, can be contained and tolerated.

What use could all our knowledge of the psychodynamics of drug dependence be in dealing with the thousands who are now said to be afflicted by the condition? Very few people, of course, will be able to have psychoanalysis, or even psychotherapy in its most limited way. Yet our understanding suggests that, if such an approach was available, it could be of great value. There are also some other conclusions that can be drawn from our psychodynamic insights. For instance, it is clear that the simple method of substituting one drug for another, which is so widely applied nowadays, is of very little use unless it is associated with supported interventions. Treatment within therapeutic community centres, which could lead to the replacement of the pathological milieu in which drug dependence thrives, is certainly well in keeping with the kind of insights which I have attempted to describe in this essay.

15 PERVERSIONS
Treatable and Untreatable*

To BE INVITED to give a Glover Lecture for a second time is an honour which is difficult to decline. It also seemed an impossible challenge considering Edward Glover's contributions to the study of sexual deviations covering a period of forty years. Atter some hesitation, I found the stimulus for this presentation in something Glover said in his paper on 'Aggression and sadomasochism' which he gave at a symposium organized by the Portman Clinic in 1963: 'it will be maintained that one of the important functions of sexual perversions is defensive in nature, a kind of organized sexual adaptation which, however, may in many instances bring a variety of ego-disorders in its train.' He added: 'the pervert protects his reality sense from gross interference' (Glover, 1964, p. 159).

Those words had been in mind for a great many years but now with my own added experience, I asked myself the question: Is that the reason why perverts are so difficult to treat? In the case of a fetishist, for instance, the psychic reality which he protects is that there are no sexual differences, a wholly illusory belief, shared by the man or woman who dresses or acts as a person of the opposite sex. Is it possible that by protecting their distorted reality sense perverts succeed in protecting some hard core of ego distur-bance, which threatens the whole of their being? It seemed that perhaps this could be a better line of understanding the therapeutic challenge we con-stantly face in this field, rather than the popular misconception that a

* This paper was given as the 10th Glover Lecture at the Royal Free Hospital School of Medicine, under the auspices of the Portman Clinic, London, on 10 November 1986. The psychoanalyst Edward Glover, 1880–1972, was the founder of the Portman Clinic for the treatment of social and sexual deviancy.

perversion is not given up because it is pleasurable. On the contrary, we know the misery of the perverts' lives as they go in search of their ephemeral satisfactions.

But there was another question which I felt needed to be answered. How does that cloud of unreality affect the therapist–patient relationship, considering that the aim of insight therapy is to promote adaptation to reality through the quest for truth? The therapist must be, *de facto*, the enemy to be defeated, a source of countless countertransference reactions.

RESULTS OF TREATMENT OF PERVERSIONS AS REPORTED IN THE LITERATURE

Looking for some answers to these problems in the relevant literature on the results of psychotherapy in the sexual deviations proved somewhat disappointing and not because of a scarcity of papers.

Many writers have reported on the success or failure of individual therapies, often a single case, adding some general comments on therapeutic issues. Though many are based on sound findings, I have in this paper chosen to discuss reports that are more extensive in their approach.

Wakeling (1979), for instance, notes that 'working within different frameworks of therapies in various centres is likely to attract, or to have referred, pre-selected groups of those individuals seeking help' (p. 24). A psychoanalyst will attract a different type of patient than a behaviour therapist, or a forensic psychiatrist. Wakeling also quotes the rate of improvement for homosexuals treated with behaviour therapy as being in the order of 30 to 40 per cent, and this is strikingly similar to that reported from the use of other psychotherapeutic techniques (Bancroft, 1974, quoted by Wakeling, p. 2). These figures could not be matched by those elicited from psychoanalytic colleagues in personal communications.

The psychoanalytic treatment of homosexuality was discussed in 1977 by an all-American panel (JAPA, 1977), when Stoller expressed his disillusionment with the treatment of effeminate homosexuals, whilst Ethel Person, also a psychoanalyst, noted how hypermasculine homosexuals were very responsive, especially because they seem to have less serious problems with their mothers. She also pointed out how differences in patients must be expressed in terms of ego integration, types of defences, object relations and personality structures. All panellists agreed on a mixed prognosis in the presence of narcissistic problems. The report, however, also shows that little distinction was made between different types of homosexuality; or even between overt and latent homosexuality.

In commenting on the results of therapy in exhibitionists, Rosen (1979) states: 'in some cases, real personality improvements had taken place, although occasional lapses in response to situational stress did occur' (p. 183). In this series of cases, some patients also showed greatly improved relationships at home and at work. This report confirms the belief that analytic psychotherapy is not efficacious in the case of severely phobic or compulsive adult exhibitionists and I would agree with it. Adolescent groups, instead, proved much more satisfactory. Rosen also points out how individual therapy for adolescents is preferable, but this, after all, is a small sample.

Stoller (1979) is also responsible for a not very encouraging report on the results to be obtained in transvestism and I have little ground for contradicting that. This, I understand, is also true in the case of behaviour therapy which, on the other hand, could, with the additional support of psychotherapy, produce good responses if the transvestites displayed marked fetishistic traits (Gelder, 1979).

To conclude this brief review of the literature, I shall draw attention to the fact that all these reports seemed to lack a clear indication with regard to the aim of the therapy. Was its primary scope the removal of the perversion? Was it directed at correcting the patient's poor adaptation to the environment? Or was it aimed at improving his or her creativity? Or was the depression so often associated with this condition responsible for the offer of help? There is no implicit criticism in asking these questions but I believe this is an important issue. A patient is often quite unable to know what he wants from therapy but this privilege must be denied to the therapist. It has occurred to me that were we to be more definite about our aims, we could perhaps be more effective in our selection of patients, and also of the type of help to be offered.

As it happens, though, not as many people who could benefit from our services turn to us in spite of the permissiveness of modern times and the relaxed ventilation of sexual problems in the media. Shame is perhaps the most important factor in this reluctance. It will always be easier to confide in a sympathetic agony uncle or aunt, on the radio, or in a magazine, than to confront another person in the confines of a consulting room. Undue pessimism on the part of our medical and psychiatric colleagues, who are often poorly informed about our methods, is another factor; but the most serious deterrent against seeking help will be the fear of what treatment entails; what anxieties will be unleashed; what, if anything, can take the place of that haven of relief and satisfaction: the perversion. In consequence, we have no accurate ways of knowing exactly what its frequency is. A French publication, a magazine called *L'Union* (quoted by Dekhlei, 1984), devoted to the subject of sexuality, some time ago analysed the correspondence with readers over ten years. It stated that it received 800 letters a month. In terms of frequency of subjects and in order of importance, the correspondence was concerned with fantasies associated with masturbation, swapping partners, homophilia, spanking, with some concern for incest, paedophilia and adultery.

All that can be said about this report is that a fairly large section of the French population is at risk, as no one could forecast when such conscious fantasies would be turned into actions. We can also confidently expect that a similar number of individuals would be found in other countries with similar social, cultural and moral backgrounds. However, I must disagree with Chasseguet-Smirgel who believes that perversions are 'a dimension of the human psyche in general, a temptation in the mind, common to us all' (Chasseguet-Smirgel, 1984, p. 1).

It must be conceded, though, that fantasies of a perverted nature may be part of anyone's psychic life; some acting out may erupt quite suddenly and we should distinguish it from those activities which facilitate orgasmic potency in men and women and which exploit the sensuality derived from the erogeneous zones in the widest sense of the term.

THE PSYCHOPATHOLOGY OF SEXUAL DEVIATION

The symptomatology of sexual deviation is too well known to require mention here. I would like to stress, though, that:

(1) they seldom appear singly;
(2) the inventiveness of human beings has no limit;
(3) we no longer subscribe to Freud's statement that the neuroses are the negative of the perversions, as we now know that they occur side by side with any other known psychological disturbance.

Whether there is a general psychopathology of sexual deviations besides what I have already alluded to (that is to say, that it is defensive in the wider sense of the word and that it attacks reality), is a matter worth further consideration. The literature of each perversion, however, is rather bewildering in view of the many different ways of examining the same phenomena. This can be shown very clearly in the case of fetishism which claims the largest number of individual and general reports. The source of this interest is probably due to the fact that it is more common than we suspect. Many fetishistic elements are part of ordinary sexuality, without being deviations in their own right. Such elements are often described as 'little obsessions' or 'certain preferences'.

It is understandable that in so far as fetishism, to all intents and purposes, occurs only in men, the stress will fall on castration anxiety as a basic aetiological factor. There are, on the other hand, other views which will be equally valid at various times. It will be said, for instance, that the fetish denies the existence of the orifice which is used in sex by the parents (McDougall, 1972); or that it is evidence of anal exchanges between mother and son (Grunberger, 1976); or that it expresses fears of aggression and destructiveness and that it is essentially pregenital in origin (Gillespie, 1964a); or that, as Greenacre (1953) has suggested, there is a disturbance of the body image in the first eighteen months of life, with further trouble developing between the ages of two and four, coinciding with the phallic phase; hence the excessive castration anxiety.

In a more recent contribution, Chasseguet-Smirgel (1984) claims that the pain for the child is derived from not being able to satisfy the mother, and to the fact that he cannot give her a child. For this author, fetishism is a denial of the double differences between sexes and generations. This is followed by a creation of an anal sadistic universe in which a child confuses his faeces with his genitals. Here we see that castration anxiety is given adequate status without ignoring the pregenital elements.

The following is a typical example of the confluence of different elements in sexual deviants. A young man whom I saw for a consultation had a compulsion since childhood to touch the legs of women who wore black stockings. As his sexuality developed, stockings had become a fully-fledged fetish. In the subsequent analysis, for which, considering his inability to use his many endowments, there was every indication, it transpired, that to achieve full gratification in his sexual life, he often wore female stockings. An interesting feature in this young man's history was that he had a very strong, supportive father who was keen to help his son, quite contrary to the belief that fathers of fetishists are ineffectual and almost non-existent in their psychic life.

Exhibitionism, too, does not lack a variety of psychopathological explanations, including the generalization that it is due to a heightened castration anxiety. Yet, Rosen (1979) has shown that the exhibitionist's activity, so common amongst all social classes, is rooted in the pregenital phase. According to this author, the oral sadistic phase has interfered with the resolution of the oedipal complex and in so doing, it has led to castration anxiety, so overwhelming as to conceal the more primitive root causes.

In so far as most exhibitionists are narcissistic, it follows that in clinical practice there will be occasions when their behaviour should be understood as being part of a desire forcibly to gain control of another person through projective identification. Should we fail to do so, we could easily miss the sadistic element of forcing someone *to look* against his or her wish. Therapeutic encounters can be deeply influenced by missing the finer points of psychopathology and I would like to illustrate this with a brief example.

An adult exhibitionist had been in once-a-week psychotherapy for some years, on account of sporadic recidivism which could always be ascribed to a different precipitating factor. In the expectation of a long holiday interruption, he had indulged in some vicious attacks on me over some weeks. His behaviour was at first interpreted as an attempt to display phallic potency against the analyst/father; later on the attacks seemed to be directed at a frustrating mother image reflected in the analyst. Much to my disappointment, upon leaving the clinic after the last session, the patient exposed himself from the street, to a lady working in a nearby office. It transpired that I had not understood that he felt unnecessarily nasty and that all he wanted was to get close to me, no matter how. Many exhibitionists do experience very strong desires to be close and are satisfied to be touched by someone's eyes, always maintaining a safe distance, of course.

The complexities we face in treating perverts have forced us to look for new solutions beyond Freud's original basic discoveries and it must be already apparent that there has been a considerable change of emphasis in our conceptualization of what takes place in sexual deviations.

Unquestionably, the majority of psychoanalysts would still regard castration anxiety as being utterly central to the establishment of a perversion and I would agree that it will account for many cases, perhaps the less severe ones. Nevertheless, we must be clear about what we actually mean when we say that someone is suffering from this particular type of anxiety. Quite often, we shall find that it is so deep as to be indistinguishable from a fear of death and disintegration. Joyce McDougall (1986) has recently stated that 'castration anxiety is nothing compared with the introjection of a damaged and a frightening sense of deadness' (p. 22). I, too, have drawn attention to the fact that transsexualism is a true challenge to many basic tenets of psychoanalytic psychology and particularly castration anxiety (see pp. 133–54 above).

Penis envy can also be a major issue in the case of female perverts. But, again, is it simply the expression of a longing for a part of the male anatomy? It could also be that at times it expresses a deep feeling of frustration at not being able to fulfil the ambition of giving mother a baby, a symbolic act of reparation for past fantasy misdeeds.

Thus the study of sexual deviations has undergone a major evolution, if not revolution, in recent years. Primarily, this change must be attributed to the fading support of the theory of phallic primacy; to our doubts about penis envy and to the constantly increasing awareness of disturbed object relations in early infancy. Such changes have occurred slowly and almost imperceptibly. Already in a 1931 paper on 'Sublimation, substitution, and social anxiety', Glover had noted how the pervert has to mask the unbearable truth of his sexual inadequacies in relation to the superiority of the father and his attributes, and especially of genitality over the anal universe. In 'A note on idealization' (1938b), he had enlarged on this statement, adding: 'the pervert idealizes part-objects, especially the ones pertaining to the anal phase . . . His geese are usually regarded as swans' (p. 94). The anality which is so often the battlefield of the relationship with mother is felt as good as genitality. The faeces which are the basis of transactions with her are as good as a penis. The fact that the pervert seldom regards his penis as being good enough to protect him from the desired and feared fantasy of fusions with the primary object is also sufficient proof of an early developmental disturbance. Also in recent years we have become much more aware of the role of aggression and sado-masochism which is seldom absent in a sexual deviation. In a state of self-idealization, the pervert will desperately try to destroy reality through the use of denial. Whilst often excelling in aesthetic appreciation and artistic endeavours, he will also use his aggressiveness to demean, spoil and pour contempt on much that is around him. Finally, once the sexualization of the aggression has been turned into sadism, it is no longer effective in keeping the aggression unconscious. In the case of homosexuals this is very apparent in the compulsive quest for a partner who will take up a complementary masochistic or sadistic role.

A similar collusive enactment is found amongst women who suffer from erotogenic masochism but its underlying pathology is a great deal more complex. Psychoanalytic exploration of these cases will often reveal that large aggressive elements have entered into the relationship with father, resulting in the introjection of a bad penis, which is feared internally and externally. The woman will compulsively test the situation, her preferred choice being that of a partner who is hostile and sadistic to the female sex. Whatever the outcome, some of her anxiety will be allayed (Klein, 1975).

A single perversion is an unusual, rather than a regular, occurrence. In my opinion the importance of sado-masochistic fantasies, conscious and unconscious, and their enactment in a kind of secondary role, perhaps, cannot be underestimated, as shown by the immense popularity of this type of pornography.

Stoller (1979), for instance, quite categorically insists on the principle that it is hurting, and therefore committing a sin, that is exciting for the pervert. He appears to find this element to be even more important than the attack on reality. There are other views concerning the insatiable quest for gratification displayed by some perverts. Glasser (1979b) has suggested that these unhappy people are attempting to establish an inner feeling of peace, to be achieved at all costs. He has summarized the situation rather admirably as follows: 'to envisage closeness and intimacy as annihilating, or separateness and independence as desolation-isolation, indicates the persistence of a primitive level of functioning' (p. 280).

This is to some extent in line with Joyce McDougall's conclusion, when she spoke of 'the pervert's fear of loss of identity, based on a shaky start in life with a dramatic compulsive way of keeping one's narcissistic self-image from disintegrating' (McDougall, 1986, p. 19). Glasser's point tallies with Masud Khan's view that the perverts attempt to personalize themselves through sexual experience. This, he feels, is part of the undoing of alienation through masturbatory practices and projective identification which is aimed at making reparation to his own idolized self. But in so doing there can be no true relating or mutuality (Khan, 1979, p. 16).

Finally, to underline the primitive nature of the identificatory processes involved in what I am describing, I shall quote from the analysis of a fetishistic transvestite, who once said: 'Mother hasn't got it in me to be able to give me warmth' (Baker, 1986).

As I was reflecting on all this, I suddenly felt that I was reaching the overriding conclusion that a perversion, after all, is not an illness but only a symptom. As a symptom it can appear at any time in the life of an individual for an infinite variety of reasons, as a state of intense excitement with a peremptory need to enact conscious or unconscious fantasies. In my view, this state of excitement is only secondary, in so far as it faintly mirrors a similar primary state of excitement that occurred in early infancy, in association with feelings of frustration and helplessness in response to overstimulation and/or emotional deprivation (Limentani, 1984). This forms the core of a syndrome which has its roots in disturbed object relations in early life, eventually surfacing as perverted acts. It should be noted that in general the original traumatic experience is subjected to disavowal. The fantasies associated with the primary excitation seldom reach consciousness but their derivatives will be found in later life.

The frustration, which I am aware has figured in many earlier formulations, promotes aggressive feelings and is the direct source of the excitations, so difficult to contain in a growing individual, Sexuality, in neutralizing aggression to some extent, assumes a soothing and calming role, to be retained throughout the individual's life. It is the amount and quality of the aggressiveness that will distinguish a deviation from ordinary sexuality.

The conviction that went with this conclusion had an odd *déjà vu* feeling. As I was checking a reference, I read again Glover's paper on 'Aggression and sadomasochism' (1964), which I have mentioned earlier, and came across the following sentence: 'It is legitimate to inquire how far the technique of sexual deviation functions as a symptom-equivalent, meaning by symptom in this connection a psychic formation arising from a combination of unconscious and pre-conscious components' (p. 150). Later in the paper I re-discovered another significant statement: 'The deeper the origin, the more likely it is that any perverted elements manifested are of a primitive nature' (p. 153).

It is regrettable that Glover did not pursue this interesting suggestion any further but, after all, that was the last paper he wrote. Certainly the symptomatology I have described does seem to be the expression of a solid defensive barrier constructed around profound, disturbed external and internal relationships, as he had suggested. I would add that giving too much prominence to the symptom by raising it to the status of an illness is likely to induce us to ignore the deeper causes which are common to all sexual deviations. Nevertheless, the symptom retains its importance, especially in relation to the attitude of the patient to it. The desire to hold on to, or be rid of the perverted behaviour, will be most valuable in assessing the severity of the underlying condition.

I would like to bring this section to a close by offering a clinical abstract from a psychoanalysis. This will illustrate how it is possible to trace current sources of excitement (secondary excitement in my terminology) back to the original and earlier situation which had given rise to protracted states of primary excitement and frustration.

A forty-seven-year-old woman was referred on account of serious problems in her personal relationships. Some years had elapsed since she had terminated a ten-year course of psychoanalysis with a senior woman colleague who had since retired. The analysis had helped to cope with the death of her young husband when she was still in her twenties; two interrupted pregnancies, as she felt unable to be a mother; some disastrous relationships with unsuitable men. She was particularly grateful to the analyst, in so far as she felt well supported in reaching the very top of her profession, in which women were notably in the minority, a fact she was to remind me of at frequent intervals. For the past ten years Mrs X had lived with a man, John, who shared her professional interests, although he was not in the same class. He was good company, boisterous, somewhat vulgar and of working-class origin, unlike her genteel, English country background. The only compensation was that he liked rough, ruthless sex, and was willing to use a mechanical aid as she could not achieve an orgasm. She did not conceal her disappointment that John was not a bit humiliated by the situation (an obvious act of dehumanization of the object, in my view, of which she was unaware). The breaking point in the relationship was reached when Mrs X fell madly in love with a male homosexual, Tim, twenty years her junior. This young man was intellectually gifted and a constant inspiration to improve her work. John could not tolerate the idea of embarking on a *ménage à trois* and soon began to have a series of love affairs with young women. This was more than Mrs X could bear but she still needed some encouragement from the referring analyst before she could make the final break which brought a host of problems in its aftermath.

When I began work with Mrs X I was struck by the intense penis envy which was obscuring the pervasive sado-masochism which was soon to occupy the centre stage. She bitterly regretted having left John who had been a source of considerable masochistic gratification. She also wondered if she had felt guilty towards him as she had given him a large sum of money just before parting, although she could ill afford it at the time. Her capacity to feel guilty was a central issue in the analysis and the suspicion that she was capable of erotizing it soon occurred to me. For instance, although her previous analyst had apparently worked very hard in an attempt to dispel her belief that she had caused her husband's death from cancer, she still felt guilty about it. The death of her father when she was around four years of age had left a deep mark and provided her with an inexhaustible source of guilt. Father had left home on his military service when she was sixteen months old, only to reappear at intervals, for brief spells, in a drunken state, 'ready to seize any opportunity to beat her'. At various times the patient brought corroborative evidence that the father had been a violent person, quite terrifying, as his sudden reappearance would interrupt the idyllic relationship she had with her mother who was in the habit of taking her into her bed. This practice came to an abrupt end with the arrival of a brother when Mrs X was two-and-a-half years old. There was no difficulty in ascertaining when the patient began to hate her mother, but I was never able to establish when the father actually died, as Mrs X mentioned at various times that this had occurred when she was three, three-and-a-half, four, or four-and-a-half years old, thus suggesting that psychically her father had died at moments of maximal rage and hate. But no sooner had she acknowledged that she felt some guilt about his death ('the sort of thing one is told in analysis') than she would promptly deny it, reminding me she had once been shown a letter in which father had expressed regret that she was not a boy. 'Do you blame me for wanting to be a boy?' she asked again and again, at the same time despairing that, as another male chauvinist, I would ever understand it, never quite realizing how much she wanted to be loved by this man.

My early impression of this patient was that, alongside deep feelings of guilt, subjected to a considerable degree of erotization, she carried a conviction of being the victim of external circumstances and adverse fate, which exonerated her from taking any responsibility for running into unpleasant situations. Thus she would say: 'With mother preferring my brother, and God, an essentially male figure, there was no protection whatsoever for me. It was a matter of avoiding the bullets; it was life in a concentration camp.' Because of sudden and frequent switches in the transference, it was impossible for me to be sure whether she hated men, with whom she 'got on ever so well', more than women, who were 'pretty useless'. On the other hand, she was very frank in rejecting the idea that she was getting something from the analysis. If I ever drew her attention to her appreciation of some work that we had done, she would become abusive, or would be late for her sessions. On one occasion I showed her that she was determined not to give me any satisfaction although she seemed to be involved with her analysis. She thought about this, quietly smiling to herself, and eventually she said that on the last night before parting, she and John had made love. She had the best orgasm of her life, though admittedly this had not been a very frequent experience for her. Working through this insight and its implications in the transference made her feel that she ought to look for a suitable heterosexual partner, especially because being so much older than Tim, it was impossible to know when he would go off for good with one of his 'queer friends', whom she disliked so much. There was a problem though, as Tim was very jealous and possessive and would not tolerate her 'taking a man into their bed'. The two of them were sharing a bed whenever possible, travelling together on business ventures, not minding about being seen together at social gatherings. Nevertheless, Mrs X did create some opportunities for herself by meeting some old friend, usually someone living abroad. But in spite of some good heterosexual experiences, she would always come back to Tim with renewed intensity of feelings, in spite of the obvious frustration involved, claiming that masturbation could well take care of it.

A sudden positive development in the transference, due to my insisting on reviewing the excessive fee she had offered to pay for her sessions, made it possible for us to look at the similarity in the relationship she had with the homosexual friend, and myself. I was then informed that, like Tim, I was now in a sort of limbo, neither male nor female. She rejected the idea that she was as frustrated with me as she was with Tim, yet this enabled us to begin to look closely at her latent homosexuality. Her hatred and contempt for lesbians had no bounds. She could not even believe that I might not share her general views on what she regarded as the inferiority of the female sex. Nevertheless the idea that she was using her homosexual friend to get rid of her own homosexuality was beginning to make some impact, and seemed to be worth considering.

The session I shall report in some detail followed a stormy period in the analysis, precipitated by her late resumption of the sessions after an annual holiday, through an illness, and her annoyance at my interpretation that she had added an extra week for good measure to punish me for being away for such a long time. My fall from limbo was immediate as she saw this as an attempt to restore my male superiority. Like her drunken father, I was beating her with my interpretations, and furthermore, not being satisfied that she had given up John to please the analyst, I now wanted her to give up Tim as well.

On the previous day, my receptionist had reported that Mrs X had gone to the lavatory after the session and had not locked the door. Someone had tried to get in and had been startled to find her there. Mrs X began the session saying that yesterday she had to use the lavatory because she had a very heavy period. She went on to mention that a funny thing had happened during the night to scare poor Tim out of his wits, as she had bled profusely, all over the bed, sheets, nightie, blood everywhere. I felt that Mrs X was gloating over Tim's dismay and also thought that the so-called funny event in the night contained a preconscious reference to the funny event during the day when she was in the lavatory. But my patient continued, saying that she now knew that she and Tim would never make love, although they were so well adjusted. She added: 'Tim is ever so amorous these days. He lies right up against me but you know he has never had an erection when he has been in bed with me. He takes care of me in every way.' As she was silent, I said that she had mentioned quite often in the past that Tim was very motherly but she never mentioned the frustration of lying against a perfect specimen of manhood as she had described him to me, especially if he was so amorous. She interrupted me abruptly to say in a slightly harsh voice: 'I know, I know, it is a kind of suffering. I am used to it. It's better than nothing, considering all the suffering in my life.' She now began a long-drawn out recapitulation of the fact that she had lost her husband so young; that she had these two miscarriages; that she spent ten years with a man who brought young women home, and so on. When I got a chance, I chose to re-open the issue of frustration which she was denying, bringing it back into the transference. I might have said nothing at all as she again immersed herself in gloomy reminiscences. 'You must have forgotten how I have suffered all my life, what with my father beating me. You never say anything about that. I had a dream last night. Tim had been menstruating at the same time as me. He said, well, now we can make love.' She was silent for two or three minutes. I then reminded her that only yesterday she had told me how she hated the thought of making love to a woman and that if she did so she feared she would lose her sense of identity. This time she was really angry. Raising her voice, she said: 'You would, too, if you had spent the first years of your life with my mother. She cuddled me to extinction until my brother was born. And I can tell you that my mother was most erotic with me. I know, as I have watched her with babies. Even now she is seductive with me until my brother comes into the room. Since I was two-and-a-half I did not let anyone touch me. By eleven I was entirely capable of running my life. But those early years I cannot forget.' I then said it was clearly so as she seemed to have a compulsive need to recreate the same situation of getting close to someone, getting excited and frustrated at the same time, perhaps hoping she could get rid of the whole thing. To my surprise she replied: 'Yes, yes it is possible. I know it is rather masochistic but how can I get out of it? That old friend I told you about wants to marry me but he is ever so dull, besides he will want me to get rid of Tim and that I do not wish to do. Anyway, last night I had another dream, one I often have. We were in a death camp; that is what I often dream about. We were eating off filthy bowls. It made me sick. I vomited a mixture of blood and phlegm. This woman must have had tuberculosis. I had all those filthy insects crawling all over me.' The alarm clock had woken her and I felt she had regretted the interruption and, unusually for her, she seemed to be upset that the session was over. Before going, with one foot off the couch, she said: 'Now you know why I am so attracted to Jewish men. I can easily picture them in a death camp. I feel so sorry for them.'

A lot of this material was old but what was new was of considerable interest, especially because, with some flashes of insight, there was also some expression of appropriate affect. The two dreams opened up a new phase in the analysis in which the patient's masturbation could be looked at in close detail. The perverted nature, centred around castrated males and females, was very much in evidence, as well as some fantasies about the phallic mother. The internalization of father's bad penis, reflected in her catastrophic relationships with men, was well in keeping with my final assessment of her predicament of being in keeping with erotogenic masochism.

SEXUAL DEVIANCY: TREATABLE AND UNTREATABLE

To decide who and what is treatable is no easy matter. The bizarre nature of the symptom can make us feel out of our depth, whilst the magnitude of the commitment can make us feel apprehensive. Most patients are likely to have hesitated a very long time before seeking help. During this waiting period they have often become depressed and vaguely anxious. Their awareness that they are defending themselves against some unthinkable pain makes them less than communicative.

The first encounter is crucial, in so far as the patient may succeed in persuading the therapist that there is little that can be done. That no one should be forced into therapy hardly requires mention. It is generally agreed that when someone's potential is not fully developed, treatment should be offered. But the imaginary threat that psychotherapy could interfere with limited sublimation may be very hard to dispel (Glover, 1964).

Quite often we are confronted by requests for intervention from very successful individuals who present themselves arrogantly, challenging, and frankly contemptuous of what we have to offer. Thus a French analyst has recently asked the question: 'What should a welfare worker say to a man who boasts about his perversion?' (Dekhlei, 1984, p. 107).

Is it, then, our narcissism, or omnipotence, which can be so often disguised by a desire to do what we can, at all times, and against all odds, that induces us to accept someone who is likely to be out of our reach, as a result of a clear absence of motivation for change?

I should point out that many perverts who present themselves in a defiant mood, could also be hypomanic. It will be only too obvious that this is a defence against the experience of depression and in all probability is a hopeful sign. These cases must not be rejected, even if it is likely that the central symptom will defeat us.

In determining suitability, we shall look at the ego organization through which the impulses operate; the mechanisms by which they are controlled, and that will include the development of the reality sense; but in the last resort the more clear-cut indications for therapeutic intervention will be found in perverts prone to compulsive re-enactments. The tendency towards taking risks and breaking the law, an added source of excitement, is sufficient for them to accept whatever is offered but they will still require careful handling in the initial stages.

Those who have committed offences always carry the danger of recidivism but the experience of having been convicted can become a very great incentive for therapy. Setbacks in life, disappointments, loss of a partner, can lead to the committing of perverted acts, which are not wholly ego-syntonic and, as such, will be very amenable to treatment. These are the cases which will demonstrate quite forcibly the relevance of castration anxiety and penis envy. Profound disorders of personality and character are doubtful propositions for psychotherapy, but not necessarily for psychoanalysis, even if we can expect that it will become interminable. The same applies to those cases which are associated with psychosomatic disturbances.

I would also be disinclined to offer analytic psychotherapy to either male or female perverts who relied on sado-masochistic enactments in order to achieve orgasm, as it may be difficult, if not impossible, to prevent the establishment of a sado-masochistic transference. On the other hand, we should not be discouraged by restrictions of ego structure and functions as those can be successfully released in the course of therapy.

In brief, I would say the best prognosis is to be found amongst those cases which, from the beginning, will show us clearly the source of suffering and conflict, also revealing the role played by the parent, especially the mother, in the formation of the symptom. Being able to establish the quality and degree of excitement, the nature of risk-taking elements involved, and the presence of depression, are all favourable pointers.

Should we then decline to intervene in the cases of countless numbers of people who tell us they have no desire to be rid of the perversion but nevertheless feel the need of help for all sorts of other reasons? It is very common, particularly for transvestites and homosexuals to come forward with such propositions when they are encountering difficulties at work or in interpersonal relations. We should never reject these potentially difficult patients but we should take particular care in assessing their conditions so that throughout the therapy we are constantly aware that we are treading on dangerous ground. In the therapeutic situation things can go wrong, irrevocably at times if, under pressure, we are caught off guard. Here is a brief example.

Whilst treating a homosexual who had stipulated that his homosexuality should be left untouched, there were some sexual murders in London involving homosexuals. Suddenly my patient became anxious and afraid I might attack him as he lay on the couch. This led me to interpret the more dangerous aspects of his perversion, showing him that he felt himself to be at risk because of his very passive behaviour towards his sadistic partners. I never saw him again, a sad end to what promised to be a good therapeutic result, as he was on the point of deciding on drastically changing the nature of his work.

It is relevant to note that there has always been considerable psychoanalytic interest in the treatment of homosexuals since Freud expressed his doubts about the possibility of altering their pathology (Freud, 1920). I would say, though, that providing we exclude the more severe cases, there is a possibility of helping some others with regard to the ambivalence towards their own sex and also the tendency to commit offences which threaten their social status and capacity to earn a living in certain professions.

SPECIAL FEATURES OF TRANSFERENCE AND COUNTERTRANSFERENCE IN THE SEXUAL DEVIATIONS

A great deal of misunderstanding arises from the assumption that nothing is happening when treating perverts unless the symptom appears in the transference and I shall now try to clarify some of the issues involved. Although we can rest assured that a patient's need to live within a sado-masochistic relationship will soon appear in the transference, it could hardly be expected that any exhibitionism or fetishism should manifest themselves in our consulting rooms. On the other hand, symbolic representation of the symptom, or its mental equivalent, will find its way into the therapy but this will occur in later stages.

Arlow (1986) has recently commented on this issue, discussing Glasser's and McDougall's papers on 'Identification in the perversions' at the last International Psychoanalytical Congress in Hamburg, when he expressed the view that 'We do not have to empathize with someone who is a fetishist or an exhibitionist. All we can do, is to empathize with feelings of fragmentation and so on' (p. 245). Although I appreciate Arlow's intention in underlining the primitive feelings involved in treating perverts, I consider that his recommendation does not go far enough, as I believe we need more than empathy in developing a transference and countertransference relationship with a pervert.

From almost our first contacts, we are struck by the pervert's tendency to treat a partner (and now the therapist) as if he or she were not a human being. This suggests that the perversion reaches out to mental representations which have an unbearable emotional overloading aggravated by intense hostility and aggression. In my view it is essential to see this dehumanization of the object as an attempt to avoid profound feelings of guilt arising from a persecutory superego. Inevitably, this state of mind will figure prominently in what is known as the perverse transference. From the very beginning the therapist is aware of being perversely treated and this will require the most careful handling, as inept responses will create a persecutory feeling in the patient. In these cases we shall hold our hand more than we would be inclined to do in treating neurotics or borderline states, who could also exhibit this particular type of transference. Furthermore, the patient's clinging to his own private psychic reality, disregarding all other kinds of realities, can also create a sense of perversity, through an inability to grasp what the analyst is saying, or even acknowledging the nature of the help being offered. In this context it is relevant to note that 'perverse' is not synonymous with 'perverted'. Whilst perverse behaviour in individuals of all ages is rooted in oral and anal sadism, perverted acts are always linked with a sexual aim, directed at facilitating genital orgasm.

Whilst all this goes on almost from the very start, we are also likely to be confronted by various manifestations directly attributable to the profound underlying anxieties, especially those concerned with separation and fear of merging. These anxieties will at times appear to have psychotic intensity and could be associated with an exacerbation of the perverted activity. The one-to-one situation, therefore, seems to play havoc with long-standing defences. Glasser has summed up the situation we encounter with the more disturbed patient as follows: 'the patient conceives the state of oneness with the object he desires and fears as a passively merging with; being engulfed by it; getting into and being intruded by it' (Glasser, 1979b, p. 280).

In my experience, most patients fight bitterly against the interpretation of these anxieties and counter-attack by erotizing every aspect of the proceedings. Hostility, and the emerging of yet more primitive feelings, are stalled for a time. Some other patients, though, react with an upsurge of sadism, showing how this is the only way they feel they can make a contact with us.

Another possible development is that the patient takes little or no notice of our interventions, calmly denying or discounting any involvement with us or the therapy. When this happens, we are concurrently forced into being more and more a captive audience, listening to the stereotyped accounts of perverted behaviour, coloured by lurid, and at times disturbing, details which create a serious challenge to our tolerance, sense of reality and deeper feelings.

Attempts to de-erotize what is claimed to be highly exciting will expose us to the risk of being judgemental, moralizing or confrontational. In any case, the patients' libidinal investment is such as to alert them to all attempts at de-erotization, increasing the resistance against abandoning what is not only erotic but also very essential to their peace of mind.

With so much eroticism pervading the sessions, it will not be unusual for a patient to unwittingly bring his or her fantasies about the parents' sex life. Should this happen, we may be forced into the position in which the patient has been as a child, a simple reverse transference phenomenon (King, 1978), not easily accepted or understood by a patient.

On one occasion, a way out of this situation occurred unexpectedly. For several months I had been listening to a patient's description of some obsessional rituals, which contained elements of voyeurism, fetishism and sadism. The ritual required the patient's wife to parade in front of him wearing underwear which allowed him to see, and not to see, her genitals. These preliminaries to intercourse could go on for hours and would only come to an end when the woman had reached a pitch of excitation and rage. In consequence, the sexual life of this couple was very limited, causing continuous violent arguments between them. My periodical interpretations that I was forced into the role of an unwilling observer, had in fact made no impression whatever. The time came when, having listened to one more account of the same old story, I yawned irrepressibly and rather loudly. The patient was extremely annoyed and accused me of destroying all his erotic pleasure. Not quite, as a lot more work was needed to make him realize that, in inducing sleepiness in me, he had recreated the sleepy state of his childhood, as he watched his parents preparing for bed at night, for the first five years of his life. This was a case treated by once-a-week analytic psychotherapy over some years. When we had to part, this couple's sexual life was much more straightforward but there was little change in their sado-masochistic way of relating to each other.

Some sexual deviations respond to therapy, in spite of the patient's fight against re-experiencing anxieties about fragmentation, fear of engulfment by, and separation from, the primary object, represented in the therapist. Good results are still obtainable, even when somatic disturbances appear in lieu of the symptom. Failure, on the other hand, is often attributed to the patient's being unable to make full use of what is offered. Over the years I have been inclined to think that stress and strain on the therapist play an important part in the outcome. To have one's efforts ignored, belittled and dismissed, hour after hour, is unpleasant, to say the least. The patient's inventiveness and capacity for springing surprises can stimulate interest at first but the continuous occurrence of re-enactments may challenge our neutrality. It is only when we can reach out to what lies behind the symptom that we feel restored to our therapeutic respect and ability. But before we get there we may react by becoming less and less involved in the relationship and finally we are overcome by despondency. At this stage, consideration should be given to referral to a colleague.

I am aware that I have only been able to offer a limited answer to my earlier question about the effect of treating patients who are constantly attacking reality.* Our efforts will be directed not only at not becoming affected by such attacks, which is too obvious, but also at not being dazzled

* At a Wednesday meeting of the Vienna Society, on 13 January 1907, there was a discussion of the sexual perversions. Freud spoke very briefly, mentioning '*Die Aufhebung der Realität* (ähnlich wie beim Theater)' as being essential for the establishment of perverse fantasies. It seems to me that the suspension of reality is a very apt description of what occurs in perversions. It is also interesting that the Concordance does not indicate that Freud made use of the expression in any writings on the subject.

by their insistence on the exquisite nature of their pleasures. Even more to the point, it will be essential for us to realize that we are not dealing with sexual madness, as it has been alleged. These patients are fighting for their survival; those who come to us for help are the more courageous amongst them. They are the representatives of a group of unhappy people who can indeed benefit from the fact that they are offered a human kind of relationship which gives them some sense of security. The value of this simple experience cannot be assessed in any way I know, and we must equally value what we have to offer.

In this presentation I have made little distinction between psychoanalysis and psychotherapy. Leaving aside all practical considerations, the choice of one or other method will be based on the patient's capacity to tolerate the intensity of the one, or the restrictions of the other. Over-stimulation can be as damaging as deprivation.

Limited therapeutic resources could induce us to concentrate our efforts in certain directions. For instance, the particular nature of the basic psychopathology I have described, could be an indication for group rather than individual therapy. I have seen some people benefit from an initial period in a group, followed by an individual approach, or vice versa. Quite often, the anxiety displayed by some patients at the first interview will dictate, there and then, what is more likely to be tolerated. Even the sex of the therapist may prove a handicap at times, or a facilitating element in what is to come.

I believe that this presentation has confirmed Glover's contention that perverted acts are defensive in nature, often associated with disorder of character and personality. I wish I could end on an optimistic note but this is an area of work where there is little room for complacency. It has been said that Freud captured the capacity of the pervert to believe in illusions, in my opinion the cornerstone of his contribution to the understanding of disturbed sexuality. But he has, to some extent, misled us into believing that the unravelling of illusions and the underlying deep-seated anxieties, would lead us to the easy relief of human suffering. Our inheritance has been hard to live up to but we shall go on working without too many illusions, but in the belief that we can be of some use to our patients.

16 VARIATIONS ON SOME FREUDIAN THEMES*

AS WE HAVE REACHED the end of a long week in the course of which most of you have been working very hard, I felt that in this address I should offer you something of a diversion. All I propose to do is to share some thoughts that have occurred to me during the last few years on all kinds of subjects that matter a great deal to all of us. I may have already published some of them in one form or another, but the majority of them are casual reflections or old annotations hurriedly scribbled on a scrap of paper in response to contributions from colleagues and patients. What I have to offer could well be regarded as somewhat iconoclastic but wisdom does not come with age, as Bernard Shaw once said. Only experience increases as we get old and that can be oppressive or liberating.

As we approach the end of the century, psychoanalysis appears to become even more difficult than we ever suspected. Some of the changes that have been introduced have certainly not been easy to accept. Yet whenever a more audacious view, possibly a challenge to classical analysis, is put forward, it is *de rigueur* to quote Freud, no matter how often he had already contradicted or altered that view himself. The haunting thought for most psychoanalysts is: What would Freud have said about this or that?

It is said that when Robert Schumann heard Chopin playing his Variations on a theme by Mozart (*Là ci darem la mano*, to be precise) he turned to a friend, saying: 'That man is a genius.' Would Freud have said anything like that of some of the innovators in our field during the last momentous

* This paper was the Presidential address at the 34th International Psychoanalytical Congress in Hamburg, July 1985.

forty years? We would like to think, though, that in the face of some real advances, even if they could have been considered variations at first, Freud might have been as generous as Tchaikovsky. 'Look at what he has done to my piece – he has altered everything,' bewailed Tchaikovsky, when the manuscript of his *Variations on a Rococo Theme* was returned to him by its first performer, Wilhelm Fitzenhagen. 'The devil take it,' then exclaimed the composer, 'let it stand as it is.' And it has for 108 years.

Freud, of course, drew the line when the variations turned out to be a real attack on the setting, as was the case with Ferenczi, whom he admired very much, as we all know. Variations should, of course, adhere to the theme as much as possible; subtle ones are very acceptable and can even go unrecognized by most people, in music or in psychoanalysis, as the case may be.

THE SETTING

I would like here to take as my first Freudian theme, the setting, which is under constant threat both by analysts and patients alike. What was a stroke of genius by Freud, who suddenly was able to create the same control situation for all our patients, has also proved the ground on which many battles are won or lost.

For some patients, psychoanalysis is like crossing the Rubicon; there is no going back. The setting facilitates the analytic process for most people, but is against it for others. In the framework we provide for the patients, they have freedom, intimacy and protection as they have never experienced before. The physical setting is the embodiment of the mental setting; its very stability and constancy invite reactions by both parties in the encounter whenever it is broken, whether this is by accident, or through interruptions that are planned in advance or are routine ones. I still remember my shock when, after six months' therapy, my first psychoanalytic patient became psychotic during the summer holidays, delaying her return. When the same long break occurred during the treatment of my second patient, I used all my powers of persuasion with my supervisor to agree that I should offer him sessions during the holiday period – and at another clinic, to boot. The patient's anxiety reached unforeseen heights, aggravated by the change to unfamiliar surroundings. The only redeeming feature was that at least I learnt not to repeat those mistakes.

If patients feel secure in the framework, it seems paradoxically inevitable that attacks should occur. Like the mother's body, the setting is attacked if it is experienced as such. This lends itself to all sorts of misunderstandings as the playful attacks of an infant are at times difficult to distinguish from true hostility, especially also when such attacks occur when the patient is getting deeper into analysis and appears secure. Attacks are also not that infrequent when a patient begins to feel separate and has to prove it to himself and the analyst. These are all areas of collusion which are so well known that they hardly need mentioning, perhaps. My only reason for doing so is that sometimes accounts of sessions create the impression that the analyst is offended if a patient is late, or if he misses sessions. The fact remains that the setting is there to be attacked, distorted and disproved.

Whilst all this is understandable in the patient, it will not be so if it originates in the therapist, as after all any attack on the framework is always likely to become an attack on the analytic process, which is unforgivable. An example of this is to be found in the analyst's persistent lateness, which is unacceptable, whilst a patient's lateness does not disturb the setting. This takes me to the much debated issues of the frequency and duration of the sessions. Unhappily, there are fewer and fewer places in the world where analysis is carried out five times a week, not even in the case of training analysis. Far too many analysts appear to subscribe to the idea that three times a week is good enough. It may be so, but again, this is one of those variations that might require a paper of its own, at the end of which I think the supporters of both views, for and against three times a week analysis, would retain their original positions, which are based on rationalizations, rigidity, etc.

But what of the duration of the sessions? Donnet (1979) deals with this issue, carefully avoiding the problem of frequency, and noting how the framework (*le cadre*) is at the same time the barrier (to incest) and the enveloping aspect (of the maternal body). He reports in a footnote as follows: 'An analysand of Lacan as he lies down begins: "At last" . . . "Good," said Lacan, terminating the session' (p. 256). Of course, anyone can see that there is something highly stimulating, provocative and capable of mobilizing a lot of heat in response to such behaviour on the part of the analyst, but what has this got to do with psychoanalysis? Is it worth discussing? We all know that we are not too sure of our reasons for fixing the duration of the sessions at 45 or 50 minutes. Some time ago, as I was having some difficulty in finding times, I decided to introduce 45-minute sessions into my practice. I thought of starting with two patients who came from countries where this arrangement was commonly accepted. I had not reckoned with their capacity to catch up with prevalent local customs.

In one instance the analysis simply did not seem to get going until the patient blurted out that he was feeling utterly deprived of his five minutes, especially since he had watched the comings and goings of other patients. What I learnt from this minor episode was that it is advisable to give exactly the same time to each analysand. What is valuable uniformity, though, becomes confused with rigidity by those who are critical of the method, or perhaps those who cannot accept its limitations and constraints.

In 1985, with the vast accumulation of our experience, we should perhaps not need to resort to quoting Freud on the topic of activity and abstinence on the part of the analyst (Freud, 1919), but from time to time it is worth remembering.

Sandler (1983) has alluded to permissible, or inevitable parameters. What does he mean, I would ask? How do we distinguish between parameters and injunctions stipulating that people should not do this or that? For instance, some variations do seem to tend to destroy the very fabric of analysis, mostly when the purely interpretative technique is abandoned. A variety of reasons are offered for the breaking away from this approach, under the pretext of the patient's psychopathology, but I often feel that such explanations tend to conceal an unadmitted need on the part of the analyst for something other than the use of words.

It is very easy, though, for psychoanalysts to introduce harmless parameters still compatible with the development and continuations of the analytic process, such as prolonging the session a little; inviting the patient to sit up; offering a tissue to a patient in distress; taking an occasional telephone call, etc. It is another matter to introduce parameters in the form of holding a patient's hand; touching his or her forehead, or any other physical contact. We do know that an infant needs contact with mother, but it does not follow that an analyst should act it out with his patients. In my view, it is for the analyst to accept first of all that the patient has every right to want to change the rules of the game and that that is a privilege which has to be denied to the analyst.

What concerns me here is that psychoanalysts still wish to claim that it is psychoanalysis when direct and persistent physical contact has been permitted. There are indeed many other approaches (which again do not have to be acknowledged even as psychotherapies) that could be used for the treatment of psychosis, or other similar conditions refractory to psychoanalysis, as we know it.

Related to this topic is the issue of social contacts between the participants in the analytic encounter. I suppose some social contact with analysands in training is inevitable in the smaller societies. Yet it would be preferable to keep such events within reasonable limits. On the other hand, frequent socializing with patients, even when it appears to be rather harmless, is seldom without complications, bitterly regretted by all in due course.

How much of the reality aspect of the relationship with the analysand should be taken up by the analyst is another matter for debate, as it leads to the introduction of parameters, but I would disagree wholeheartedly with Greenson (1965) who insisted we should go out of our way to do so. This is the very argument used by our patients to avoid the full impact of the transference which evolves in a setting that tends to favour unreality of perceptions, fantasy development and the reliving of old desires side by side with present ones.

This should not be taken to mean that I deliberately favour ignoring the reality aspects of the analysand's life experiences, his way of existing and his interactions with the external world (cf. Bollas, 1983).

What price do we pay for preserving the setting? It seems to me that the analyst's attitude is even more important than the physical framework at times. What is the point of never smiling, never shaking hands with patients, never laughing with them? This shows that the setting can be idealized. As it is linked with reality, ignoring it is an assault on it and can induce hallucinatory states. But when we consider, however carefully, this aspect of our work, we shall always conclude that only words matter, and words can fail and frustrate an analysand as much as they do us.

THE TRANSFERENCE

If the introduction of a stable setting can be regarded as a stroke of genius, the discovery of the transference must surely be looked upon as the most revolutionary development in the treatment of the mentally ill and in the understanding of interpersonal relationships. Its validity is often challenged, belittled, ridiculed, mishandled and feared by vast numbers of people. Psychiatrists spend much time trying to discount it and warning their junior colleagues against it, as if it were an infectious disease. Basically it has stood the test of time.

Yet, not all is well with the transference. That this is so, is clearly demonstrable by the fact that any discussion on the transference nowadays has to start with the author's definition of it, something I am deliberately refraining from doing. The situation has become somewhat worse since psychoanalysts have familiarized themselves with the challenge of presenting detailed descriptions of sessions, showing exactly what they do. This often provides our colleagues with the opportunity of presenting their own views on what is and what is not the transference. Thus the Congress Hall corridors resound with statements such as: 'He or she missed the transference altogether; he misunderstood the transference', and so on. What is missing in these comments is the appreciation that no matter how accurate the report is, the transference is not easily conveyed to an audience or even an intimate friend, as it is an emotional experience, stretching over a fleeting moment, or weeks, or months. The state of intimacy created by the transference is not for public consumption, neither is it possible to convey the atmosphere of the setting and the innumerable details which are seldom, if ever, mentioned. How often are we told in detail of the physical setting which forms the background to sessions, so carefully reported? How often is it mentioned whether a patient has access to a bathroom? How often are we informed of the arrangements which are made to prevent an analysand coming in contact with another? Does the analyst take notes or, indeed, is a tape-recorder used?

The rush of definitions and counter-definitions continues. As late as 1970 Sandler and his co-workers could mention no less than five different ways in which transference could be used by psychoanalysts. These included the use of the term interchangeably for the therapeutic alliance; the emergence of infantile feelings and attitudes in new form; the transference of defence; all inappropriate thoughts, attitudes, fantasies, etc., which are revivals from the past and experienced in relation to the analyst, which means seeing all that occurs in the consulting room and in the patient's associations as an expression of the patient's involvement with the analyst.

In a paper by Betty Joseph (1985) entitled 'Transference: the total situation,' we read: 'transference . . . by definition must include everything that the patient brings into the relationship. What he brings in can best be gauged by our focusing our attention on what is going on within the relationship and how he is using the analyst, alongside and beyond what he is saying' (p. 448). A very sweeping statement which is likely to ensure that the broadening of the transference is here to stay, just as it is most unlikely that the importance of the here-and-now interpretations will ever be lost to practising analysts. But what appears to be a final statement is open to challenge, as it essentially relies on the ubiquitous, much abused use of interpretations based on the mechanism of projective identification. This brilliant contribution from Melanie Klein is, in my opinion, being allowed to lose its impact. Let us assume, as few would doubt, that this way of communication between mother and child is closely reproduced between analyst and patient. Should it not change, or at least alter after years and years of analysis? And if it is also prevalent in some form of mental disorders, as it unquestionably is, should it also never be modified? But is it ever likely to alter if the analyst insists on understanding everything that takes place in the consulting room in those terms? I for one regard this as another passing phase in analytic technique, comparable to the outbreak of pathological envy that we witnessed throughout the sixties and early seventies. Again I would like to predict, and I do so entirely because I have complete faith in the prevalence of good reason amongst analysts, that the all important here-and-now, or shall I say you-and-me, interpretations will in time lose the mechanical flavour which is so much in evidence in some analyses at present.

Towards the end of her life, Paula Heimann held similar views, which she expressed even more forcibly. Bollas (1983) quotes her as saying: 'There are those who insist that all the patients tell us in analysis is a metaphor of the patient–analyst relationship. That, she said, is not interpreting the transference . . . It is a translation, not an interpretation' (p. 264, my translation). As the stress on here-and-now interpretation in conjunction with the widespread use of projection identification has been pioneered by the Kleinian school, it would be wrong to assume that all Kleinians subscribe to the rather extreme picture which has been presented here. Abuses are in fact to be found mainly amongst the imitators of that school and the less experienced right across the psychoanalytic spectrum.

Nevertheless, Kleinians do claim to have a particular interest in pregenital happenings and very early object relations, insisting that they are badly neglected by others (an unjust allegation, in my view), and they must take a great deal of responsibility for encouraging the increasing length of analyses. The situation has been very adequately summed up by Rossi (1985), a contributor to a discussion on 'Reconstruction' recently held by the European Psychoanalytical Federation. He said:

We contribute to the excessive strength of the nostalgia for the lost object that everyone brings into analysis . . . The nostalgia referred to here is considered, in current psychoanalysis, as being stimulated . . . by a situation linked with maternal reverie. The intolerable parts of the self find a suitable and available container . . . that refers back to the mother–child relationship. Interpretation of this can stimulate dependence to an excessive extent, and this might perhaps explain the enormous prolongation of the duration of analysis which we so often see nowadays. (p. 39)

I can think of few other areas in our work where it is more apparent that theory can be adopted as a result of weakness in one's own temperament.

This takes me to my next major Freudian theme, the countertransference, which at the moment of writing is plagued by uncertainties, confusions, dogmatic statements and equally dogmatic counter-statements.

THE COUNTERTRANSFERENCE

'I have been struck by the widespread belief amongst candidates that the countertransference is nothing but a source of trouble. Many candidates are afraid and feel guilty when they become aware of feelings towards their patients and consequently aim at avoiding any emotional response and at becoming completely unfeeling and detached' (Heimann, 1950, p. 81). In common with many other great discoverers, Paula Heimann, whom I have just quoted at length, did not realize the nature of the impact on future generations of practitioners of her statement that the countertransference could in fact be an asset, if properly used to monitor feelings generated in the analyst by the patient's associations and behaviour. It has now become commonplace for candidates, following the example of their elders, indiscriminately to attribute everything that evolves in the consulting room to their patients. Supervisors must indeed find it increasingly more difficult to direct the candidate's attention to the possibility that some of his emotional responses are in the realm of his or her own pathology. In group supervision, it is not unusual nowadays to encounter a collusive tendency between all the members of the group, including the seminar leaders, to attribute all sorts of things to the patient's influence. Should the group fail to decipher an extremely difficult piece of material, the chances are that the general consensus of opinion is that the patient is paralysing everyone's mind, via the reporting analyst (cf. Joseph, 1985). I am not sure whether there is an idealization of psychoanalysis here, or a reluctance to admit that we may not know something. Of course, such phenomena as I have briefly described could well occur in exceptional circumstances, but what is a remarkable piece of insight in the hands of an experienced analyst is subject to imitation that can spread like wildfire in psychoanalytic institutions.

In so far as what the analyst experiences is currently almost always attributable to the projective identifications originating from the patient, it is quite in order to disclose all that the therapist is feeling. Pontalis (1975) wrote sceptically about these disclosures several years ago, warning us that 'we could not in all truth talk about the countertransference, or say the truth about it. The stringency of this proposition is not attenuated by public exercises of the pretended auto-analysis by the analyst.' 'Ah,' laments Pontalis, 'these carefully distilled fragments, purified, displaced upwards (as if having reached our psychoanalytic maturity we only dream of Freud), how suspect is their moving frankness.' 'And,' he continues, 'what is more paradoxical than the presuppositions that: I see my blind spots, I hear what I am deaf to, the only thing I am sure of is that I have no preconceived ideas, and (furthermore) I am fully conscious of my unconscious' (p. 74, my translation). Harsh words, but not to be ignored, as the curiosity about what goes on in the analyst's mind is inexhaustible.

Let us now turn our attention to what is required of the analyst if he or she is to perform adequately during the sessions. The reliance on free-floating attention has not been altogether discarded but seems to belong essentially to classical analysis. This is logical if the therapist is constantly engaged in monitoring his reactions to the patient's projective identifications. Great stress is given on the other hand to Bion's (1970) recommendation that we should enter the session without desire, memory, understanding or preconceived ideas. All this seems quite reasonable, but if I understand Bion correctly we should approach each session with an empty mind, which is not the same thing as saying that no special weight should be given to the previous session. Also, I gather that, if we are tired we should not allow that to influence us; that 'we should not think of the end of the hour, or the week, or going on holiday' (Bion, quoted by Carpelan, 1981, p. 158).

In addition, another writer advises that 'the facial expressions (of the analyst) generally reflect the response of an internal object of the patient to the latter's material . . . placed outside . . . that is to say projected on to the analyst' (Racker, 1968, p. 27). An odd assumption, because if it were correct, it would make the use of the couch unnecessary, or perhaps contra-indicated. It would indeed be unfair to deprive the analysand of such valuable information about his inner world.

It strikes me that we are in danger here of attempting to create a super-human analyst, an effort likely to lead to unwholesome countertransference reactions. Research into the state of mind of the therapist is very necessary in order to establish with some degree of certainty what is pathological and what is an emotional response to the analysand's behaviour and associations. What to do with the source of information thus obtained is a matter which we shall not go into here. Briefly, though, I shall say that I only make a mental note of a sudden and passing emotional response to the patient's material and I only tend to deal with any such response when it is extended over several hours of analytical work. I could not ignore here the view of a small minority which proposes to share with the patient what has been experienced in the 'countertransference'. I believe this to be a pernicious practice since only very few people could take this kind of confrontation in their stride. There must be other ways and means that can be used to convey an analyst's personal experience to the patient without burdening the latter with the task of analysing us.

In common with many psychoanalysts, I have my idiosyncrasies about this controversial aspect of our work. For instance, I cannot accept the idea that the countertransference is the *transference* of the analyst to the analysand. The transference is a recapitulation of all that someone has experienced in his past and present life, internally and externally, all of which is relived in the here-and-now. As I recall it, the transference can be an invigorating or debilitating state of mind, stimulating or paralysing according to circumstances. How could that experience be compared to what occurs when we treat patients? How could we work if we were so affected in relation to eight or even ten persons in the course of a day's work? Only occasionally we encounter elements obviously reminiscent of a *transference*, and that is when the emotions of love and/or hate towards the patient have become unmanageable.

In my opinion, the term countertransference should be restricted to those instances when the analyst's pathology influences the understanding and management of the therapeutic situation. An example of this is when it impedes the unravelling of what originates from the patient himself or his internal objects which can at times too closely resemble those of the analyst.

In all other instances, I prefer to use the term 'emotional response' – a reflection, in my view, of what is occurring in the therapist, who will note it as being either appropriate or not. In both instances the responses will become the guiding line to the correct interpretation. I also feel that the use of the term underlines the importance that we should attach to the appraisals and verbalization of the affects which pervade the analytic encounter.

With such vast literature covering this basic Freudian theme, and so many variations in understanding and handling it, we can lose sight of the fact that many 'countertransference' problems originate in a lack of capacity on the part of the analyst to be alone. Psychoanalysis, as everyone knows, is one of the most solitary professions. Should the therapist feel too lonely in the course of the day, all sorts of complications may arise; amongst them is the possibility of the analyst becoming intrusive, pouring out interpretations.

Psychoanalysis is an art and for this reason it needs discipline – which is possibly the best rational explanation for the so-called training analysis.

TRAINING ANALYSIS

The training analysis – or, as some would say, the personal analysis of a future analyst – is an important and perhaps the worst example of a variation of the method; but, as it was Freud who thought of it, we have been able to accept it without demur for a very long time. However, rumblings of discontent about it have recently become more noticeable. Because I believe that in taking someone into a so-called training analysis, we perpetrate a devastating attack on the setting, quite apart from creating transference and countertransference problems, I am not amongst those who regard it as being indistinguishable from ordinary therapies. The complexities of training are such that for several years, the International Psychoanalytical Association has been forced to make special arrangements to discuss it at the time of the Congress. This is not the place or the time to enter into a detailed argument of the pros and cons for training but I shall limit myself to some random comments on what has appeared to me to be of relevance in making some distinction between the two types of psychoanalysis.

It is a paradox, for instance, that when an analysand is in training, it induces in us a strong urge to become therapeutic in both our attitude and approach. Casual remarks about our analysands, which we pick up here and there, mobilize our attention to some neglected area, at the same time threatening our self-esteem. We are also concerned at the prospect of sending someone into the professional world with crippling symptoms.

According to Pontalis (1975, p. 85) a pre-countertransference is implicit in our work, derived from instinctual and narcissistic sources, well beyond any identification with our analyst. We can also safely assume that some feelings will be mobilized in response to someone who intends to do exactly what we do, well before the analysis has got going in some instances. We are then forced to assume that the training analyst is a person who is well able to look after himself, by reason of considerable clinical experience, familiarity with theoretical and technical problems; all essential prerequisites if he has to meet what is a very challenging experience.

But what about the candidate-patient? I suppose he can escape the impact of the new situation in the early stages, although some complications will arise when he or she applies for training, having already introjected Freud, Klein, Bion or Winnicott and formed identifications with any of them. We all know, of course, how to handle intellectualizations. The more serious problem is that the candidate may come into his training analysis with a pre-transference condition, with a solid idealization of his analyst, having familiarized himself with his writings and areas of special interest. I am much less confident of our overall capacity to deal with that kind of idealization.

There are other major difficulties for the candidates to deal with, which are spared to analytically unambitious patients. For instance, on entering the Institute, candidates are confronted by the concretization of sibling rivalries. Meeting analytical brothers and sisters creates problems as serious as those created by the internal families they carry around within themselves. But all that is grist to the mill and eminently analysable. The real reckoning comes at the end of the training when a candidate expects that someone is going to find out what he has done with his analysis and this can become highly persecutory. Should such persecutory feelings escape analysis, there will be an interference with the candidate's adjustment within the Society. Some other analysands end up by identifying with the aggressors located in the teaching organizations, and not excluding their analysts. Within the transference, certain disturbances of identification are revived, at times leading to difficulties in functioning as an analyst and, later, identity problems. Worst of all are those cases which end up with pseudo-identification or frank imitation (Gaddini, 1984); eventually these people make the most of scientific criticism of psychoanalysis under the appearance of being original researchers with something valuable to say. Our French colleagues refer to them as the 'psychanalystes comme', the 'as if' psychoanalysts who have used mechanisms not unlike those to be found in Winnicott's false personality types.

I hope I shall be forgiven for having presented such a lopsided account of the outcome of training analysis. But my intention was to show that claims that there is no difference between training and ordinary analysis are, in my opinion, groundless.

The purpose of training is to foster the establishment of an appropriate psychoanalytic identity. I have read somewhere that for an analyst to establish his identity on ideology or on a technical or theoretical model is likely to lead to disaster. I agree with this notion, but only in a general way because I do believe we do need some model or models. Analysts, on the other hand, are particularly prone to be taken in by certain models and to incorporate them in a static manner. In a recent report on psychoanalytic thinking in Latin America, a group of Brazilian psychoanalysts write: 'We are without personality, peripheral to the influence which comes from outside . . . We are Kleinians, Bionians, Winnicottians, Lacanians, Kohutians, Hartmannians, Fairbairnians, Frankfurtians, etc.' Note the absence of Freud in that long list, but, as Winnicott once told me, we 'are all Freudians'. But let us not detract from what is a genuine *cri de coeur* from our Brazilian colleagues, who are probably less than aware of similar problems in other parts of the world. Although I sympathize with their appeal for 'urgent decolonization of the thinking of Latin American psychoanalysts' (Barreto *et al.*, 1984, pp. 628–9), I cannot agree with their suggestion for dealing with the dominance and plethora of variations of the Freudian method. Their recommendation is that we should rely on present-day currents which utilize the development of French structuralistic thinking based 'around the magisterial work of Lacan' or leaning more towards the existentialism of Heidegger and Jean-Paul Sartre. As all these are beginning to be somewhat outdated positions there is a danger here of adding more intractable variations. On the other hand, their call for new translations of Freud's writings is now fast becoming a matter which is treated with urgency throughout the internal community.

Is life as a psychoanalyst as grim as I may have unwittingly represented? It is true, of course, that we are more restrained in our behaviour than our early predecessors used to be. No one would think of celebrating a good interpretation by getting up to light a cigar, as Freud used to do; or reading a long, complex but very useful interpretation on a Monday, after a very difficult week, as Melanie Klein is reported as having done on at least one occasion (verbal statement by Dr W. Clifford M. Scott at an English-speaking Conference in London). Some of the older generation still with us do seem to have behaved much more supportively towards their candidates than we would dream of doing now.

We may well ask ourselves the question, whether we could, in fact, go back to the method as Freud first discovered it. I doubt that it would be possible; indeed, it would be unwise.

Some of the variations I have touched upon in this address are certainly here to stay and one day they will be so deeply incorporated into the theory and technique of psychoanalysis that they will no longer be regarded as variations as such. It is also my impression that a great deal of what is written nowadays is less intended to say anything particularly new, than to explore why we are doing certain things and whether there are different ways of doing them.

At times I even ask myself a rather unfair question. How would some of these remarkable contributions compare with say: Freud's early statement on the dynamics of transference (1912); or Melanie Klein's paper on the origins of transference (1952); or Strachey's simple statement on the mutative interpretations (1934); or Heimann's comments on the countertransference (1950)? I would suggest that reading those papers again induces a feeling of pleasure and satisfaction, only comparable to the exhilaration we experienced in listening to a great piece of music for the very first time in our lives.

BIBLIOGRAPHY

All books are published in London unless otherwise indicated.

Aarons, Z. A. (1962) 'Indications for analysis and problems of analysability', *Psychoanal. Q.* 31: 514–31.

Abe, K. and Moran, P. A. P. (1969) 'Parental age of homosexuals', *Br. J. Psychol.* 115: 313–18.

Abraham, K. (1926) 'The psychological relation between sexuality and alcoholism', *Int. J. Psycho-Anal.* 7: 2–10.

Anouilh, J. (1941) *Eurydice*, in *Pièces noires*. Paris: La Table Ronde, 1958.

Anthony, E. J. (1970) 'Two contrasting types of adolescent depression and their treatment', *J. Amer. Psychoanal. Assn* 18: 41–59.

Arlow, J. (1986) 'Discussion of papers by J. McDougall and M. Glasser. Panel on identification in the perversions', *Int. J. Psycho-Anal.* 67: 245–50.

Asch, S. S. (1976) 'Varieties of negative therapeutic reaction and problems of technique', *J. Amer. Psychoanal. Assn* 24: 383–408.

Bachrach, H. M. (1983) 'On the concept of analyzability', *Psychoanal. Q.* 52: 180–204.

Bak, R. C. (1970) 'Psychoanalysis today', *J. Amer. Psychoanal. Assn* 18: 3–23.

Baker, R. (1986) 'Psychoanalysis as a lifeline'. Unpublished paper, p. 8.

Balint, M. (1935) 'Critical notes on the theory of pregenital organization of the libido', in *Primary Love and Psychoanalytic Technique*. Hogarth, pp. 49–73.

Bancroft, J. H. J. (1974) *Deviant Sexual Behaviour: Modification and Assessment*. Oxford University Press.

Barreto, C. A., Lacombe, F., Pelegrino, H., Lima, J. and Chebabi, W.

(1984) 'Corrientes actuantes en el pensamiento psicoanalitico de l'America Latina', *Rev. Psicoanal.* 41: 625–32.

Bégoin, J. and F. (1979) 'The negative therapeutic reaction. Envy and catastrophic anxiety', *Bull. European Psychoanal. Federation* 16: 21–31.

Bene, E. A. (1965) 'On the genesis of female homosexuality', *Br. J. Med. Psychol.* 111: 815–21.

Benedek, T. (1936) 'Dominant ideas and their relation to morbid cravings', *Int. J. Psycho-Anal.* 17: 40–56.

Bergler, E. (1951) *Neurotic Counterfeit Sex*. New York: Grune & Stratton.

Bion, W. R. (1970) *Attention and Interpretation*. Tavistock.

—— (1976) 'Evidence', in *Clinical Seminars and four Papers*. Reading: Fleetwood, pp. 239–46.

Birtwistle, H. (1986) *The Mask of Orpheus*. Opera, libretto by P. Zinovieff. Universal Edition, 1987.

Blos, P. (1962) 'The concept of acting out in relation to the adolescent process', in Rexford (1978), pp. 153–62.

Bollas, C. (1983) 'La révélation de l'ici et maintenant', *Nouvelle Rev. Psychanal.* 27: 262–72.

Bonaparte, M. (1954) 'The fault of Orpheus in reverse', *Int. J. Psycho-Anal.* 35: 109–12.

Bougard, P. (1934) 'L'interprétation psycho-analytique du mythe d'Orphée et son application au symbolisme musical', *Rev. Fr. Psychanal.* 7: 320–71.

Boyd, P. (1972) 'Adolescents – drug abuse and addiction', *Br. Med. J.* 4: 540–3.

Brenner, C. (1959) 'The masochistic character: genesis and treatment', *J. Amer. Psychoanal. Assn* 7: 197–226.

Brierley, M. (1951) 'Affects in theory and practice', in *Trends in Psychoanalysis*. Hogarth, pp. 41–56.

Calef, V. (1976) 'The psychoanalytic process'. Panel discussion, Association for Child Psychoanalysis, Kansas City.

Camus, M. (1958) *Black Orpheus*. Film.

Carpelan, H. (1981) 'On the importance of the setting in the psychoanalytic situation', *Scandinavian Psychoanal. Rev.* 4: 151–61.

Chasseguet-Smirgel, J. (1980) 'Loss of reality in perversion with special reference to fetishism', *J. Amer. Psychoanal. Assn* 29: 524–36.

—— (1984) *Creativity and Perversion*. Free Association Books, 1985.

Cocteau, J. (1949) *Orphée*. Film and poetry. Paris: La Bonne.

Cohen, P. S. (1983) 'Unconscious factors in the violent act: a sociological perspective'. Portman Clinic Symposium on Violence, London.

'Controversial Discussions' (1967) *Bull. British Psycho-Anal. Society* 53: 1–293.

Craft, M. (1966) 'Boy prostitutes and their fate', *Br. J. Psychol.* 112: 1111–14.

Dekhlei, K. (1984) 'Civilité du sexe moderne', *Nouvelle Rev. Psychanal.* 29: 102–10.

De Quincey, Thomas (1822) *Confessions of an English Opium Eater*, in *Collected Writings of Thomas De Quincey*, vol. 3. Edinburgh, 1890, pp. 209–449.

de Saussure, J. (1979) 'Narcissistic elements in the negative therapeutic reaction', *Bull. European Psychoanal. Federation* 16: 33–44.

Deutsch, H. (1963) 'Problems of acting out in the transference relationship'. Discussion of P. Greenacre in Rexford (1978), pp. 235–45.

Dewhurst, K. (1969) 'Sexual activity and urinary steroids in men with special reference to male homosexuality', *Br. J. Psychol.* 115: 1413–15.

Donnet, J.-L. (1979) 'Sur l'institution psychanalytique et la durée de la séance', *Nouvelle Rev. Psychanal* 20: 242–59.

Eisnitz, A. J. (1974) 'On the metapsychology of narcissistic pathology', *J. Amer. Psychoanal. Assn* 22: 279–91.

Ekstein, R. (1966) 'The Orpheus and Eurydice theme in psychotherapy', *Bull. Menninger Clinic* 130: 207–24.

—— (1972) 'On psychoanalytic education: authoritarian, anti-authoritarian and authoritative?', *Psychiat. Opinion.* 9: 14–21.

Erle, J. B. (1979) 'An approach to the study of analyzability and analyses: the course of forty consecutive cases selected for supervised analysis', *Psychoanal. Q.* 48: 198–228.

Erle, J. B. and Goldberg, D. A. (1984) 'Observations on assessment analyzability by experienced analysts: report on 160 cases', *J. Amer. Psychoanal. Assn* 32: 715–37.

Fairbairn, W. R. D. (1958) 'On the nature and aims of psychoanalytical treatment', *Int. J. Psycho-Anal.* 39: 374–85.

Feldman, W. S. (1977) 'The transsexual imbroglio', *J. Legal Med.* 4: 157–61.

Fenichel, O. (1945a) 'Drug addiction', in *The Psychoanalytic Theory of the Neurosis*. New York: Norton, pp. 377–9.

—— (1945b) 'Neurotic acting out', *Psychoanal. Rev.* 32: 197–207.

Flournoy, O. (1980) 'Sigmund Freud–Melanie Klein: une querelle dépassée', *Rev. Fr. Psychanal.* 5–6: 912–16.

Freeman, T. (1955) 'Clinical and theoretical observations on male homosexuality', *Int. J. Psycho-Anal.* 36: 235–48.

Freud, A. (1943) 'Discussion of "The nature and function of phantasy" by S. Isaacs' in 'Controversial Discussions' (1967), pp. 1–167.

——— (1952) 'A connection between the states of negativism and of emotional surrender', *Int. J. Psycho-Anal.* 33: 265.

——— (1954) 'The widening scope of indications for psychoanalysis', *J. Amer. Psychoanal. Assn* 2: 607–20.

Freud, S. (1905a) *Three Essays on the Theory of Sexuality*, in James Strachey, ed. *The Standard Edition of the Complete Psychological Works of Sigmund Freud*, 24 vols. Hogarth, 1953–73. vol. 7, pp. 125–231.

——— (1905b) 'On psychotherapy'. *S.E.* 7, pp. 257–71.

——— (1910) 'Leonardo da Vinci and a memory of his childhood'. *S.E.* 11, pp. 59–128.

——— (1911) 'Psychoanalytic notes on an autobiographical account of a case of paranoia'. *S.E.* 12, pp. 3–80.

——— (1912) 'The dynamics of transference'. *S.E.* 12, pp. 97–101.

——— (1913a) 'On beginning the treatment'. *S.E.* 12, pp. 121–44.

——— (1913b) *Totem and Taboo. S.E.* 13, pp. 1–162.

——— (1914) 'Remembering, repeating and working through. (Further recommendations on the technique of psycho-analysis, II)'. *S.E.* 12, pp. 145–57.

——— (1916) 'Some character-types met with in psychoanalytic work'. *S.E.* 14, pp. 309–33.

——— (1918) 'The history of an infantile neurosis'. *S.E.* 17, pp. 3–123.

——— (1919) 'Lines of advance in psychoanalytic therapy'. *S.E.* 17, pp. 57–169.

——— (1920) 'The psychogenesis of a case of homosexuality in a woman'. *S.E.* 18, pp. 145–74.

——— (1921) 'Group psychology and the analysis of the ego'. *S.E.* 18, pp. 65–140.

——— (1923) *The Ego and the Id. S.E.* 19, pp. 3–68.

——— (1924) 'The economic problem of masochism'. *S.E.* 19, pp. 157–73.

——— (1930) *Civilization and its Discontents. S.E.* 21, pp. 59–145.

——— (1932) 'Why war?' (Einstein and Freud). *S.E.* 22, pp. 199–218.

——— (1933) *New Introductory Lectures on Psychoanalysis. S.E.* 22, pp. 5–158.

——— (1937) 'Analysis terminable and interminable'. *S.E.* 23, pp. 209–55.

——— (1940) 'An outline of psychoanalysis'. *S.E.* 23, pp. 141–208.

Friedman, A. M., Kaplan, H. I. and Sadock, B. J. (1972) *Modern Synopsis of Psychiatry*. Baltimore, MD: Williams & Wilkins.

Gaddini, E. (1969) 'On imitation', *Int. J. Psycho-Anal.* 50: 475–84.

—— (1981) 'Precocious defensive fantasies and the psychoanalytic process'. Paper read at 4th Conference of European Psychoanalytic Federation.

—— (1984) 'Changes in psychoanalytic patients up to the present day', in R. Wallerstein, ed. *Symposium on Changes in Analysts and their Training.* International Psychoanalytic Association Monograph Series no. 4. New York: International Universities Press, pp. 6–22.

Gallwey, P. L. G. (1979) 'Symbolic functions in the perversions – some related clinical problems', *Int. Rev. Psycho-Anal.* 6: 155–61.

Gamill, J. (1982) 'Quelques souvenirs personnels de Melanie Klein'. Memorial meeting for Klein, Paris. Unpublished paper, pp. 1–19.

Gelder, M. (1979) 'Behaviour therapy for sexual deviations', in I. Rosen, ed. *Sexual Deviations.* Oxford: Oxford University Press, pp. 351–73.

Gillespie, W. H. (1964a) 'The psychoanalytic theory of sexual deviations with special reference to fetishism', in I. Rosen, ed. *The Pathology and Treatment of Sexual Deviations.* Oxford University Press, pp. 124–45.

—— (1964b) Symposium on homosexuality, *Int. J. Psycho-Anal.* 45: 203–9.

—— (1980) 'Review of *Klein* by H. Segal', *Int. J. Psycho-Anal.* 61: 85–8.

Gitelson, M. (1952) 'The emotional position of the analyst in the psychoanalytic situation', *Int. J. Psycho-Anal.* 33: 1–10.

Glasser, M. (1979a) 'From the analysis of a transvestite', *Int. Rev. Psycho-Anal.* 6: 163–73.

—— (1979b) 'Some aspects of the role of aggression in the perversions', in I. Rosen, ed. *Sexual Deviations.* Oxford: Oxford University Press, pp. 278–305.

Glover, E. (1926) 'The neurotic character', *Int. J. Psycho-Anal.* 7: 11–30.

—— (1931) 'Sublimation, substitution, and social anxiety', *Int. J. Psycho-Anal.* 12: 263–97.

—— (1932) 'On the etiology of drug addiction', *Int. J. Psycho-Anal.* 13: 298–328.

—— (1938a) 'The relation of perversion formation to the development of the reality sense', *Int. J. Psycho-Anal.* 14: 486–503.

—— (1938b) 'A note on idealization', *Int. J. Psycho-Anal.* 19: 91–6.

—— (1954) 'The indications for psychoanalysis', *J. Ment. Sci.* 100: 393–401.

—— (1964) 'Aggression and sadomasochism', in I. Rosen, ed. *The Pathology and Treatment of Sexual Deviations.* Oxford: Oxford University Press, pp. 146–61.

Gluck, C. W. (1762) *Orpheus.* Opera, libretto by R. Calzabigi. English version by E. Dent. Oxford: Oxford University Press, 1941.

Graves, R. (1960) *The Greek Myths*. 2 vols. Harmondsworth: Penguin.

Greaves, S. (1985) 'Starting off on a life of crime', *The Times*, 10 May.

Green, A. (1973a) *Le Discours vivant, la conception psychanalytique de l'affect*. Paris: Presses Universitaires de France.

—— (1973b) 'Some comments on psychoanalytic training', *Bull. European Psychoanal. Federation* 3: 6–12.

—— (1975) 'The analyst, symbolization and absence in the analytic setting', *Int. J. Psycho-Anal.* 56: 1–22.

Green, R. (1974) *Sexual Identity Conflict*. Duckworth.

Greenacre, P. (1948) 'Symposium on evaluation of therapeutic results', *Int. J. Psycho-Anal.* 29: 11–14.

—— (1950) 'General problems of acting out', *Psychoanal. Q.* 19: 455–67.

—— (1953) 'Certain relationships between fetishism and faulty development of the body image', *Psychoanal. Study Child* 8: 79–98.

—— (1956) 'Re-evaluation of the process of working through', *Int. J. Psycho-Anal.* 37: 439–45.

—— (1963) 'Problems of acting out in the transference relationship', in Rexford (1978), pp. 224–35.

—— (1975) 'On reconstruction', *J. Amer. Psychoanal. Assn* 23: 693–712.

Greenson, R. R. (1965) 'The working alliance and the transference neurosis', *Psychoanal. Q.* 34: 155–81.

—— (1966a) 'That impossible profession', *J. Amer. Psychoanal. Assn* 14: 9–27.

—— (1966b) 'A transvestite boy and a hypothesis', *Int. J. Psycho-Anal.* 47: 396–403.

—— (1968) 'Dis-identifying from mother', *Int. J. Psycho-Anal.* 49: 370–4.

Grunberger, B. (1976) 'Essai sur le fétichisme', *Rev. Fr. Psychanal.* 40: 235–64.

Grunert, U. (1979) 'The negative therapeutic reaction as a reactivation of a disturbed process of separation in the transference', *Bull. European Psychoanal. Federation* 16: 5–19.

Guttman, S. A. (1968) 'Indications and contra-indications for psychoanalytic treatment', *Int. J. Psycho-Anal.* 49: 254–5.

Hall, R. (1926) *The Well of Loneliness*. Virago, 1982.

Hamburger, C., Strup, G. K. and Dahl-Iverson, E. (1953) 'Transvestism: hormonal, psychiatric and surgical treatment', *J. Amer. Med. Assn* 152: 391–8.

Hartmann, H. (1925) 'Kokainismus und homosexualität', in *Zeitschrift für*

Psychiatrie und Neurologie 95: 79–94.

Hays, H. R. (1963) *In the Beginning.* New York: G. B. Putnam.

Heimann, P. (1950) 'On counter-transference', *Int. J. Psycho-Anal.* 31: 81–4.

Hoerig, J. and Kerna, J. (1970) 'Social and economic aspects of trans-sexualism', *Br. J. Psychol.* 117: 163–72.

Hopper, E. (1981) *Social Mobility: A Study of Social Control and Insatiability.* Oxford: Basil Blackwell.

Horney, K. (1936) 'The problem of the negative therapeutic reaction', *Psychoanal. Q.* 5: 29–44.

Isaacs, S. (1943a) 'The 1943 "controversial" discussions', in 'Controversial Discussions' (1967), pp. 1–168.

—— (1943b) 'Reply to the discussion on "The nature and function of phantasy" ', in 'Controversial Discussions' (1967), pp. 1–168.

—— (1948) 'The nature and function of phantasy', *Int. J. Psycho-Anal.* 29: 73–97.

James, M. (1964) 'Interpretation and management in the treatment of pre-adolescents', *Int. J. Psycho-Anal.* 45: 499–512.

JAPA (1977) 'Panel discussion on the psychoanalytic treatment of homosexuality', *J. Amer. Psychoanal. Assn* 25: 83–201.

Joffe, W. G. and Sandler, J. (1968) 'Comments on the psychoanalytic psychology of adaptation with special reference to the role of affects and the representational world', *Int. J. Psycho-Anal.* 49: 445–54.

Jones, E. (1915) 'War and sublimation', in *Essays on Applied Psychoanalysis,* 2 vols. Hogarth, 1951. vol. I, pp. 77–88.

—— (1929) 'Fear, guilt and hate', *Int. J. Psycho-Anal.* 10: 383–97.

—— (1931) *On the Nightmare.* Hogarth.

Joseph, B. (1985) 'Transference: the total situation', *Int. J. Psycho-Anal.* 66: 447–54.

Jung, C. (1940) *Integration of the Personality.* Kegan Paul.

Kallman, F. J. (1952) 'Comparative study on the genetic aspect of male homosexuality', *J. Nerv. Ment. Dis.* 115: 223–98.

Kantrowitz, J. L. (1987) 'Suitability for psychoanalysis', in R. Langs, ed. *The Yearbook of Psychoanalysis and Psychotherapy.* London/New York: Gardner, pp. 403–16.

Kanzer, M. (1957) 'Acting out, sublimation and reality testing', *J. Amer. Psychoanal. Assn* 5: 136–46.

Kernberg, O.F. (1970) 'Factors in the psychoanalytic treatment of narcissistic personalities', *J. Amer. Psychoanal. Assn* 18: 15–85.

—— (1974) 'Contrasting viewpoints regarding the nature and

psychoanalytic treatment of narcissistic personalities: a preliminary communication', *J. Amer. Psychoanal. Assn* 22: 255–67.

Khan, M. M. R. (1962) 'The role of polymorph-perverse body-experiences and object-relations in ego-integration', in Khan (1979), pp. 31–56.

—— (1963a) 'Silence as communication', in Khan (1974b), pp. 68–181.

—— (1963b) 'The concept of cumulative trauma', in Khan (1974b), pp. 42–59.

—— (1964a) 'Ego-distortion, cumulative trauma and the role of reconstruction in the analytic situation', in Khan (1974b), pp. 59–69.

—— (1964b) 'The role of infantile sexuality and early object-relations in female homosexuality', in Khan (1979), pp. 56–120.

—— (1968) 'Reparation of the self as an idolized internal object', in Khan (1979), pp. 11–17.

—— (1969) 'Vicissitudes of being, knowing and experiencing in the therapeutic situation', in Khan (1974b), pp. 203–19.

—— (1970) 'Fetish as negation of the self. Clinical notes on foreskin fetishism in a male homosexual', in Khan (1979), pp. 139–77.

—— (1972) 'The use and abuse of dream in psychic experience', in Khan (1974b), pp. 306–16.

—— (1974a) 'Ego-orgasm in bisexual love', in Khan (1979), pp. 185–97.

—— (1974b) *The Privacy of the Self*. Hogarth.

—— (1979) *Alienation in Perversions*. Hogarth.

King, P. (1978) 'Affective response of the analyst to the patient's communications', *Int. J. Psycho-Anal.* 59: 329-34.

Klein, M. (1932a) 'The effects of early anxiety situation in the sexual development of the girl', in Klein (1975), vol. 2, pp. 194–240.

—— (1932b) 'The effects of early anxiety situation in the sexual development of the boy', in Klein (1975), vol. 2, pp. 240–74.

—— (1935) 'Contribution to the psychogenesis of manic depressive states', in Klein (1975), vol. I, pp. 262–90.

—— (1946) 'Notes on some schizoid mechanisms', in Klein (1975), vol. 3, pp. 1–25.

—— (1952) 'The origins of transference', in Klein (1975), vol. 3, pp. 48–56.

—— (1957) *Envy and Gratitude*, in Klein (1975), vol. 3.

—— (1975) *The Writings of Melanie Klein*, 4 vols. Hogarth.

Klein, M. and Rivière, J. (1975) *Love, Guilt and Reparation and Other Papers*. Hogarth.

Knapp, P. H., Levin, S., McCarter, R. H., Werner, H. and Zetzel, E. (1960) 'Suitability for psychoanalysis: a review of one hundred supervised analytic cases', *Psychoanal. Q.* 29: 459–77.

Kuiper, P. C. (1968) 'Indications and contra-indications for psychoanalytic treatment', *Int. J. Psycho-Anal.* 49: 261–4.

Langs, R. (1976) *The Therapeutic Interaction.* New York: Jason Aronson.

Laplanche, J. (1975) *Life and Death in Psychoanalysis,* J. M. McReaman, trans. London/Baltimore, MD: Johns Hopkins University Press.

Laplanche, J. and Pontalis, J.-B. (1973) 'Object relationships', in *The Language of Psycho-Analysis.* Hogarth, pp. 277–81.

Levin, S. (1960) 'Problems in the evaluation of patients for psychoanalysis', *Bull. Philadelphia Psychoanal. Assn* 10: 86–95.

Lewin, B. (1965) 'Reflections on affect', in M. Schur, ed. *Drives, Affects, Behaviour,* vol. 2. New York: International Universities Press.

Limentani, A. (1973) 'Psicoanalisi e dipendenza dalla droga nei giovani', *Enciclopedia.* Istituto della Enciclopedia Italiana, Roma: 403–16.

—— (1984) 'Towards a unified conception of the origins of sexual and social deviancy in young persons', *Int. J. Psychoanal. Psychother.* 10: 383–409.

Loch, W. (1988) 'Reconstruction, constructions, interpretations: from the self-ego to the ego-self', *Symposium on Constructions in Psychoanalysis,* European Psychoanal. Federation, February 1988, Sweden.

McDougall, J. (1972) 'Primal scene and sexual perversion', *Int. J. Psycho-Anal.* 53: 371–94.

—— (1974) 'The psycho-soma and the psychoanalytic process', in *Plea for a Measure of Abnormality* (1980). New York: International Universities Press, 1980, pp. 337–97.

—— (1982) 'The narcissistic economy and its relation to primitive sexuality', *Contemp. Psychoanal.* 18: 373–96.

—— (1986) 'Identification, neoneeds and neosexuality', *Int. J. Psycho-Anal.* 67: 19–31.

Malinowski, B. (1926) 'The role of myth in life', *Psyché* 24: 29–39.

Margolin, C. G. (1954) *Recent Developments in Psychosomatic Medicine.* Pitman.

Marks, I., Gelder, M. and Bancroft, J. (1970) 'Sexual deviants. Two years after electrical aversion', *Br. J. Psychol.* 117: 137–85.

Matter, J. (1951) 'Le mythe de Narcisse dans l'Orphée de Jean Cocteau' *Psyché* 6: 236–57.

Mitchell, J. (1976) 'A review of *The Transsexual Experiment* by Robert Stoller', *Int. J. Psycho-Anal.* 57: 357–60.

Moran, P. A. P. and Abe, K. (1959) 'Parental loss in homosexuals', *Br. J.*

Psychol. 11: 319–21.

Morrison, B. (1963) 'Psychosomatic symptomatology'. Unpublished paper.

Nacht, S. and Lebovici, S. (1955) 'Indications et contre-indications de la psychanalyse', *Rev. Fr. Psychanal.* 19: 135–88.

Namnum, A. (1968) 'The problem of analysability and the autonomous ego', *Int. J. Psycho-Anal.* 49: 271–5.

Numberg, H. (1938) 'Homosexuality, magic, and aggression', *Int. J. Psycho-Anal.* 19: 1–16.

Offenbach, J. (1858) *Orphée aux Enfers*, Opéra-féerie, libretto by Crémieux and Halévy. Paris: Au Ménestrel.

Olinick, S. L. (1964) 'The negative therapeutic reaction', *Int. J. Psycho-Anal.* 45: 540–8.

Ostow, M. (1953) 'Letter to the Editor', *J. Amer. Med. Assn* 152: 458.

Ovid (1955) *The Metamorphoses*, M. M. Innes, trans. Harmondsworth: Penguin.

Pare, C. M. B. (1956) 'Homosexuality and chromosomal sex', *J. Psychosom. Res.* 1: 247–51.

Pontalis, J.-B. (1975) 'A partir du contre-transfert: le mort et le vif entrelacés', *Nouvelle Rev. Psychanal.* 12: 73–86.

——— (1979) 'The negative therapeutic reaction. An attempt at definition', *Bull. European Psychoanal. Federation* 15: 19–30.

Racker, H. (1968) *Transference and Countertransference*. Hogarth.

Rado, S. (1926) 'The psychic effects of intoxicants', *Int. J. Psycho-Anal.* 7: 396–413.

Randell, J. H. (1959) 'Transvestism and transsexualism', *Br. Med. J.* 2: 1448–52.

Rangell, L. (1967) 'Psychoanalysis, affects and the human core', *Psychoanal. Q.* 36: 172–202.

Rapaport, D. (1953) 'On the psychoanalytic theory of the affects', *Int. J. Psycho-Anal.* 34: 177–98.

Rexford, E. N. (1963) 'A developmental concept of the problems of acting out', in Rexford (1978), pp. 1–14.

Rexford, E. N., ed. (1978) *A Developmental Approach to Problems of Acting out.* New York: International Universities Press.

Richards, A. (1988) 'Review of *Forty-two Lives in Treatment. A Study of Psychoanalysis and Psychotherapy* by R. S. Wallerstein', *Int. J. Psycho-Anal.* 69: 140–5.

Rivière, J. (1936) 'A contribution to the analysis of the negative therapeutic reaction', *Int. J. Psycho-Anal.* 17: 304–20.

Rosen, I. (1979) 'Exhibitionism, scopophilia and voyeurism', in I. Rosen, ed. *Sexual Deviations.* Oxford: Oxford University Press, pp. 139–94.

Rosenfeld, H. (1949) 'Remarks on the relation of male homosexuality in paranoia, paranoid anxiety and narcissism', *Int. J. Psycho-Anal.* 30: 36–45.

—— (1960) 'On drug addiction', *Int. J. Psycho-Anal.* 41: 467–75.

—— (1964) 'An investigation into the need of neurotic and psychotic patients to act out during analysis', in *Psychotic States.* Hogarth, 1965, pp. 200–16.

—— (1975) 'Negative therapeutic reaction', in P. Giovacchini, ed. *Tactics and Techniques in Psychoanalytic Therapy*, vol. 2. New York: Jason Aronson, pp. 217–28.

Rossi, R. (1985) 'Myth and tragedy: the past and the present in interpretation'. Discussion of a paper by R. Riesenberg Malcolm, *Bull. European Psychoanal. Federation* 25: 31–40.

Roustang, F. (1982) *Dire Mastery*, N. Luckacher, trans. Baltimore, MD: Johns Hopkins University Press.

Rycroft, C. (1962) 'Beyond the reality principle', *Int. J. Psycho-Anal.* 43: 388–95.

Sandler, J. (1972) 'The role of affects in psychoanalytic theory', in *Physiology, Emotion and Psychosomatic Illness.* Ciba Foundation Symposium 8, new series. Amsterdam: Elsevier–Excerpta Medica, pp. 31–56.

—— (1979) 'The negative therapeutic reaction: an introduction', *Bull. European Psychoanal. Federation* 15: 13–18.

—— (1983) 'Reflections on some relations between psychoanalytic concepts and psychoanalytic practice', *Int. J. Psycho-Anal.* 64: 35–47.

Sandler, J., Dare, C. and Holder, A. (1970a) 'Basic psychoanalytic concepts: the treatment alliance', *Br. J. Psychiatry* 116: 555–88.

—— (1970b) 'Basic psychoanalytic concepts: transference', *Br. J. Psychiatry* 116: 667–72.

—— (1973) *The Patient and the Analyst.* Allen & Unwin (and Maresfield Reprints).

Sandler, J., Holder, A. and Dare, C. (1970) 'Basic psychoanalytic concepts. VII. The negative therapeutic reaction', *Br. J. Psychiatry* 117: 431–535.

Sashin, J., Eldred, S. and Van Amerangen, A. (1975) 'A search for predictive factors in institute supervised cases: a retrospective study of 183 cases from 1959 to 1966 at the Boston Psychoanalytic Institute and Society', *Int. J. Psycho-Anal.* 56: 343–59.

BIBLIOGRAPHY

Scott, W. C. M. (1951) 'Indications for and limitations of psychoanalytic treatment', *Br. Med. J.* 2: 597–600.

Segal, H. (1957) 'Notes on symbol formation', *Int. J. Psycho-Anal.* 38: 391–7.

—— (1962) 'The curative factors in psychoanalysis', *Int. J. Psycho-Anal.* 43: 212–17.

—— (1964) *Introduction to the Work of Melanie Klein.* Heinemann.

—— (1978) 'On symbolism', *Int. J. Psycho-Anal.* 59: 315–19.

—— (1979) *Klein.* Fontana Modern Masters, F. Kermode, ed. Collins.

Silverberg, W. (1955) 'Acting out versus insight: a problem in psychoanalytic technique', *Psychoanal. Q.* 24: 527–44.

Socarides, C. V. (1970) 'A psychoanalytic study of the desire for sexual transformation. (Transsexualism: the Plaster of Paris Man)', *Int. J. Psycho-Anal.* 51: 341–9.

Solomon, G. F. (1987) 'Psychoneuroimmunology', in G.F. Adelman, ed. *Encyclopedia of Neuroscience*, 2 vols. Boston: Birkhauser.

Spillius, E. (1979) 'Clinical reflections on the negative therapeutic reaction', *Bull. European Psychoanal. Federation* 15: 31–9.

Stoller, R. J. (1969) *Sex and Gender.* Hogarth.

—— (1975) *The Transsexual Experiment.* Hogarth.

—— (1979) 'The gender disorders', in I. Rosen, ed. *Sexual Deviations.* Oxford: Oxford University Press, pp. 100–38.

Stone, L. (1954) 'The widening scope of indications for psychoanalysis', *J. Amer. Psychoanal. Assn.* 2: 567–94.

Strachey, J. (1934) 'On the nature of the therapeutic action of psychoanalysis', *Int. J. Psycho-Anal.* 15: 127–59.

—— (1943) 'Memorandum on current theoretical controversies affecting matters of training'. Archives of Br. Psycho-Anal. Society. Unpublished paper. 1–6.

Sullivan, H.S. (1955) *Conceptions of Modern Psychiatry.* Tavistock.

Szasz, T. S. (1957) 'On the theory of psychoanalytical treatment', *Int. J. Psycho-Anal.* 38: 166–82.

Thorner, H. A. (1949) 'Notes on a case of male homosexuality', *Int. J. Psycho-Anal.* 30: 31–45.

Tsoi, W. F., Kok, L. P. and Long, F. Y. (1977) 'Male transsexualism in Singapore: a description of 56 cases', *Br. J. Psychiatry* 131: 405–9.

Valenstein, A. F. (1973) 'On attachment to painful feelings and the negative therapeutic reaction', *Psychoanal. Study Child* 28: 365–92.

Wakeling, A. (1979) 'A general psychiatric approach to sexual deviations', in I. Rosen, ed. *Sexual Deviations*. Oxford: Oxford University Press 1979, pp. 1–29.

Waldhorn, H. F. (1960) 'Assessment of analysability: technical and theoretical observations', *Psychoanal. Q.* 29: 478–506.

Walker, B. G. (1983) 'Orpheus', in *The Woman's Encyclopedia of Myths and Secrets*. San Francisco: Harper & Row, pp. 745–8.

Wallerstein, R. S. (1972) 'The futures of psychoanalytic education', *J. Amer. Psychoanal. Assn* 20: 591–606.

—— (1986) *Forty-two Lives in Treatment. A Study of Psychoanalysis and Psychotherapy*. New York: The Guildford Press, p. 784.

—— (1987) 'The assessment of analysability and of analytic outcomes', in R. Langs, ed. *The Yearbook of Psychoanalysis and Psychotherapy*. London/New York: Gardner, pp. 417–26.

Watson, J. P., Annear, J. M. and Yagge, M. (1977) 'Aspects of the psychopathology of sexual behaviour', *Procs Royal Soc. Med.* 70: 789–92.

Weber, J. J., Bachrach, H. M. and Solomon, M. (1985) 'Factors associated with the outcome of psychoanalysis. Report of the Columbia Psychoanalytic Center Research Project', *Int. Rev. Psycho-Anal.* 12: 127–41.

Weissman, P. (1962) 'Structural consideration in overt male bisexuality', *Int. J. Psycho-Anal.* 43: 159–68.

Williams, T. (1953) *Orpheus Descending*. Harmondsworth: Penguin, 1961.

Winnicott, D. W. (1945) 'Primitive emotional development', in Winnicott (1975), pp. 145–57.

—— (1949) 'Mind and its relation to the psycho-soma', in Winnicott (1975), pp. 243–55.

—— (1952) 'Anxiety associated with insecurity', in Winnicott (1975), pp. 97–101.

—— (1956) 'The antisocial tendency', in Winnicott (1975), pp. 306–16.

—— (1958) 'The capacity to be alone', *Int. J. Psycho-Anal.* 39: 416–21.

—— (1974) 'Fear of breakdown', *Int. Rev. Psycho-Anal.* 1: 103–7.

—— (1975) *Through Paediatrics to Psychoanalysis*. Hogarth.

Zetzel, E. (1968) 'The so-called good hysteric', *Int. J. Psycho-Anal.* 49: 256–60.

Zilboorg, G. (1952) 'The emotional problems and the therapeutic role of insight', *Psychoanal. Q.* 21: 1–24.

Zimmerman, D. (1982) 'Analysability in relation to early psychopathology', *Int. J. Psycho-Anal.* 63: 189–201.

INDEX